Busted

Nova Scotia's War on Drugs

Vernon Oickle

NIMBUS
PUBLISHING LTD

Nimbus Publishing Limited
P.O. Box 9301, Station A
Halifax, NS B3K 5N5
(902) 455-4286

Design: Zab Design & Typograpy Inc
Printed and bound in Canada

Canadian Cataloguing in Publication Data
Oickle, Vernon L.
Busted.
ISBN 1-55109-227-1
1. Drug traffic—Nova Scotia. 2. Narcotics, Control of—
Nova Scotia.
I. Title.
HV8079.N3052 1997   364.1'77'09716   C97-95-147-4

Contents

"DRUGS ... THEY'RE ALL AROUND YOU. They're in our communities. They're part of society. If there's a way to get the stuff into the country so they can sell it, then you can damned well be sure that somebody out there somewhere will try to figure out how to do it. There's good money in drugs, and a lot of people out there want to get a piece of the action. The law can do whatever it wants to, but you ain't gonna stop it. It's too big. There's just too much money involved for anyone to think they're ever gonna stop the drugs. If there's a drug out there and someone will pay for it, then this war will never be over ... it's a war that neither side can win!"

—*A confessed drug dealer*

For Kellen and Colby
my inspiration

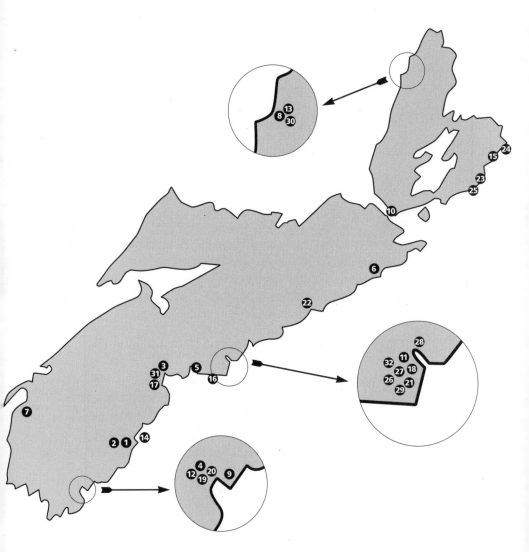

THIS MAP SHOWS THE LOCATIONS OF SOME OF THE MAJOR DRUG
SEIZURES IN NOVA SCOTIA FROM THE EARLY 1970s TO 1997.

1   October 1975, Liverpool: 245.4 kg hashish

2   May 1977, Beech Hill: 823 kg hashish

3   May 1977, Chester: 5.85 tonnes marijuana

4   May 1980, Shelburne: 22 tonnes marijuana

5   July 1980, St. Margarets Bay: 4.5 tonnes hashish

6   August, 1982, Wine Harbour: 39.4 kg hashish

7   September 1982, Corberrie: 8.2 tonnes marijuana

8   (exact date unavailable) 1985, Chéticamp:
     undisclosed quantity of hashish

9   May 1985, Lockeport: 13.2 tonnes hashish

10 June 1985, Port Hawkesbury: 294.5 kg marijuana

11 June 1985, Halifax: 91 kg marijuana

12 June 1986, Shelburne: 176 kg marijuana

13 October 1986, Chéticamp: 17.4 tonnes hashish

14 May 1990, Ragged Harbour: 35 tonnes hashish

15 July 1990, Baleine: 27 tonnes hashish

16 May 1991, Prospect Bay: 1.5 tonnes hashish

17 October 1991, near Chester: 7 tonnes hashish

18 Fall 1991, Halifax: 11 tonnes hashish

19 June 1992, Shelburne: 22.7 kg hashish

20 February 1994, Shelburne: 5,419 kg cocaine

21 March 1994, Halifax: 753 kg cocaine

22 November 1994, Sheet Harbour: 700 kg cocaine

23 September 1995, near Louisbourg: 3.6 tonnes hashish

24 September 1995, near Scatarie Island: 3.5 tonnes hashish

25 September 1995, Capelin Cove: 45.4 kg hashish oil

26 November 1995, Halifax: 7,500 kg hashish

27 December 1995, Halifax: 484 kg marijuana and 72 kg hashish

28 February 1996, Dartmouth: 30 kg hashish

29 March 1996, Halifax: 8.6 tonnes hashish

30 October 1996, Chéticamp: 10 tonnes hashish

31 December 1996, Gold River: province's largest indoor marijuana-
     growing operation busted and 506 plants seized

32 May 1997, Halifax: 92 kg cocaine

Preface

GROWING UP IN LIVERPOOL, a rural coastal community on Nova Scotia's South Shore, I had a rather idyllic view of our friendly little town. By the time I reached high school in the mid-1980s, I had seen drug exchanges between other kids many times. But I could not have imagined the extent of the drug trade that had already moved into the Liverpool region.

Years later, when I became a reporter for Liverpool's weekly newspaper, *The Advance*, I began to understand that ours was a community facing many challenges, some a direct result of the drug trade. Saddened for my community, yet intrigued by the nature of this pervasive problem, I came to the conclusion that Liverpool was like many small communities in North America dealing with a similar difficulty—but unlike the others in one significant way: since the early 1970s, Liverpool, indeed, the entire South Shore, has become a prime target for drug smugglers.

In my job I have had many opportunities to investigate the drug trade at the local level, and questions naturally arose. Where did the drugs come from? Where did they go once they got here? Which local people were involved? Who was behind the conspiracies that brought millions of dollars' worth of drugs to Nova Scotia's shores? What impact are drugs having on our communities, and what are we doing to counter their negative effect—can the drug trade be stopped, and by whom?

Many questions, few answers. That is the nature of the issue—its complexity, and its subterfuge. But I kept asking questions, and at long last amassed enough material to write a book—which is my attempt to answer these and other questions about narcotics smuggling. No matter what the topic, undertaking a book is a daunting task, which requires a major commitment and a great deal of insight and help from others. I have had the distinct pleasure of working with Dorothy Blythe, managing editor of Nimbus Publishing, and have received a great deal of guidance from book editors Liane Heller and Dean Jobb, who gave me an honest and thorough review of several versions of my manuscript.

The staff at Nimbus has my sincere gratitude and respect. There were many other people who gave me information, advice, and helpful criticism. Two significant individuals are retired RCMP officer Gary Grant and RCMP Sergeant Bill Parker, both of them valuable resources for the research material and personal perspectives they provided on the drug trade in Nova Scotia; both of them exceptionally cooperative and generous with their time.

I would especially like to mention Marg Hennigar of Lighthouse Publishing. Along with Ralph and Lynn Hennigar, she agreed to accommodate my writing time when I began working for Lighthouse as editor of *The Bulletin* in 1994; and as an award-winning weekly newspaper editor and publisher, she was able to bring insightful suggestions and constructive criticism to the reading of my manuscript, which she graciously worked in to her busy schedule. Her support was vital to bringing this project to fruition.

As a newspaper editor, I should also mention the good papers in this province that became a valuable source of information; in particular the weeklies in communities along the South Shore, including the Yarmouth *Vanguard*, Shelburne *Coast Guard*, Liverpool *Advance*, Bridgewater *Bulletin,* and Lunenburg *Progress Enterprise*, as well as the Halifax dailies, The *Chronicle-Herald/Mail-Star* and *The Daily News*. These publications helped fill the void left by police reports, court documents, and official reports, helping me to piece this story together.

I would also like to thank the Nova Scotia Department of Education for providing me with financial assistance through its Assistance to Established Writers program, without which the many months of research and writing would not have been possible.

Probably the most important form of support and encouragement for this project since its beginnings as an idea born in 1990 has been the unwavering faith and love of my family. My wife Nancy and our two sons were my rock and my inspiration; they appreciated the importance of this project and understood that completing it quickly became a passion for me. Even though our family life often suffered in my travails, they consistently helped me to keep going; and it is no exaggeration to say that while my name appears on the cover, this book is as much theirs as mine.

The users, pushers and victims of drugs—and the undercover law enforcement personnel who tracked the deadly cargo they prized—were also crucial to the project. They were the keys that unlocked the doors to the underground world of drug smuggling in Nova Scotia; without their stories to bring this book to life, its pages would offer only lists of facts and figures. The true identities of these individuals are not revealed here, and some circumstances have been altered to further protect them; and the narration of their accounts clarifies their need for anonymity— on either side of the law, the men and women involved in the narcotics trade would be in very serious danger indeed, were their real names to be revealed. To speak more specifically of those who have participated in the trade, or made use of its booty, these are people who, despite their fear of public persecution or criminal prosecution, nevertheless were brave enough to relate the horror and pain of their experiences. And it is their stories, not their names, which are important; they have made many sacrifices to enable the public to learn from their mistakes. For their personal safety, their identities must remain undisclosed.

If I have one wish for this book, it is that it will make a difference in someone's life; if these stories have a positive influence on even one person, then I will have accomplished my goal. The drug trade is a serious business, in Nova Scotia and throughout North America: crime, personal hardship, and even death are its consequences. This is an issue that demands and deserves society's immediate and unswerving attention, but if current trends are any indication, the situation will continue to deteriorate. A sad commentary, indeed.

VERNON L. OICKLE

The Big Picture

IT WAS AFTER 5:00 P.M. when Ray Martin got home to his three-bedroom bungalow in the quiet South Shore fishing village. Weeks had gone by since the thirty-seven-year-old father of three had first heard from the men whose offer of $25,000 in exchange for a couple of days of his trucking services changed his life forever. He was still unsure what he was going to tell his contact, Larry, when the call came that evening. His future hung in the balance: on the one hand, he could just say no to the trio of drug-smugglers, as he now knew them to be; or he could take the terrifying plunge into the netherworld of narcotics trafficking—and buy himself some precious time with his children.

As it was, Ray hardly ever saw the kids. Since he and Shirley had separated, shortly after the birth of their third child, he had spent just about every waking hour on the road in his rusty '83 Ford half-ton, trying to make ends meet and scrape together a little extra to support his family. It was never enough to keep Shirley satisfied, never enough to buy Jessica the sneakers all the other kids in school were wearing—and most of all, never enough to allow him to take the day off that would be necessary for a visit; Shirley had moved to another town, and now the telephone was his only link to his family.

The money Larry and his partners Tobias and Paul dangled before him would transform all that. But the price he would have to pay—Ray still didn't know for sure exactly what the men's cargo was, but he had found out enough, in their first, fateful meeting in the smoky tavern back in April, to know that it was drugs.

He was frightened. Not only because he might be caught, but also because he knew the deadly commodity would at some point end up in the hands of kids—children no older than his Jessica, who'd just turned eleven!

As he agonized over his dilemma, Ray could hear his friend Dan's words from earlier that afternoon: "If you get caught, you'll lose everything you've got." He had always appreciated Dan's honesty and insight,

1

but things weren't so simple this time. He was up against the wall as it was, and if he accepted the deal, he could take care of his immediate financial obligations and still have money left; in particular, to get the things his children wanted. That would make him feel good.

The phone rang around 6:30. Ray shot out of the living-room sofa where he had been sitting, brooding ever since he'd come home. "Hello! Who's this?" His manner was so abrupt, it was almost rude; the stress was getting to him, big time.

"Hey, bud. It's Dan. Just called to see how things are going. You seemed pretty much out of it this afternoon when you left the garage; like you were really mixed up or something. Are you all right?" Ray paused, trying to get his bearings. "Yeah, man! Everything's fine. Sorry about that. I didn't know it was you."

"That's okay, bud. What'cha do this afternoon after you left my place?" Ray shrugged: "Not much—drove around a bit, did some thinking. It's hard to figure things out. I almost wish this hadn't come along. It's real tempting."

"So what have you decided? Are you going to get involved with these guys?" Ray knew Dan was genuinely concerned; if he was contemplating some type of drug deal, Dan wanted to make sure he had thought it through—covered all the angles, considered all the consequences. "You really don't think these guys could be running anything else other than drugs, do you? What's the chance of that?"

Again Ray paused. He didn't want to offend Dan. "Not much chance of that. It can't be anything else. But, like I told you this afternoon, I ain't made up my mind. I don't know what to do. If I turn these guys down, I could be blowing a real good chance to get back on my feet. I can't ignore that. I can't just turn my back and walk away from a deal that would pay off my worries. I can't do that without thinking about it. What would you do if you were me?"

The silence lasted a long time. "Well, bud, I really don't know what to say. We've all got lots of money problems," he finally said. "If I was offered a chance like you, I'd be going through the same thing. Guess I can't really know what you're up against, but like I said this afternoon, you could get yourself in some really serious trouble messin' with these guys. We've been through a lot together. I'm worried about you. I don't want to see you go and do something stupid that you're going to regret for the rest of your life. Money's not everything."

Ray's response was quick. "Thanks, Dan. But you don't know what it's like to have this carrot just dangling there in front of you. My back's against the wall. It just ain't that easy to walk away from this kind of offer. I know there's risks. But, hell, everything has risks." Ray couldn't believe he'd just spoken the same words to his best friend that Paul, another of the smugglers, had used on him when they'd all finally met in the smoky bar the previous night.

"Maybe you should stall for time. Things might look different if you wait awhile," Dan suggested, only half-believing what he was saying. "I've been waiting one hell of a long time for things to get better. They ain't gonna look much better than they do right now," Ray argued—not mentioning that Paul, Larry, and their ringleader Tobias had only given him until tonight's call to finally decide. "I'm sinking over here. If I don't get some cash quick, I'm gonna lose the house—lose everything else I've worked for. It ain't much, but it's all I got. I got to hang onto it if I can. You would do that, Dan, if it was you. You can't tell me you'd pass up a chance to get yourself out of debt. It's tough living like this, wondering where the next cheque is coming from. I'm running out of hope—I'm running out of time. I've got to find some money real fast."

Again the two men fell silent. It was obvious they both knew what was right—not to go through with the deal—but neither could say it out loud. "Well, bud, guess I should let you get back to whatever you were doing," Dan said at last. "But hey, take it real careful. This could be big-league stuff. You 'n' me, we're little leaguers. If you need anything—need to talk or anything—give me a call. You know I'm always here, at the garage."

"Yeah, thanks, Dan. I appreciate that." The phone went dead, and for a few minutes Ray sat, holding the receiver, the dial tone in his ear as his mind raced over his options yet again. There were still no easy answers. It was nearly 7:00 when the ringing phone snapped Ray back to reality again. Reluctantly, he picked up the receiver; a woman's voice screeched in his ear. Great, Ray thought. Just what I need right now. "What do you want, Shirley?" he snapped.

"What makes you think I want something?" his ex-wife retorted sarcastically. "Because you don't call unless you do." Ray's voice was sharp. "Well, I don't this time. Jessica said you phoned last night. I was just returning your call." Ray could tell by her tone that she was annoyed by his brusque manner: "Sorry," he said, listlessly. "Didn't mean to snap. I've got a lot on my mind."

"Well, don't take it out on me if you've had a bad day," she said. If she only knew! And this conversation wasn't improving matters.... But rather than continue the verbal sparring, he asked about the kids.

3

"They're fine," Shirley replied. "Jessica's having some kind of trouble in school. She says the other kids don't like her. I don't know why; she's a great kid. I think it's because she's new in school, maybe. Brian's doing great, though, and the baby's fine ... we're all fine. You don't have to worry about us."

Ray knew the reason Jessica was unhappy—peer pressure was what it boiled down to—but he didn't bother telling Shirley; she didn't like him asking too many questions, even about the kids. "Well, I worry about them, you know," he said simply. "They're my kids too. I miss them."

Shirley hesitated, then let him have it: "You're the reason things are the way they are. It's not like I set out to plan it this way."

"Drop it, Shirley. All's I'm saying is that I miss the kids and wish I could see them more. I'm still supporting them, remember?" "How could I forget? I wondered when you'd start throwing that up. I can't talk to you any more, Ray, without you bringing money into it. You got to bring money into everything. That's all it is to you, isn't it? Money. I wonder if you'd care so much about these kids if you didn't have to help support them."

She'd meant to hurt him; Ray exploded with pain: "That's bullshit, and you know it! You ain't got no reason to say that. You always gotta turn it around to me. I'm the one who always gets the blame. It ain't all my fault. I wasn't the one who left. I wasn't the one who wanted excitement. I wasn't the one who got tired of living here as a family. You left me. You took my kids. I'm paying support for these kids because I want to, not because of you, remember that. And yes, I talk a lot about money because I ain't got much of it. Is that a crime? If it is, there's a hell of a lot of people in trouble these days." Predictably, Shirley began to cry. When they first met, Ray admired her emotionalism and considered it a sign that she was a caring person. Now he couldn't stand her crying whenever they argued; to him it was just a way to make him feel guilty—and there was a time when it had worked. But not now. He simply grimaced as she whimpered: "All we ever do is fight. Even on the phone, we end up fighting. I'm just not going to talk to you any more." With that, she slammed down the phone.

Bewildered, Ray hung up too, shaking his head and wondering what had just happened. The conversation made no sense. Then again, conversations with Shirley rarely did these days. But as he sat thinking, the irony of certain words Shirley had said began to dawn on him. She was right; he did think a lot about money—and with less than an hour to go before Larry's call, he still had to do a lot more thinking about it.

4

He was still wavering when the phone rang at 8:03. "Hello!" No-one seemed to be there. "Hello! Anyone there?"

This time, a voice with a French accent responded. It was Larry. "Ray? You in or out? We need an answer now. Are you in—or should we find somebody else with a truck?"

Although he had thought about nothing else for hours, Ray still didn't know how to answer. "What's the cargo? Where's it at, and where's it going?" It was a futile attempt to buy time, and Larry's response was predictable. "You know I can't tell you anything, Ray. As much as I'd like to, I can't. If you're in, I'm sure you'll know it all soon enough."

Ray desperately pressed on: "Is the cargo heavy? Maybe my truck can't handle it." But Larry was intractable. "Ray, we need an answer now. I gotta have it right now."

He could hardly believe his next words. "Well ... yeah, I'm in. What now?"

"Good," Larry sounded sincerely pleased. "You don't do anything. You just sit tight. We'll be in touch." Ray, dissatisfied, probed further: "When's that gonna be?" "It could be a couple of days. It could be a couple of weeks," Larry said. "Just be ready when we call you."

"Well, give me some notice, will you? And listen, what about the ten thousand up front?" "Soon," Larry assured him. "Remember, don't talk to anyone about this, or the deal's off." Angling for any scrap of information about his mysterious new associates, Ray asked: "Where *are* you guys, anyway? How can I reach you if something comes up?" Ray thought he could make out the background noises associated with long-distance connections, but that didn't tell him much. Nor did Larry. "Don't call us. We'll call you," he said. "You just be ready when we do." With that, the phone went dead.

Almost all night, Ray sat in the dark, thinking. Had he really said yes? The words had come out of nowhere, as if someone else had been talking.

Too late now to try figuring that one out. Intentionally or not, Ray Martin—with a simple "I'm in," had gone from a South Shore trucker struggling to pay the bills, to a pawn in the multibillion-dollar narcotics-smuggling game. He was joining a fraternity that has a long history in Nova Scotia.

Illegal importation has been a reality on the South Shore of the province since the late 1800s. The methods used by smugglers, and their primary motivation of greed, have changed very little over the years; only the cargo is different today—narcotics have supplanted alcohol.

Rum-running along the southern coast peaked during Prohibition, in the late 1920s and early 1930s, when public consumption of liquor was illegal in both Canada and the United States, and strict regulations governed production levels. During the thirteen years of U.S. Prohibition which ended in 1933, hundreds of vessels of all shapes and sizes moved up and down the Atlantic coastline, distributing the sought-after commodity to communities throughout North America, but especially along the American east coast—at least until 1930 when U.S. defence efforts against smugglers intensified.

At that point, ports in Nova Scotia and other Maritime provinces became prime off-loading areas for alcohol destined for distribution in large Canadian cities and in the United States. Liverpool was one of the most popular locations, and others included Halifax, St. John's, Newfoundland, Saint John, New Brunswick, and the island of St. Pierre. Smuggling became a major Maritime industry, creating sizable economic benefits for some provinces.

By 1941, rum-running was all but history—which would repeat itself in an altered, and even more lucrative form, starting about thirty years later. Once again, Nova Scotia was the focus, and in particular the picturesque South Shore. The smuggling of this new contraband—marijuana, hashish, cocaine, hallucinogens such as LSD, and other illicit substances—unfortunately shows every sign of flourishing much longer than its Prohibition forerunner. Today's drug trade is a multibillion-dollar industry employing thousands of Canadians, from small-time truck drivers like Ray Martin to kingpins, in often elaborate schemes to get narcotics from around the world into the eager hands of users on the streets of Toronto, Montreal, New York, Boston, and, yes, idyllic communities along Nova Scotia's lovely—and largely unprotected—coastline. Right back into the hamlets and villages where the contraband first landed, literally tonnes of cannabis products and cocaine are carried, some of it worth hundreds of millions of dollars in a single shipment packed into the hold of a huge cargo vessel.

But why Nova Scotia? Why has this province gained the dubious distinction of drug-smuggling capital of Canada? Statistics speak for themselves: proportionally based on population, more illegal narcotics have been seized in Nova Scotia than anywhere else in the country according to RCMP. Ironically, the enchantment and allure of the province's spectacular coast has been the very attraction for smugglers, generation upon generation, first with their kegs of black-market cognacs, whiskies, and wines; then in small, ill-formed collaborations of individuals seeking to make an easy buck off much-demanded cannabis products; finally by highly organized, dangerous international and national cartels, whose predilection for the more compact and infinitely more valuable contraband of cocaine has once again changed the cargo of the sea's black-market transport, but not its basic geographic processes.

Landing at any number of utterly deserted, well-protected coves and inlets dotting the South Shore, and, to a lesser but regular degree, the equally remote harbours of the North Shore and Cape Breton, those who come bearing their contraband by sea find waiting for them an equally deserted, remote series of access roads leading into the province's largely unpopulated coastal counties, and thence to major centres across Canada—Halifax, Montreal, Toronto, Vancouver—and large U.S. metropolitan areas such as New York, Boston, Chicago, and drug-hungry southern California.

Sergeant Bill Parker, a twenty-five-year veteran of the RCMP who was appointed the province's drug coordinator in September 1994, says smugglers appreciate the value of the province's coastline. "The province's geography really is a problem for the police in trying to deal with drug smugglers," he says. "You can go to any of these coves and look for miles without seeing a house or any sign of population. It's no wonder that smugglers look at Nova Scotia because they know we can't be everywhere. They can sneak into those areas, unload their goods, and be gone before we even know they were here. We've heard of this happening many times."

Lunenburg Police Chief, Brent Crowhurst, also twenty-five years with the RCMP before his new posting—nine of them in drug-law enforcement—agrees with this assessment. "All you have to do is look at the map and you'll see two reasons why Nova Scotia is so popular for smugglers. First, the South Shore of Nova Scotia is on a direct line from the northern coast of Colombia on the Atlantic Ocean. All these drug ships have to do is get out into the international shipping lanes and stay there until they get to their destination, which, in recent decades, has been Nova Scotia because of the enforcement practices of the Americans. The second reason the province is so popular is because of its vast, unprotected coastline." The coves and inlets are the big attraction, Crowhurst says, echoing Parker's notes. "Once they get their shipment in to the coast, they can practically drive their trucks down to the water and unload their shipment. Furthermore, they can work largely undetected by authorities because the coastline provides them with that protection. We're talking about several hundred miles of craggy coastline—what better place to run a drug operation?"

Indeed, in the 1960s and early 1970s, drug smugglers to North

America had an even easier route—from the North Atlantic coast of Colombia, a major source of both cannabis and cocaine, to virtually any community along the Eastern Seaboard of the United States. However, by 1977, the Americans were beginning to enforce zero-tolerance policies against illegal drug imports and unleashed a series of tough laws and regulations aimed at keeping narcotics smugglers out of the country. The Americans set up drug units and gave wider powers—and extensive resources—to their Coast Guard. American authorities were given the green light to enforce the strict new laws: the era of the multibillion-dollar war on drugs had begun in the United States.

For the traffickers, these moves created new challenges, to which they responded by seeking alternative routes, marking for Canada—especially Nova Scotia—the dawn of the drug-smuggling era. Although a number of earlier shipments signalled this change, authorities say it became completely clear by 1980 that Nova Scotia was the preferred entry point, when the first major shipments were intercepted. Smuggling operations, usually led by the Americans, sprang up across the province, most notably on the South Shore, from Yarmouth to Halifax. However, remote areas of the North Shore, such as Sheet Harbour, and the hills and inlets of Cape Breton, also provided a desirable setting for the illegal activity. Since the early 1970s, Cape Breton—like other areas of the province— has witnessed many seizures, as smugglers have doggedly sought out new areas offering protection and seclusion for their illicit enterprises.

But certain locations have proved to be perennial favourites, and two decades of police records reveal a pattern that points to Queens and Shelburne Counties as smugglers' preferred destinations. Two of Canada's largest record-breaking drug seizures took place here in these two counties. The marked prevalence of secluded coves on the southernmost tip of Nova Scotia and the vast expanse of unpopulated territory make these counties ideal targets for this type of activity. Since the 1970s, drug seizures in Queens and Shelburne Counties have represented the largest level of illicit substances seized in Nova Scotia.

It took a quarter of a century for the geographic patterns of drug-smuggling in Nova Scotia to fully emerge, and the illicit activity itself had been going on for several years before the public and authorities became aware of the activity spreading through their once-idyllic communities. Before the 1980s, few people were aware that narcotics were arriving in their towns and villages on huge ships and being whisked down back roads to their waiting customers. Local people just didn't talk about drugs in their small South Shore communities; they kept a close eye on what was going on around them, but that had more to do with neighbours watching out for neighbours than bothering themselves with any strangers who might be in town for a few days, or a week, and then gone. The police fought drug trafficking in their own communities, but the question of smuggling just didn't arise; no one—the authorities, the government, the community at large—was discussing the issue, or had any idea of its vast ramifications for the region, the province, and, indeed, the country.

This ignorance was an opportunity the smugglers embraced with considerable enthusiasm. By the 1970s, with drugs like marijuana and hashish starting to become available on the streets of towns like Liverpool and Shelburne, first through local pushers then via the criminal element, loose bands of smugglers, organized crime syndicates, and biker gangs all saw an increased opportunity—a growing marketplace as well as conduit system—to enhance their illegal transport of narcotics into and through Nova Scotia. The public, still largely ignorant of the major-league piracy taking place on their deserted, rugged shorelines—or in the skies above them, as some smugglers used aircraft to make drops of narcotics, especially cocaine, to waiting trucks on some of the province's many abandoned airfields—did start to become aware, at least, of the presence of drugs in their communities.

Gradually, recalls Bob Brogan, high sheriff of Queens and Lunenburg Counties and a retired RCMP officer, communities, not only on the South Shore but throughout Nova Scotia, and Canada, began to realize they had a serious problem on their hands. Authorities began to arrest, with increasing frequency, pushers who hailed from other provinces, or local dealers and truckers who, like Ray Martin, were being used as go-betweens. More alarming still, they observed that drug users were emerging from every age group, but particularly among teenagers and young adults; narcotics—particularly marijuana, at first—were even turning up in the local schools. Police began to crack down on drug use and peddling, but they could not contain—and still did not realize—the scope, or the true source, of the problems they were dealing with. Throughout the 1970s, and into the 1980s and 1990s, Nova Scotia gradually became the major pipeline through which dealers siphoned their drugs into the North American underground market, often planning their shipments—and transshipments by vehicle or aircraft—with meticulous detail in order to escape detection. Of the hundreds of cannabis shipments that have landed on Nova Scotia's shores, often attracting front-page headlines because of the sheer volume and staggering value of the narcotics confiscated, one of the most striking examples was the 1990 seizure in the tiny South Shore community of Ragged Harbour, Nova Scotia, in which thirty-five tonnes of hashish with an estimated street value of more than $400 million—a Canadian record that still stands—was confiscated, and a group of six conspirators from Indonesia and the Netherlands were eventually brought to justice.

In the early 1970s, before the Colombian and other international cartels and crime syndicates forced their way into the Nova Scotia conduit system, smugglers usually worked in small, independent groups, mostly importing cannabis products. Through the decade, and into the 1980s, larger, richer, more powerful, and more dangerous consortiums of drug importers got involved in the lucrative smuggling market, occasionally using some of the many remote airstrips throughout the interior of the province before loading up their trucks in the wee hours of the morning, but mostly arriving by sea with multi-tonne shipments of marijuana and hashish often worth tens, even hundreds of millions of dollars. Major source countries supplying Canada's thriving cannabis market—and its Maritime conduit system to the United States—include Colombia, Jamaica, Mexico, Afghanistan, Pakistan, Lebanon, and Thailand. With the growing popularity and relatively higher value of cocaine products, this '90s drug of choice began to turn up more and more on Nova Scotia shores. Much in demand, particularly on the mean streets of inner cities of the United States and Canada—including Halifax—those who provide the supply are only too happy to comply. Not only does cocaine yield a better return on investment, it is less bulky than cannabis, therefore easier to transport; fewer people are required in the operation, and unlike marijuana or hashish—which require a ship to hold the amounts of drugs that make a smuggling operation worthwhile to kingpins and their henchmen—cocaine can be transported in small vessels or planes. And because of its density, the drug's offloading process takes less time, inviting less chance of being caught.

And as the decade continues, heroin, hallucinogens such as LSD, illegally obtained prescription drugs, the deadlier form of cocaine known as crack, and an even more dangerous methamphetamine called Ice, continue to turn up along the Nova Scotia coastline and in remote airfields and on the streets and in the schools of communities across the country. Yarmouth, Nova Scotia, for example: on May 31, 1996, RCMP officers in that coastal community completed a year-long undercover investigation, arresting and charging thirty-four people. Ninety drug-related charges were laid following the early-morning raid that involved

10

almost forty police officers from Yarmouth, Shelburne, and Digby Counties. RCMP seized $35,000 in drugs, three vehicles, and several thousand dollars in cash. The confiscated drugs included morphine, Demerol, mescaline, marijuana, and hashish.

Other disturbing new trends in the illegal marketplace include the growing presence of West African couriers using Canada as a conduit for heroin bound for the United States. This activity was first reported in 1991, says J.J. Coutu, RCMP director of drug enforcement.

During 1993, Canadian authorities seized 153.94 kilograms of heroin, a 30 per cent increase over 1992, according to the RCMP's 1994 National Drug Intelligence Estimate. Throughout the year, the world's traditional poppy-growing regions in Myanmar and Afghanistan continued to produce an abundance of opium; the bumper crops of heroin resulted in record single seizures made in Vancouver and Toronto, and the purity levels of the drug remained very high. As a result, RCMP say the number of heroin-related deaths continued to rise over the same period. "As well, the use of crack cocaine has spread outside the main centres of Montreal and Toronto," he says. And this includes Nova Scotia, from larger centres such as Halifax and Sydney, Cape Breton, to coastal communities such as Yarmouth and Lunenburg.

Meanwhile, Maritime cannabis smuggling operations continue to expand exponentially, despite the headline-making seizures. For example, of all the hashish confiscated in Canada in 1995, 90 per cent of it originated with these schemes.

"Traffickers are continually developing new smuggling routes and methods in an attempt to avoid law enforcement detection and reap sizable profits," says Coutu. "Drug trafficking organizations are better structured and better financed than ever before, and are flexible and mobile in their methods of operation."

Since 1981, says Coutu, the illicit drug trade in Canada has undergone such expansion that today it is a serious global problem: money-laundering (disguising the proceeds of criminal activity through legitimate avenues, usually international banking systems); illegal drug routes that crisscross the world; and drug production centres ranging from South America to the Middle East—all proof that no country is immune. And Canada is definitely vulnerable—increasingly so. For example, federal authorities' alarm about the escalation of the cocaine problem is underlined by political and legislative trends in source countries, and the participation of new countries. Tougher laws in Colombia, says Coutu, have contributed to the decentralization of the cocaine trade.

The weakening of the Medellin cartel in the early 1990s, for example, has prompted other South American organizations in such countries as Brazil and Venezuela, as well as Italy and the Asian nations, to take advantage of opportunities to produce and traffic cocaine, which is expected to further increase the amount of cocaine on the Canadian market in the future. More recently, the number of seizures in South Africa recorded by 1996 indicated to police that this country, too, is taking on the role of global shipper of narcotic contraband—heroin, cannabis, and cocaine—to Europe and North America, following a route through poorly watched African ports and airfields that puts the smugglers at less risk of detection than direct shipments from Colombia or Thailand. In 1995, 136 known drug syndicates were operating in South Africa, half of them internationally.

The unprecedented seizures of cocaine in the early 1990s—culminating in the record 1994 confiscation of $1 billion worth of the drug off Shelburne, Nova Scotia—suggest to police that cocaine smuggling into Canada has been restructured again and again, increasing the difficulty of breaking the rings. From using couriers to import a few kilograms of coke, illegal importers have moved to shipments of hundreds of kilograms, hidden in legitimate commercial imports, as they were in the Shelburne seizure—cocaine tucked into a load of steel aboard a ship. As well as the ever-shifting politics of the Colombian drug cartel dynamic, police also face domestic organizations in Montreal and Toronto, Jamaican trafficking groups known as "posses," many of which have links with Colombian groups and other Jamaican organizations in the United States. As well, groups within the Chilean, Italian, Eastern European, Chinese, and Vietnamese communities, and outlaw motorcycle gangs are also involved in the cocaine trade. In British Columbia, Chinese street gangs have developed cocaine distribution networks, as have East Indian groups and members of the Russian community. Internationally, the RCMP has found that Ecuadorian cartels may also be targeting Canada with large shipments of cocaine, and that cocaine processing is apparently taking place in Peru and Bolivia, where the bulk of the region's coca leaf is cultivated—more competition for the Colombians, more likelihood that the trans-border trafficking between Canada and the United States, which police have observed for years, will continue to thrive.

Based upon RCMP projections, the future of the drug trade in Canada looks strong. Bumper crops in many source countries have ensured an abundance of heroin, cocaine, and cannabis well into the future. As well, domestic supply networks are making their presence felt in the drug trade; developments in hydroponics technology are making the climate less of an issue for marijuana cultivation in Canada, which now supplies an estimated 20 per cent of the marijuana market in this country — another twist in the already complicated problem of the Canadian illegal drug market. Yet another dimension to the issue, created by the new participation of hitherto uninvolved source countries, has been Canada's emerging role not only as a continental conduit of illegal narcotics, but an international one as well.

While Canada is a known pipeline through which the drugs flow into the United States, authorities are also discovering that international trafficking organizations may be using the country as a transit point to smuggle multi-tonne cannabis shipments from source countries into Europe. Federal statistics show that Canadian-related cocaine seizures in foreign jurisdictions increased 64 per cent between 1989 and 1990, and show every sign of continuing on the upsurge.

In 1993, cannabis derivatives, in particular marijuana and hashish, remained the mainly used illicit drug across Canada, whether originating domestically or arriving from overseas — mostly the Caribbean, Mexico, Asia, and the Pakistan-Afghanistan region. And over the past few years, small communities all over Canada, like those in Nova Scotia, continue to battle an escalating drug problem — once again, despite the spectacular seizures. Case in point: A twenty-six-year-old Lunenburg man was sentenced to five months in jail March 26, 1996, for possession of marijuana for the purposes of trafficking; his home had been searched in May 1995, after police received a tip that he was selling drugs. The man had been buying hash and marijuana obtained in Bridgewater and selling in Lunenburg for about two years.

He said he was supplying two to ten people per day and making a profit between $400 and $500 per month. On March 1, 1996, two men in Sydney, Cape Breton, were charged on counts of possession for the purposes of trafficking after police found 52 kg of hashish and 2 kg of marijuana stashed behind the back seat of a vehicle. Total value: more than $1 million.

The chemical drug trade has also developed into a multibillion-dollar industry in Canada. Chemical drug traffickers have become increasingly active in the 1990s, with more seizures reported by the RCMP in 1991 and 1992 than in previous years; in June 1992, a particularly well-trafficked drug group, anabolic steroids, was reclassified to controlled drug status in order to curb its trafficking. Other widely abused substances on the black market include LSD — the most prevalent hallucinogen — along with illegally produced narcotics such as ersatz methaqualone manufactured from bulk Diazepam (commonly known as Valium). Courier services and the post office, along with sea and air transport, are increasingly used to import certain drugs into Canada—LSD and anabolic steroids, for example. Police investigations show that distributors, including outlaw motorcycle gangs, are expanding their activities in the chemical trade from production and distribution of methamphetamines, PCP, and LSD, to obtaining and trafficking anabolic steroids.

Despite the range and prevalence of drugs being smuggled into Canada, authorities have had some success battling the problem over the years: sensational, multimillion-dollar seizures such as the ones in Ragged Harbour and Shelburne. Provincial drug coordinator Parker indicates police are intercepting more of the contraband and arresting the latter-day pirates—even though, during the 1980s, only 5 per cent of Canadian drug enforcement resources were being put into Nova Scotia operations. "We are getting some," he says; however, "statistics indicate that the drug smugglers have more success getting into the province than we have catching them. That's the way police work goes; you win some, you lose some."

Indeed, the figures on seizures of illegal drugs show why Parker's determined but philosophical attitude is appropriate: RCMP estimate that of every ten shipments that hit the province's coastline, police make a seizure in only one of those cases. This is a ratio authorities are using all their power to alter. But it is a difficult fight. Dealers are protected by syndicates operating openly under the mask of legitimate investment— also known as money laundering. The drug trade is the largest component of Canada's underground market, and the drug traders pull all the strings.

Illicit drugs are worth an estimated $8 billion to $10 billion in Canada. After twenty years of development and diversity in the drug trade, users can now get whatever they want, wherever they live—whether Liverpool and Bridgewater or Vancouver and Toronto.

"The drug trade is a major industry, and many people are getting rich off it," says retired RCMP staff sergeant Peter Williamson, a veteran narcotics officer. "This thing's way out of control because there's so much money in it. If you had a million dollars to invest, you could put it in the drug trade and multiply it a hundred times. That's why people do it— because they're greedy."

Aside from the direct profits generated by selling smaller and smaller amounts of drugs at higher and higher base prices by the time they reach the street, powerful drug lords also pump their illegal booty back into the mainstream economy through ever-sophisticated methods: bank accounts established in foreign tax havens; investment in Canadian and American banking and financial-institution systems; import and export contracts involving legitimate goods.

Even real estate acquisitions are involved. Since the early 1980s, for example, real estate agents in seaside communities say a great deal of Nova Scotia's seafront has been purchased as residential property or as investments; the sale of coastal real estate has become a multibillion dollar industry, and at least some of this speculative activity is related to elaborate schemes by smugglers to infiltrate a community by allaying residents' concerns that they are anything but honest, would-be home-owners establishing themselves on Nova Scotia's idyllic coast. No one knows exactly how much money is generated by such laundering proce-dures of drug money, but RCMP-case-generated information suggests as much as $10 billion dollars of illicit funds per year are redirected in various ways in Canada each year.

The National Drug Intelligence Estimate classifies money laundering operations into three categories—proceeds of drug trafficking in Canada that are laundered within the country; proceeds redirected, as profit, by parent organizations located in source countries; and proceeds generated abroad and moved into Canada for laundering and investment.

Under the RCMP Anti-Drug Profiteering Program, begun in 1981, seizures and referrals to other agencies in 1991 amounted to $15.2 million in cash and other assets. That year, $51 million was seized, emphasizing the extent of this underground economy. By 1992, RCMP estimate that $200 million in cash and assets had been confiscated or referred to other agencies. To support the investigation and prosecution of money-laundering cases, an act under the Proceeds of Crime legislation dealing directly with money laundering by governing financial transaction-record-keeping was enacted in 1991, and three policing units governing anti-drug profi-teering were set up a year later in Toronto, Montreal, and Vancouver, under Canada's Drug Strategy. The origins of these ever-toughening laws dealing with profiteering from illegal drug money were the Proceeds of Crime legislation itself, passed in 1989 in order to separate offences dealing with the possession and laundering of proceeds of drug crimes from other charges under the Narcotics Control Act and the Food and Drugs Act.

The Proceeds of Crime legislation has somewhat improved the ability of law enforcement agencies to hit drug traffickers where it hurts them most—in their wallets. The billions of dollars of drug profits are not only integrated into the Canadian economy through money-laundering operations; they are also used by drug dealers to invent increasingly sophisticated methods of importing and distributing drugs.

Besides the domestic efforts to combat money laundering, Canada continued bilateral negotiations throughout the 1990s on Mutual Legal Assistance Treaties with Austria, Brazil, Germany, Japan, Korea, Portugal, Switzerland, Venezuela, France, Australia, the Bahamas, Mexico, the United Kingdom, Hong Kong, and the Netherlands. The multilateral initiatives undertaken by the international community since the 1980s culminated in 1991 with the establishment of the Financial Action Task Force, convened by the 1989 G-7 Economic Summit as a freestanding organization chartered by its members to evaluate the progress made by member countries, facilitate cooperation between agencies, and evaluate new proposals.

Despite its ongoing efforts, however, Canada has been under pressure from the United States to tighten its money-laundering laws, in particular because the Canadian regulations require only recording of profiteering, not reporting to authorities. Canadian officials, too, want tougher regulations. To dismantle big crime organizations it is necessary to undermine their infrastructure and empty their wallets completely. Since the late 1980s, authorities have mounted major campaigns on other fronts to fight this nationwide plague. Canada's National Drug Strategy, which, along with anti-profiteering measures, also funds police forces and other community-based organizations in their battle against drugs, was established in 1987. Along with programs initiated by Health and Welfare Canada, it has done much to heighten Canadians' awareness of the dangers of illicit drugs. Indeed, about 70 per cent of the strategy's fund of more than $200 million is devoted to education, treatment, and rehabilitation, a slow process exacerbated by the constantly evolving complexities of the drug trade. While education is an important strategy in the drug war, so is policing; the remaining 30 per cent of the drug fund is dedicated to law enforcement.

In Nova Scotia, too, authorities—especially on the South Shore—have waged an ongoing war against the pushers and dealers. Since the early 1990s, police have targeted the people who bring the drugs into the community and make them available to young people. In a sense, the authorities—not just in Nova Scotia, but across the country—got a slow start in the war on drug smugglers. In the 1970s, recalls retired RCMP officer Gary Grant, "No one was talking about a drug war, and no one was talking about drug smuggling. We just were not aware of what was happening along the coast, and you can't enforce something that hasn't been recognized as a problem." Communities such as Liverpool were just beginning to accept that they had a drug problem at all, Grant explains. "Drugs were still new to everyone in those days. It was our job to go in to the communities and clean them up. We didn't really stop to think about the source or where these drugs were coming from."

It is impossible even to guess how many drugs passed through the province before authorities began noticing how they were being imported, but, says Grant, "We're talking about massive amounts. Even today, we still don't have any idea how much is getting through. We do know, though, that the seizures we do make are only a small portion of the total picture. In the 1970s, Nova Scotia was like a sieve for drugs—we'd suck it in and pass it through without any resistance."

By the mid-1970s, however, after a number of cannabis seizures from ships, and faced with a growing drug-use problem among young people— who often purchased marijuana and hashish on the streets of towns like Liverpool and Shelburne, police responded strongly, with a no-nonsense, zero-tolerance approach to the drug trade.

"We believed that if you wanted to get rid of a tough problem, then you had to get tough," recalls High Sheriff Brogan. "And we did." The growing drug trend resulted in a rise in the local crime rate, so RCMP mounted a full-scale war on drug users and pushers. Officers in the Liverpool detachment were instructed to lay as many charges as they could and to get the dealers on as many offences as possible.

"We didn't accept any explanations or excuses; if you had drugs and you got caught, then you were going down," Brogan says. "We had no other choice, because people were getting frightened by what was happening in their own community. You have to remember, this was happening at a time when drugs were just arriving in this part of the world, so people were not used to hearing about this problem in their community."

But local crackdowns weren't enough to stem the tide of smugglers arriving in little coves all along the South Shore, and police realized further action was necessary—especially as the U.S. war on drugs swung into full action in the late 1970s and under the administration of then U.S. President Ronald Reagan in 1980. Smugglers simply saw Nova Scotia as a safer route to bring contraband into North America. "We couldn't watch all the shoreline and do our job in other areas," Grant says. "It just wasn't realistic back then, just like it isn't realistic today to ask police to watch the entire coastline of Nova Scotia. It's just not possible."

It was then, Grant explains, that the idea surfaced of getting the public involved in watching the coastline for unusual activity during a series of discussions at the Liverpool detachment. "We came up with the idea of having members of the community be the eyes and ears for us." This was early 1970s and once the idea was suggested, RCMP officers merely began talking with local residents and stressing the need for their involvement. "Basically, we told people that in order for us to do our job, we needed their help. We needed them to tell us when they saw something that just didn't seem right. And we told them that we needed them to be willing to share their information with us without being fearful of us. It took some time, but eventually we began seeing people coming forward to talk to us."

"That was the beginning of the Coastal Watch Program, which has evolved into what we have today—an effective tool in which the public can become involved in the fight against drugs."

Grant emphatically supports the Coastal Watch concept because he says without the public's involvement, it would be impossible for the police to do their job. "The drug trade is just too massive and there are huge, gaping holes in our coastline that the police cannot cover. Coastal Watch is a very low-cost, but effective way to counteract the drug trade. From the public's point of view, it allows them to take an active role in protecting their community by doing something positive to fight crime. Coastal Watch is a valuable tool for the police. The thing about the program is that over the years it has been proven that it works." The record-breaking hashish seizure in Queens County in May 1990 resulted from a Coastal Watch tip.

Programs like Coastal Watch; the development of extensive cooperative undercover investigation between local police, the RCMP, and members of the public; and new, tougher initiatives introduced over the years through Canada's Drug Strategy have helped authorities vastly improve their efforts in stopping the contraband before it hits the shores of Nova Scotia. More recently, a controversial piece of proposed new legislation, federal Bill C-7, has been introduced to provide the Canadian enforcement and justice system with a wide new set of measures to control and suppress the unlawful import, export, production, or distribution of controlled substances. The law addresses the seizure of any property intended to be used in committing these offences.

The legislation would consolidate Canada's drug policy to fulfill its international obligations under the Single Convention on Narcotic Drugs, the Convention on Psychotropic Substances, and the relevant portions of the United Nations Convention against Illicit Traffic of Narcotic Drugs and Psychotropic Substances, repealing the former Narcotic Control Act and parts of the Food and Drugs Act.

Bill C-7 also provides a framework for the control of import, production, export, distribution, and use of substances that can alter mental processes and that may produce harm to personal health and social stability when distributed or used without supervision. As well, it establishes mechanisms to ensure that the export, import, production, distribution, and use of internationally regulated substances are confined to medical, scientific, and industrial purposes.

Canadian authorities are keenly aware that their neighbours to the south take an even tougher, no-holds-barred attitude to international drug smuggling—an attitude that has persisted since the inception of the American's war on drugs in the 1970s. "They go about things in a different way, putting more people into their efforts and more money behind them," say the RCMP's Gary Grant. "They have a high level of intensity and a visible commitment to stop drugs from entering their country. Anyone who breaks that security can expect to pay big time if they get caught." He points to a 1980 example of a successful interception of $50 million worth of marijuana aboard a ship, the *Patricia*, that had been headed up the U.S. Eastern Seaboard with a planned destination of, most likely, Boston. But U.S. Drug Enforcement Agency officials kept close to the suspicious vessel, whose crew, aware of the tough American penalties for smuggling, decided to put in towards the Nova Scotia coast, off Shelburne. There, working together—twenty RCMP officers on instructions from their American counterparts—the U.S. and Canadian officers successfully nabbed the American captain, and the all-Colombian crew, who were later deported. The captain was successfully prosecuted in the United States. Canada could not prosecute as the vessel was intercepted in international waters.

To Grant, the case demonstrates how tough American laws against smugglers force more and more of them into Canadian—specifically, Nova Scotian—waters. "Back in the early 1980s, when Canada was just waking up to the drug trade, the Americans were already into the war big time. They were very professional and serious in their efforts to get these guys before they could get that junk into their country, and that's the way they continue to operate today." However, Grant points out, while the resources in the two countries vary greatly, the officers are alike in many ways. "Our guys may not have as much money or as many fancy weapons at their disposal as the Americans, but they're all professionals and hard workers; they're dedicated to their jobs, and they believe in what they're doing or they wouldn't be doing it. They wouldn't be putting their lives on the line if they didn't want to make a positive impact."

Former RCMP Commissioner Norman Inkster, in referring to the major drug seizures in Nova Scotia, says the proportions of the situation can seem overwhelming to the public. "However, to most of us, the drug problem has become hauntingly familiar. The language of illicit drugs is common currency, where trafficking, money laundering, IV use, and crack are the words that shape today's headlines."

Today, says Brogan, the public too is becoming disturbingly blasé about illegal narcotics. "Even though people still want the drugs cleaned up, they seem to tolerate it more; almost like we've just kind of accepted the inevitable. They don't seem to get all that alarmed if you arrest someone for possession of drugs. It wasn't that way in the '70s, I can tell you. When you arrested someone back then for doing drugs, it was big news. Now, we're lucky if we make the news at all."

Yet the drug trade in Nova Scotia is serious business—more than ever. RCMP staff sergeant Peter Williamson agrees that the public may be getting complacent about the issue, and wonders whether, as Inkster points out, their indifference might be due to the prevalence of drugs. "It's almost like drug dealing is the accepted form of bootlegging today. What was unacceptable ten years ago almost goes overlooked today."

From a law enforcer's point of view on the smuggling problem—the drug problem in general—the greatest challenge today is public aware-ness and involvement. "Realistically, we can't do any more to police this province than we already do. We need the public to stand up and say 'Enough is enough,' when it comes to drugs. The police are doing as much as we can right now. It would be nice to have more resources, but I have no doubt that we're getting the most out of what we have right now."

If the public is impressed by major seizures, like those in Ragged Harbour and Shelburne, then, Williamson says, they can express their gratitude by doing their part. "Through efforts like the Coastal Watch Program, people can make a difference."

But does the public get involved? Sometimes yes, often no. One Shelburne County man, speaking anonymously because he fears his safety in the often-volatile and sometimes violent drug world, says that over the past decade he has witnessed most of the seizures in the local area—and his attitude is that it is best to keep silent about such activities. "You hear so much stuff about the drugs and the killings and all, so I just as

soon not give my name," he says. "But that don't mean I haven't got anything to say. Drugs are big in this part of the country—I guess you might
say it's becoming kind of famous as the drug capital of Canada—and I'm
never surprised when I hear of another bust or something going down.
It's not really something to be proud of, I don't suppose, but it does show
how serious the problem is around here. But what really surprises me is
that these guys [the smugglers] keep coming back for more. You'd think
that after awhile they'd get the message, wouldn't you?"

As a fisherman who has spent much of his life on the open seas, the
forty-seven-year-old man says that he has seen many strange activities
in and around the coastline of Nova Scotia over the years. "But we all
just keep our mouths shut. After awhile, you learn to look the other
way." One time, he recalls, he and another man helping him on his boat
watched for hours as the crews of two boats, tethered together, passed
"bundles of stuff" from one vessel to the other. "I can't really say for sure
if they were drugs, but what the hell would they be? You ain't going to
stop way out there in the middle of the Atlantic Ocean for a social call. I
never saw either of those boats before that day, and I never saw them
again afterward; don't know where they came from, and I don't know
where they went. And we never found out for sure what the bundles
were, so we're only guessing." And he prefers not to speculate further—a
common attitude in the area, he says. "I don't think you'd get too many
people to talk about what they've seen out there, but we're only thinking
about what's best for us and our families. You don't really want these
guys doing this sort of dangerous stuff, but there's not a whole hell of a
lot you can do about it, so you just may as well accept it. I guess that's
what people around here have done."

He continues: "From my own perspective, I am concerned that this
stuff happens here. I have three kids, and it scares me that these drugs
are coming into our community. If that stuff is coming in here, I can't
help but think about the kind of people who are coming here with it. It
does bother me, but after awhile you just kind of grow used to it; you
may not like it, but there isn't much you can do about it."

It is precisely this kind of indifference that enforcement and health
authorities are trying to change. The public must face facts: drugs seized
in remote parts of Canada, such as rural Nova Scotia, are destined for
Upper Canada and the United States—but some of them return to the
rural communities through which they entered the country. It is for that
reason that junior-high-school students in towns such as Liverpool are
arrested for selling drugs to younger children. It is the reason petty

thieves break into their neighbours' homes searching for money to pay for their habit.

In April 1994, an eighteen-year-old Lunenburg County man was video-taped by police, selling hashish at a local high school. Police watched as the suspect met a second man; they split up a 10 gram piece of hashish, and the first man was seen going from group to group and car to car out-side the school, selling the drug for $20 per gram. In December, he was sentenced to three months in jail and two years' probation; his defence—he was a drug addict who had turned to selling narcotics to support his habit.

Canada's escalating crime rate is a direct result of the drug trade, say the RCMP. Drug-related arrests are rising at a critical rate, reflecting a growing problem and signalling that the war on drugs is being lost, despite the millions of dollars, thousands of hours, and hundreds of arrests that have gone into combating the problem.

Illegal drugs affect every age and social group in the country. Drug-related charges were once associated with young people—between eighteen and twenty-five—and with certain racial or social groups; but such patterns no longer apply. The problem knows no age, social, gender, educational, or racial barriers. However, statistics show a particularly dramatic increase in the number of younger users, creating especially challenging situations for police in contemplating arrests of school-aged children for pushing drugs. As well, there have been marked increases in the use of hard drugs such as cocaine, heroin, and hallucinogens—the demand reflected in the ever-growing supply, often arriving in the coun-try via the Nova Scotia coastline.

Canada's former solicitor general, Doug Lewis, says that behind the statistics of drug abuse lurks a frightening story of human misery that affects every segment of society. Sexual abuse, family violence, robbery, murder—all too often drugs, or abuse of drugs, are factors in these crimes.

Besides these effects, however, there is the staggering cost of dealing with the social consequences of drug abuse. Reduced productivity in the workplace, increased absenteeism in the work force, higher insurance costs, and higher health care expenses are all by-products of the drug culture. "And perhaps," says Inkster, "the most tragic costs of all are the thousands of people, particularly our young people, who fall prey to drugs. Their loss is our loss, for the future well-being of the nation depends upon the health and welfare of the people who comprise it."

Current research suggests that the use of hard drugs has increased among adolescents in Canada and the U.S. in the 1990s. These young people seem disturbingly nonchalant about the physical and emotional hazards of the substances they're using. Marijuana and other soft drugs have not regained the popularity they enjoyed in the late 1970s and 1980s; however, the cannabis that is being used is as much as ten times more potent than what was available to teenagers a generation ago. Research also shows that fewer young people worry about the risks of trying crack or other forms of cocaine, while use of LSD is quickly approaching the user levels of the 1970s. Locally, police are particularly concerned about the types of drugs appearing in Nova Scotia. In the past, the drugs of choice were marijuana and hashish, but the presence of hard drugs along the South Shore—especially cocaine—is particularly alarming, because of these narcotics' addictive qualities. Research into drug abuse in Canada, according to Health and Welfare Canada, is still in its infancy; however, it is clear that the problem directly affects a significant number of Canadians.

On May 25, 1987, the federal government formally launched the component of the National Drug Strategy known as Action on Drug Abuse, a program, still in existence, aimed at providing individuals, families, and communities with information and treatment to combat abuse of alcohol and other drugs.

Despite its slight decline, figures show that the illicit drug most frequently used by young people is cannabis—marijuana or hashish; one Gallup poll revealed that 44 per cent of Canadians aged 12 to 29 had used cannabis. Indeed, cannabis is the most-used illicit drug in Canada: 23.2 per cent of Canadians have used the drug at some time in their lives. It has also been found that young people's involvement with illicit drugs increases with school level, and that young men are more likely to use illicit drugs than young women. For example, the use of stimulants is highest among males in the 15 to 24 age group. Surveys also reveal that young users of illicit drugs, whose numbers far exceed parallel usage rates among young adults, are also most likely to use tobacco and alcohol. As well, frequency and quantity of alcohol consumed directly affects the use of marijuana and tobacco. Cannabis and cocaine are the drugs of choice in the 15 to 24 age group, while their cocaine use is double that of the general population. By comparison, cocaine or crack cocaine have been used by 3.5 per cent of adult Canadians, while 4.1 per cent of adult Canadians have used LSD, speed, or heroin.

In November 1995, Health Canada released the results of Canada's Alcohol and Other Drugs survey, which paints a grim picture of the drug trade going into the future. Since 1989, the use of LSD, speed, and heroin has risen 0.7 per cent. More than a quarter-million Canadians (1.1 per cent) are users of LSD, speed, and heroin, an increase from 0.4 per cent in 1989. Current use is reported at 7.4 per cent as of 1994, compared with 6.5 per cent in 1989. Lifetime use remains almost the same as in 1989— 23.1 per cent in 1994, compared with 23.2 per cent in 1989.

Herb Gray, Canada's Solicitor General, said in the RCMP's 1994 National Drug Intelligence Estimate, that legislation and enforcement are only part of the solution; prevention, too, is an essential component. The social issues contributing to drug abuse "cannot be addressed by the police alone. [The situation] calls for a concerted effort by all of us— teachers, parents, politicians, social workers, health-care specialists; in fact, all concerned members of society."

Prevention and partnership are key elements in the federal government's efforts to curb not only drug abuse and drug trafficking, but also criminal behaviour in general, he explained. He also noted that these twin ideas form the foundation of The National Crime Prevention Council, founded by the government in July 1994, as an answer to the crying need for action, and attempt to unify crime-prevention efforts across the country. "It will bring together individuals with a variety of professional and cultural backgrounds, creating a national network of knowledge and experience ... for dealing with both the underlying causes that contribute to drug abuse, and the criminals who run the illegal drug trade."

In 1987, the RCMP launched its nation-wide Drug Awareness Program, which employs twenty-four coordinators across the country. The program has already seen the development of delivery strategies for all RCMP officers and a renewal of the force's commitment to community policing.

In 1994, in response to Nova Scotia's growing drug problem, the Nova Scotia Department of Health's Blueprint Committee recommended that communities be given greater authority to identify and fund addiction services on the local level. "The community development model has shown us the kind of benefit that can be realized when we involve the family, the community, and volunteers in planning and delivering services," said committee chairman David MacLean. Among the committee's recommendations: core funding for addiction treatment services and a consistent level of treatment for addicts in all regions of Nova Scotia; money to facilitate community health board planning of addiction services and prevention programs; a greater emphasis on prevention, promotion, and education; and development of standardized methods of evaluating services provided. "Aggressively promoting good health and openly talking, especially to our young people, about the dangers of addictive substances and activities will help reduce the number of people who become addicted. This means providing teachers, police officers, support groups, and volunteers with the support they need to develop effective programs at the community level." The committee also recommended the government examine policies on the availability and marketing of addictive substances to ensure they reflect Nova Scotia's health goals. "There is a need for measures to be taken in areas such as advertising, taxation, access to addictive substances enforcement, and legislation, so that the health of the community is both protected and promoted," MacLean says.

The issue of addictive substances, such as alcohol and tobacco, that retain their legality while garnering an increased level of criticism from health-care workers, the government, educators, and the public, also invites discussion of yet another thorny issue in the complex situation of narcotics usage. This question is the legalization of illicit drugs—particularly cannabis—or at very least its decriminalization. Dr. Neil Boyd of the School of Criminology at Simon Fraser University in Burnaby, British Columbia, one of Canada's strongest proponents of legalization, points out an inherent hypocrisy in Canada's drug laws: more than fifty thousand North Americans die each year as the result of alcohol and tobacco consumption, yet these products are legally sold. "The criminalization of drugs may be the blame for more deaths, but the use of drugs themselves is not as big a threat as people are led to believe by police and politicians. Authorities and lawmakers are trying to scare the public with their talk about the so-called war on drugs, but I think that it is the laws themselves which must be fought."

Indeed, it is the very illegality of drugs, Boyd says, that results in high crime rates. "Because of the laws which prohibit the sale of drugs and make them hard to get, you have people selling their bodies and committing thefts as well as other violent crimes so they can get money to buy drugs. If these laws did not exist, then these types of activities would not be necessary. So instead of having all these other crimes, all you would have would be the sale of the drugs themselves, which could be regulated. I don't think you can leave it wide open, but drugs could be sold under a controlled method, like tobacco and alcohol. It's no more harmful to smoke a joint than it is to drink a glass of wine or smoke a cigarette."

Scare tactics is how Boyd describes current drug laws, which, he says, are outdated. "The current approach is not working. I believe the only way to change the situation is through the decriminalization of all drugs in Canada. The decreasing use of tobacco has shown that legalized but controlled selling can be a positive response to the problem."

Other supporters of legislation, a movement that has been promoted in Canada for almost thirty years—without success—question lawmakers' motives of health concerns as the impetus towards tougher laws. According to the Institution of Canadian Health Promotion, public aims have always been secondary to the primary objective of establishing new methods of social control. "The obscuring of penal law priorities with respect to drugs persists to the present. Public fear predominates because of a massive misinformation campaign, maintained by a number of groups invested in continuing this 'war on drugs.' The public accepts proactive drug-detection programs and drug testing in the workplace, without ever demonstrating any serious resistance. It accepts police as major actors in school drug programs—parents, educators, and other interveners cannot or dare not oppose these strategies, which are largely based on social control and not on health promotion."

Law enforcement personnel disagree with Boyd and other advocates of decriminalization; improving access to drugs would only perpetuate the problem. As well, they point out, the public can learn from the mistakes made about alcohol and tobacco; it has taken many years for people to finally get the message about the dangers of these drugs. So why not take a more hard-hitting, all-encompassing approach with other drugs? They also point out that even if some drugs were legalized, a black market would continue to thrive for other illegal substances.

Retired RCMP officer Gary Grant and Sergeant Bill Parker, Nova Scotia's RCMP Drug Coordinator, emphasize the need for public education. "I really believe the only way we're going to see a change is by continuing to drive home the point that drugs are harmful and that they kill," says Grant. It's a tough process—there's no question about that—but legalizing drugs is certainly not the answer. That'd be like giving someone a gun and declaring open season on anything that moves." Adds Parker: "We know that some people think we are losing this battle, but just because we have not yet won the war does not mean that we should give up the fight. We are making inroads in the drug trade because of the pressures that have been applied over the years; now is not the time to quit."

Staff Sergeant Peter Williamson, who retired from active RCMP duty in the spring of 1995, advocates maintaining tough laws against pushers. "If anything, instead of legalizing the sale of drugs, we should be getting even tougher. If we had the money and manpower, I'd say we should throw even more resources behind the effort, but since we don't, I guess we'll have to make do with what we have. But certainly, this is the time

26

to keep up the pressure; to let these drug dealers know that we aren't going to be pushovers in this province. If we back off now, we could unleash a problem that could be just too big to handle."

Already, across the province and the country, thousands of people of every age, background and socio-economic status are struggling—often tragically without success—against addictions to the myriad illicit substances reaching Canada from around the world. It seems more pressing to provide them with the help they need—and to prevent countless others from travelling down the same path—than to spend tax dollars on legislative bickering over legislation, decriminalization, and the various forms such new laws could take. The story of a fifty-four-year-old alcoholic and drug addict named Arthur is a heartbreaking case in point.

A chain smoker and a functional illiterate, to compound those other problems, Arthur appears to have complete disregard for his health and well-being, lighting one cigarette after another and tossing the butts into an already overflowing ashtray. "Who really cares, anyway?" Arthur remarks, adding that if he doesn't die from cigarettes, either the drugs or the booze will kill him; like the cigarettes, drink and drugs are a daily habit, and he has no intention of quitting. "It's just the way things are," he says. "I gave up caring about what happens to me a long time ago. Life has been the shits, and I know it ain't getting any better for me."

Arthur can't recall exactly when he started drinking and smoking dope. "It must be thirty or forty years ago. I can't really remember a whole hell of a lot; everything's a bit cloudy ... kinda like my life." He was born in rural Nova Scotia; he knows that much, and he attended a two-room schoolhouse that combined classes from primary level to Grade 8. "But I never got that far; I never got past Grade 6." He stayed in the small community and managed to find odd jobs, then made his way to the coast and hired onto fishing boats. "I'd work for a few months, then I'd be off for a couple of months, drawing unemployment. That's just the way I liked it, because it gave me some money to live off of."

For Arthur, living meant having money to buy drugs and alcohol—nothing more. He thinks his stained, forest-green coat came from a friend about eleven years ago. As for a place to live, "I don't got no regular home. I stay here for a few months, and then I go there for awhile; I kinda go back and forth like that. That's how things go." Today, he subsists on the meagre disability pension he started receiving about twenty-five years ago after being injured on a fishing boat. "Damn near lost my whole hand," he says with a sly smile, holding his left hand in front of his ravaged, whiskered face. "I lost two of my fingers and almost all of this thumb."

27

The day he was injured, Arthur was drunk and stoned. "Me and the other guys had been drinking a lot the night before, and when I got up that morning, I had me a few puffs to clear the head because I was still drunk from the liquor. Guess it didn't work," he jests, making light of the misfortune that ended his fishing career. His pension money usually runs out two weeks before the next cheque arrives, so he begs for money to support his habits. "I've done just about everything you could think of to get money, 'cept for selling my soul to the devil. I've collected beer bottles out of garbage cans; I've stolen money and stuff like that. But usually I just come right out and ask people for money. Some people are good; others are mean sons'a'bitches. Guess they don't figure they owe me anything."

Getting the booze is no problem; he begs for some if he has no money. But sometimes the drugs he also craves can be hard to come by. "I don't have no regular supplier or anything like that, but I do know a couple of guys who can get me what I want. I have to pay for it up front, because they don't give me any credit. And they don't take kindly to people who try and cheat them."

Once, he was short a few dollars on a drug buy, but convinced the pushers he could get them the money in a few days. When he wasn't able to keep his promise, "They beat me up real bad; beat the shit out of me and left me on the side of the road, they did," he recalls. It wasn't the first time Arthur had woken up in a ditch. "It happens a lot. When you're drunk and stoned out of your head, you don't really care where you end up." He bears no ill will towards the pushers; the week after his beating, he was back to dealing with them again. "I had no other choice, really, because I couldn't get it nowhere else." Besides, he says, dealers are basically ordinary people—at least on the surface. "You think they're some kind of thief or something, or organized criminals? Well, most of the guys I know who sell the stuff are guys who live and work right here where I live. They're your everyday kind of guys, and they're people you would never think were pushers."

Arthur estimates that over the years he has spent thousands of dollars on drugs. "You can't say how much for sure. I bet I spend about fifty dollars a week; something like that. Some weeks it may be more, it may be less. I don't bother to keep count, because it don't matter none. I just buy what I want when I have the cash and don't think about it much any more."

Arthur knows someday the drugs and booze will kill him. "But I don't really care what happens in the future. All's I care about is what happens today; right now. If it kills me, then it kills me. And so what if it does? I ain't got a whole lot to lose, you know, and there ain't going to be anyone crying over me."

Nor do people involved in the illicit drug trade at the supply end fare much better than addicts like Arthur. Except for the fabulously wealthy kingpins at the top of the smuggling heap—the cartel bosses and their senior henchmen—individuals who work in narcotics contraband seem as desperate, and as pathetic, as Arthur. Their motives may be slightly different; while an addict's self-destructive abuse of drugs is often the only perceived means to escape a lifetime of pain and disappointment, the "employees" of drug-smuggling rings are more often motivated by simple greed, or by some urgent financial crisis to which there appears to be no answer other than this "quick fix" of illegal activity. Police, however, have seen enough of who constitutes the crews of smuggling ships to know that these men aren't living a life of ease.

In many cases, crews on drug ships are entangled in smuggling schemes without even having a financial investment; they view the venture as an opportunity to earn a bit of money and get free transportation to North America. Once on board, they are seen as cheap labour and often treated like slaves, denied even the basic amenities like decent food or even water. As for the go-betweens in the ports of call—those who transport, sort, and finally push the drugs on the streets, the apparently good money they receive in exchange for their services rarely seems adequate compensation if the scheme is intercepted by police. As Ray Martin's friend Dan had tried to tell him on the phone the fateful evening he decided to accept the smugglers' offer, it would not be the ringleaders going down if there were a bust. It would be the likes of Ray Martin.

Between a Rock and a Hard Place

THE DAYS THAT FOLLOWED Ray Martin's fateful acceptance of the smugglers' offer to pay him handsomely for transporting narcotic contraband along the back-roads of the South Shore were filled with painful contemplation. Over and over, in excruciating detail, he played and replayed in his mind the events that led to his decision. And, reaching even farther back, he faced the earlier influences that also had shaped his difficult choice. How had it all begun—and where? As he went over the sequences yet again, he saw himself sitting in his rusting 1983 Ford half-ton, watching customers coming and going from the town's only tavern. As he peered through the bug-smeared windshield, he saw many familiar people on their way inside the sleazy, run-down bar. How had he arrived at this crossroads? Why was he taking the risk of coming to talk with people he had never met about some kind of suspicious-sounding trucking deal? The offer promised good, quick money; sounded like a chance worth taking, although he assumed something illegal was involved—and his vague doubts were fast becoming second thoughts. This meeting could change his life; his ship could be coming in, or ...

Ray kept trying to shrug off the nagging feeling that something wasn't quite right—something he couldn't quite put his finger on. But he did know at least one reason for his discomfort. This was a small town; people talked about each other's business. The men he was about to meet had obviously chosen this location so they could get lost in the crowd; the only problem was, this crowd consisted of mostly people he knew. That's why he had arrived half an hour before the meeting, which had been set for 6:30. He wanted to check things out; to at least try to keep his back covered.

Usually, Ray at age thirty-seven had learned to pay attention to his inner voice. Intuition had gotten him by for most of his adult life, and kept him out of serious trouble. This time, though, he knew he was throwing caution to the winds for a chance at big money, a chance to finally stop worrying about the bills.

Ray's life hadn't gone exactly the way he had planned. As he waited, listening to the country music station, his mind drifted. The soothing melody of the love song took him away from the present and elicited a flow of memories—and questions. Why was he even contemplating participation in some illicit deal with people from God knows where? Whatever had happened to all his teenage dreams? When had the dreams ended and the reality of life begun? How had everything become so complicated?

Growing up in a small rural community on the South Shore of Nova Scotia had its good points, but to Ray, these were also its problems. The people in these parts were friendly to a fault, caring more about the well-being of strangers than themselves. They were hard-working folk, steeped in tradition, living off the land and the sea. Young men were usually groomed to work on their fathers' fishing boats or to join their families working in the fish plants, often before they had even finished high school. Life in the fishing industry was hard, but honourable; it was the only job Ray's father ever had, and it had enabled him to raise seven children. Although life was a struggle for his parents, and although Ray and his siblings didn't have many luxuries, their basic needs were always met. As a child and teenager, Ray hadn't recognized his father's dedication to the family; as an adult with children of his own, however, he had a clearer understanding of that commitment.

Childhood, for Ray Martin, was one big contest. As a child, vying with four brothers and two sisters for his parents' attention, Ray never settled for second best; he always had to be the best, regardless of the games or activities. This trait gave him a competitive edge as a young person; and when he became an adult, he was even more demanding. He wanted something better than a life on the fishing boats. He didn't want to spend forty or fifty years busting his ass working for someone else, as he liked to put it. He wanted to be his own boss. He wanted to chart his own future—preferably one involving a good job where he made big money without working very hard.

Truth was, Ray tended to be a schemer, always thinking about how to make the next big profit. Like most of his contemporaries in the dozens of fishing villages dotting the region, Ray hadn't finished high school. Instead, at sixteen, he accepted his destiny—at least temporarily, he told himself—and went to sea on the fishing boats. Like his dad always said, if you quit school, you go to work. It was far from the glamorous lifestyle he longed for, but he believed that if he worked hard and saved his money, he could get off the boats and start a better life. Ray truly felt he could control his own destiny by carefully plotting a specific course: he would fish for three years, save all his money, then take his earnings and invest in a truck—the start of his own business. Within ten years, Ray figured, he would have a fleet of trucks on the road and an army of drivers working for him.

It was a good plan—and it might have worked, if he'd stuck to it. He had made good money on the scallop draggers, but like most young fishermen, he hadn't summoned the discipline to save any of it. For the first time in his life, Ray was tasting freedom—and enjoying it. Like most young people earning a pay cheque for the first time, he spent his money freely—bought new clothes, partied, drank, and treated his friends at the bar. And there were women to impress, of course. It doesn't take long for the earnings to disappear when you're having a good time....

The music stopped and the announcer's voice droned on. Ray stared blankly through the dirty windshield, remembering those days with regret; if he had banked his money, as originally planned, he wouldn't be sitting here waiting to talk with three strangers about some suspect venture. Ray's qualms intensified; he briefly considered just driving away—but he just couldn't seem to turn the key in the ignition. The promise of money was too strong a pull.

Ray didn't know much about the men he was supposed to meet, in a few minutes now. He had only spoken with one of them, and that had been four days before, when a man called him at home, asking if he knew anyone who had a panelled truck or van that he and his partners could rent for a week. Someone on the wharf had told him to call Ray, the guy said in a pronounced French accent; there were some goods to move and the pay would be worth his while, but he had to promise not to talk about the "rental" to anyone.

That would be easy. Ray lived alone; his wife Shirley, had moved out six months ago with their three children, and now lived in another town. Married life had not been easy for either of them; it seemed Shirley was never satisfied, no matter how hard he tried. Things hadn't always been that way: when they met and married—Ray was twenty-one, Shirley a year younger—there was the promise of a long, happy future. The happiness lasted only four years; by the time their third baby had arrived, the bills were piling up and the romance was wearing down.

Shirley wanted to be more than just a cook, housekeeper, and babysitter. She didn't like staying at home alone with the kids for days on end, while Ray was on the road delivering cargo from one town to another. But trucking was his livelihood; although the money wasn't much, it was a steady income and it put food on the table. But for Shirley, it was never enough. He soon found himself staying away from home more frequently, making up excuses. It was easier to stay away and avoid the inevitable arguments over money than to go home and fight with her. After all, he reasoned, he did the best he could. She couldn't blame him if things didn't turn out the way they'd planned.

When the marriage finally fell apart, Shirley took the children, then demanded support—even though she knew Ray wasn't making enough to support two households. Not with the mortgage and all the other bills to pay. He sent her what he could, when he could, especially for the children's sake. And he missed those kids desperately. The trucking business wasn't enough to enable him to cover all the bills, but it still kept him on the road almost all the time—away from home six out of seven days, usually. There wasn't time to visit his children. So he just kept sending whatever support money he could. There may have been no love left between him and Shirley, but his kids—that was something else again.

He shivered with a chill of loneliness. Please let this deal work out, he pleaded silently. That would show Shirley. And, more to the point, he could see his children again. That was why he was still there, why he hadn't been able to drive away.

This wasn't the first time Ray Martin had dealt in contraband—he'd hauled black-market cigarettes and liquor—but this seemed much more serious, especially because he wasn't at all sure what he was getting into. All the secrecy was disturbing, but Ray was a discreet man, by nature; he didn't make it a habit to talk to other people about his business. Still, he didn't like being told to keep quiet; it bothered him. But what the hell, he told himself; just about anything was bearable if there was enough money at the other end.

Being naturally cautious, on his guard even with people he knew and trusted, his natural reticence built quickly into suspicion during the four days between the phone call and tonight's meeting. Just what were these goods that needed transporting? The caller had refused to be specific— wouldn't give his name or say where he was calling from. The man determined that Ray did have a truck, then after setting the date and location for them to meet, hung up without leaving a phone number that Ray could call in case he had to cancel. To compound the mystery, Ray couldn't find anyone at the local wharves who had talked to a stranger about him. Just how did the caller get his name, then? Ray didn't like these unanswered questions; he had known for a long time that loose ends lead to trouble—and this was definitely a loose end. Ray had lived

33

in this close-knit community all his life, and he had a good reputation as a hard worker and dedicated family man—the divorce obviously hadn't changed his commitment to his children. Ray's friends knew he was having money troubles, and they often recommended him for jobs that came along. Surely someone would have said something if a stranger had been around asking about him.

All this aside, Ray kept on waiting. There was the promise of a big payoff; and he was just plain curious to find out who these guys were and what they were up to. He had to stay.

From behind the steering wheel of his truck, Ray watched a blue car pull into the parking lot. Nice car, Ray thought. Probably a rental. As the driver parked, Ray slid further down in his seat behind the dashboard; he wanted to avoid any contact with the men until they were inside, on his turf. Ray had sealed many deals over a beer in that tavern and took some comfort in the fact that it had been chosen for this meeting. He would feel more at ease inside the crowded bar than outside in a shadowy, cold parking lot. The people he knew inside would just assume he was working on another deal; they would ask no questions.

He watched the three men climb out of the car; they seemed strikingly different, enough to make them stand out from the crowd. The driver was unshaven, but otherwise good looking; dark, about six feet tall, sharply dressed in jeans and a brown suede jacket over a white turtleneck shirt. About thirty, Ray thought—give or take a year or two. Although it was nearly dark, he slipped on a pair of sunglasses. The passenger in the front seat was a short, heavy-set man with sandy-coloured hair. He wore brown slacks, a green bomber-style jacket, and white running shoes. His receding hairline and bulging belly marked him at about forty, Ray figured. As he slowly closed the car door, his eyes nervously scanned the parking lot, pausing at each vehicle in the lot as if expecting trouble. The third man was dark and ruggedly handsome, in his mid- to late thirties, Ray decided. Class, Ray thought, eyeing with some envy the black jacket and light-grey slacks, the well-groomed, thick dark hair. He got out of the back seat and motioned for his companions to join him at the rear of the car.

The three men huddled for a few minutes, then went inside the tavern. Once again, Ray thought about leaving. They hadn't seen him, after all. Maybe they'd wait ten or fifteen minutes, then leave and look for somebody else to do the job—whatever it was. But once again, he stayed. Ray needed the cash; he had to take the chance. Torn between conscience and desperation, he finally came to a decision—opened the door, walked across the parking lot, and entered the tavern. The three strangers were sitting at the corner table near the jukebox; two had beers, the third a Coke. Since they didn't know what he looked like, he felt he had the upper hand, for the moment at least. Rocking back on the heels of his well-worn steel-toed work boots, as if to gather inner strength, Ray summoned an air of self-confidence and headed towards them.

"I'm Ray. You guys here to see me?"

Without a word, the men motioned for Ray to join them; there were no handshakes, no introductions. He dropped into the empty chair, taking in the man still wearing sunglasses; the good-looking model type; the pudgy, nervous guy. Ray felt as if he'd just entered the set of some Grade B movie; his discomfort increased as the three men eyed him up and down. He wished he'd taken off when there was a chance, but now he would just have to make the best of it.

He asked the men if they had names; the question met with silence and an exchange of looks, then the good-looking guy nodded approval for the others to speak—clearly, this was the boss.

The stocky man introduced himself as Larry; the moment he spoke, Ray recognized him as the man who'd phoned to arrange this meeting. In turn, Larry introduced the fellow behind the sunglasses as Paul, and the third man—the leader—as Tobias.

Continuing to speak for the trio, Larry thanked Ray for coming. "We can't really tell you too much right now," he said. "Basically, we just wanted to meet you, see if you'd be interested in some trucking work."

"I'm always interested in making money." Ray shrugged, feigning calmness; he was far from feeling comfortable, but didn't want to seem intimidated. "But making good money usually means you gotta do some-thing that's, well, maybe underhanded—even illegal. Is that it? What kind of goods have you got to move?"

No one answered. Just as Ray thought he had blown it, Paul answered. "It doesn't matter to you what we've got to move, does it? All we gotta know from you is if you got a truck you can drive for us for a week. We gotta move some stuff, we need a truck, and we figure it'll take a week. We pay good. That's all you gotta know. Are you in or not?"

Sensing tension building between Paul and Ray, Larry jumped in to deflect trouble. "The cargo's delicate," he said. "It will take a few days to move it all. If you're not interested, we can find someone else."

"Wait a second," Ray shot back. "I didn't say I wasn't interested. All I want to know is what risks are involved. I got a right to know what I'm getting into. I got a right to know. It's my ass on the line."

"You gotta expect risks," Paul snapped, leaning in closer, his muscles flexing. Ray leaned back, symbolically removing himself from the conversation. At 6'2" and 230 pounds, Ray seldom backed down from anything or anybody: Paul didn't scare him, but he didn't want to cause a scene before he found out what this deal was all about, so he backed off, letting Paul think he'd won this round.

Minutes passed in silence, which Ray finally broke, trying again to elicit some hard facts from these men. "Say, how'd you guys find out about me, anyway?" he asked, glancing around the table for a reaction. Again Larry spoke for the trio. "Actually, Paul got your name from a friend who suggested you'd be discreet, and said you needed some cash. This is a good deal. We'll cut you in—provided we can trust you. We need some help; you can help us. What we don't need is somebody who wants to put his nose in where it doesn't belong."

Ray wasn't satisfied, but decided to let it go. Paul would just jump in again if he felt Larry was being pumped for information. "Where you guys from, anyway?" Ray asked, looking at Tobias. Once again, Larry quickly jumped in, as if to protect his companion from any direct questions. "We're from away. That's all you gotta know. It's not important where we're from." That was the final straw. Ray's temper flared: "Hey, listen, you guys. You want me to work with you, you gotta trust me. I got a truck; you need a truck and a driver. But either you ease up, or I'm outta here. No more shit. Cut me some slack, or I'm walking—and finding another truck won't be easy."

"He's right," Tobias replied quickly—his first words since Ray had joined them. "Let's not forget what we came here for. We can tell him some of what he wants to know. He'll have to know everything eventually, if he decides to join us." Like Larry, Tobias spoke with an accent, but Ray couldn't place it.

"I'm from Toronto," Larry volunteered. "Paul's from the States." Nodding towards Tobias, he added, "He's from overseas, but even we're not exactly sure where." "That wasn't so tough, was it?" Ray grinned, feeling more in control. The information was minimal, but it was something. "Now what do you guys want from me?"

Taking over the conversation again, Larry briefly outlined the plan. "We're expecting a shipment soon. When it arrives, we'll store it on shore, then, over a week or so, move it out. We don't want you involved until it's time to move, then we want to use your truck to move it. You got the truck; we want it for a week."

"What are we talking about?" Ray asked, although he felt he already knew the answer—drugs of some sort. "Hash? Grass? It must be something big if it takes a week to move it." Paul smiled wryly. "I think you know enough for now. Are you in or not?" "How much?" Ray asked, mimicking Paul's grin. Paul pushed himself back from the table; whether Paul was angry, or whether he was enjoying the verbal sparring, was unclear. Ray prided himself on his ability to pick up people's signals, but he couldn't get a fix on this guy.

Larry answered the question. "Enough. It is risky for you. We'll make it worth your while." He glanced at his partners for assent, then continued. "We'll pay $10,000 up front. After the move's completed, you'll get another $15,000." Ray reflected on the figure. "You're offering me $25,000 just to use my truck for a week, right?" Larry nodded agreement. The group fell silent. "Do you need an answer now, or can I sleep on it? And one more thing: I have to know the cargo before I agree to anything." The men exchanged glances. Then Paul resumed his enforcer role. "We can't wait long, Ray. We'll need an answer by tomorrow night. If you're out, you won't get a second chance, but breathe a word of this to anyone and you answer to me. We need a truck and we're willing to pay you good for it. It's your decision, but the offer stands—$25,000. Take it or leave it."

Ray decided Paul enjoyed antagonizing people. He bit his lower lip to control his temper. "Thanks for the offer. How do I reach you?"

"I'll call tomorrow night," Larry said; the three men stood to leave. "Expect my call around eight. We'll expect your answer. If you're in, you'll find out the cargo when you accept the first payment." With that, the three men were gone. Ray sat quietly for a long time, thinking. He motioned to the waiter for a Schooner. It was going to be a long night. This was the toughest decision of his life—if this plan went sour, he'd be caught in the middle. It didn't matter to him what other people thought, but his kids might suffer as a result.

On the other hand, he thought, as he pulled his truck into the muddy driveway that ran alongside his empty three-bedroom bungalow, the way his finances were, he didn't have much of a future to offer them. He had stayed at the tavern for less than an hour; the noise was getting to him. He needed to be by himself; he needed a quiet place to think. Now that Shirley and the kids were gone, his house was the quietest place he knew. What was once a beehive of activity now seemed like a morgue. It wasn't quite nine o'clock when he opened the front door to the sound of the telephone ringing.

Ray groped his way through the darkness, cursing under his breath as he tripped over a pair of shoes he'd tossed aside earlier. He had been meaning to replace the light bulb in the front hall for weeks, but never seemed to get around to doing things like that any more. Story of his life, he thought. Breathlessly, he picked up the phone just in time to hear the line go dead. Damn! He hated that. What the hell, he thought, reaching around a corner for the lamp on the hall table. Might as well give Shirley a call and ask to speak to the kids. It was Thursday night; she should be home. He dialled the number, hoping the sound of their voices might help him make the right decision.

"Hello," a child's voice answered.

"Hi, Kim, this is Daddy. How's my girl?" Kim was three and a half, the youngest of his three children. Ray pictured her infectious smile and long brown hair as he coaxed her to talk; Kim giggled a lot, but didn't say a word. Then, much to his disappointment, Ray heard her scurrying away, letting the receiver drop to the floor.

Then another child picked up the phone; Ray heard his elder daughter scolding her sister. Jessica was just eleven and very mature, but to Ray she was still his baby. "Hello," she said. "Who's this?"

"Jess? It's me, Daddy. How ya doing?"

"Fine. Mom's not here right now. She's gone to a movie with some guy she met at work or something."

This didn't really surprise Ray. "That's okay, baby. I didn't want to talk to her anyway. Who's watching you guys while Mommy's out?"

"Aunt Sandy. Do you want to talk to her?"

"No. I'd rather talk to you and Brian." His son was eight and already showing all the signs of becoming a rugged young man. Ray was proud of all of them: if he accomplished nothing else in his life, at least he had three great kids—and that was a positive contribution to the world. Yet he worried about them, too; they seemed to be coping well with the divorce, but he felt that it was a surface acceptance and that, inside, they must be struggling to understand what had happened to the family. There were no answers, Ray knew. He himself had trouble fully comprehending the end of a marriage that had begun in such happiness. All he could do was continue to try his best to be a good father; Ray had won his children's affection early in their young lives, with a strong but caring approach to parenting. But now they were being raised by their mother alone.

"Well, Brian's not home either," Jessica said. "He's staying over with some friends. It's a birthday party or something, I guess. He's going to school from over there tomorrow. But I'll tell him you called; he'll be sad he missed you."

"Thanks, honey," Ray responded. "I just called to see how you're all doing. How's school?"

"Fine, I guess."

Ray sensed a problem. "Fine, you guess? What's the problem, honey? Everything not all right at school?"

"Yah, everything's fine. It's just that ... well, there's these sneakers that everyone's wearing and I want a pair, but Mom says we can't afford them. I don't understand why I can't have the same things all the other kids at school have. It's just not fair." Ray could hear the anguish in her voice as she fought back the tears; to an eleven-year-old trying to fit in, peer pressure can be overwhelming. "Nothing's ever gonna be the same again now that you don't live with us any more, is it, Daddy?"

Ray spoke quietly, sympathetically—but with directness. "No, Jess. I guess things will never be back the way they were. I'll be down to see you as soon as I can, and we'll talk about those sneakers. Okay?"

There was a sudden silence, then Jessica's voice again. "Daddy? Good, you're still there. Aunt Sandy says it's soon time to get ready for bed, so I gotta go. When you coming down to see us again?"

"Don't know, baby. I got a lot of things on the go right now. Things are getting really busy with the truck. It may be a few more weeks before I can get clear. But it will be soon, I promise. Then we'll see about those sneakers you're talking about."

"Okay, Daddy. Listen, I gotta go. Love ya. 'Bye."

"Love you, too, honey. Tell Kim and Brian I love them too. 'Bye." Ray hung up reluctantly, pangs of loneliness biting at his heart.

Over the next few hours, Ray roamed aimlessly through the empty house, thinking, trying to decide what he should do, weighing the pros and cons of the offer, over and over, torn between his reluctance to get involved and the promise of a good payoff.

Greed is the powerful weapon people use against men like Ray, who constantly struggle to survive: the promise of $25,000 was good bait. But years of hard work—years of clawing to get ahead—had taught Ray caution. What if they got caught? What if he took the rap and ended up in jail? What then? He thought about Jessica. He wanted his children to experience the pleasures of the world, but luxuries, even small ones like brand-name sneakers, are expensive. Ray already owed a lot of money, and there wasn't enough coming in to meet all his financial obligations. But drug-smuggling? Was that perhaps more than he was willing to do in order to make ends meet, and give his kids a few treats?

Sure, Ray knew the men he'd met at the bar were running drugs. This was the mid-1980s and drug-smuggling along the southern coast of Nova Scotia was commonplace. He read the papers. He watched the news. He spent a lot of time on the docks, where the fishermen often talked about big drug shipments, and the big bucks involved. This was no small-town running of contraband cigarettes and liquor. This was the big leagues, and Ray wasn't sure he wanted to play.

Sometime in the wee hours, exhausted by his warring thoughts, he drifted into a fitful sleep.

* * *

Ray was feeling worn out as he drove his white 1981 Chevy cube van—his second vehicle he used in his business—down the highway. He had been up at 5:00 A.M., and on the road by 6:00, to deliver a load of scrap metal to a recycling yard in the Annapolis Valley. You had to be on the road at daybreak to beat the commuter traffic to Halifax—and Ray wanted to make sure he was home as early as possible. It was common for residents of Lunenburg and Queens Counties to drive to the city for work; Ray himself had spent years making the trip along Highway 103, the main route from the South Shore to the city; with any luck, he'd be home by lunch time—even with the slower pace along Route 12 to the Valley.

This was the day of reckoning for Ray. Although he could think of nothing else but the $25,000 offer the three strangers had made the night before, he still hadn't decided to accept it. There was a lot at stake—not that his life was worth much these days, what with a broken marriage and a struggling business; but at least he wasn't breaking the law. Ray kept thinking about the drugs he was sure the offer involved—and he couldn't help feeling that to help these guys move their illicit cargo of drugs was almost as bad as trafficking, and that bothered Ray. He hated the idea of children no older than Jessica having access to drugs he'd delivered. But, even so, the allure of the money he so badly needed—well, it was the chance of a lifetime. As he drove along, Ray tried to convince himself that any part he would play in this scheme was insignificant; besides, if he didn't help these men, they'd find another way to ship their goods, and someone else would get the money.

Ray's mind raced as he tried to recall everything he had ever heard about the drug trade in Nova Scotia. He remembered newspaper accounts of drug seizures in recent years along the coast. He recalled the dockside tales of offloads at sea, of huge shipments arriving right under the noses of the authorities. He knew that many of these operations were carried out successfully every year in this part of the province; but some did fail....

After unloading the scrap metal, Ray headed back to the South Shore. He felt good: for a while, at least, he had managed to think about something else other than the tough decision he still had to make. It had been a profitable trip—$267 from the recyclers—not enough to meet all his bills, and a far cry from the $25,000 offer, but at least he had earned it honestly. He thought about how far the money had to stretch: some should be put towards the mortgage payment, and then there were the power and oil bills, and the truck needed new tires, and Jessica's sneakers. He couldn't forget about those. Well, he'd have to buy a pair of second-hand tires—the truck just had to be kept on the road—and what was left would go towards the mortgage. The rest would just have to wait, even Jessica's sneakers.

There were times when Ray had thought about selling the house and freeing himself from the financial burdens that went with it, but he hadn't been able to do it. Instead, he continued to scrape by every month, barely managing to make the necessary payments. It was tough, but he felt he had to hang onto something from his past. Shirley had the kids; all he had was the house. As difficult as it was to maintain, it provided some stability in his life—a connection to his past. As he drove along the winding secondary road that cut through the centre of the province to join the South Shore with the Annapolis Valley, Ray continued his silent deliberations.

Ray understood how money can lure people into criminal activity. Except for a few minor indiscretions over the years, Ray considered himself an honest, law-abiding citizen. He wasn't a churchgoer or anything like that, but he was a good person who worked hard to eke out a respectable living.

Two years ago he would have said no—without hesitation. He might even have considered going to the police. But things were different now: his money problems seemed insurmountable—almost unbearable. After Shirley left, he had contemplated suicide, until he remembered his children, and realized he couldn't do that to them. Not that he was suicidal now, but his life seemed a shambles, and he believed that money woes were the cause. That $25,000 would go a long way to easing them. So what if there were some risks? Wasn't life itself a risk? Other people took chances, and ended up wealthy.

He thought again about the men he'd met the night before. Paul, now he came on strong, but Ray didn't scare easily. He could hold his own against the Pauls of the world. Larry and Tobias worried him more, because he couldn't read them. It wasn't at all clear where Larry fit in.

41

The pudgy little man had done most of the negotiating, but seemed nervous, almost as if he was intimidated by his partners, or maybe afraid someone might be listening or watching him. And who knew what Tobias was all about? At any rate, if these men were running drugs, they were used to pulling people's strings, and Ray would have to watch his step if he took them up on their offer. These weren't people one could trust; Ray was sure of that.

It was nearly 12:30 when Ray pulled into his driveway. After a quick sandwich, he headed out to buy a pair of good used tires at Dan's garage. Dan was almost like a brother to Ray; they were only two years apart in age, and they'd grown up watching out for each other. They had been through good times and bad times together. Quite apart from the good tires Dan would sell him at a fair price, Ray knew his friend would lend a sympathetic ear to his troubles. Ray needed to talk to someone, and Dan had always been there for him, through the divorce, through the painful separation from his children. For his part, Ray had provided emotional support for his friend when one of his children was killed in a car accident a few years back. They had always been each others' sounding boards—and that's what Ray needed right now, a sounding board.

Pulling up in front of the run-down garage with two service bays, Ray found his friend working on the engine of his candy-apple red Ford Mustang. "Just about shot," Dan sighed, acknowledging Ray's presence without taking his head out from under the hood. "Maybe it's time to retire her and get a real car," Ray joked, knowing that would get his friend's attention. "This here car and me have been through a lot together," Dan shot back defensively. "Won't be long now before she's purring like a kitten again. What ya up to today?" "Been to the Valley," Ray explained. "Took a load up. Pretty good haul this time. Now, I need a good pair of tires. Got any around real cheap?"

The long-haired, scruffy-looking Dan, grease up to his elbows, stopped to think for a minute. His eyes scanned the inventory laying around his cluttered garage. "Think I might have something over there," he finally said, pointing towards the second service bay where dozens of used tires were strewn about.

"Someday you gotta clean this place up," Ray jokingly suggested, stepping over car parts and tools scattered around the garage floor, on his way to the second bay. Dan returned to the Mustang, leaving his friend to sort through the tires. About ten minutes later Ray yelled, "What ya want for these?" holding two tires for Dan to inspect. "Forty bucks and they're yours."

Ray knew that if Dan could have afforded it, he would have just told him to take the tires, but times were tough and Ray gladly paid his friend. Anyway, forty dollars was a hell of a lot cheaper than buying new ones. "All this tire talk's got me thirsty. Got time for a quick beer?" Although Ray hadn't told him he wanted to talk, Dan knew when his friend showed up for a beer in the middle of the afternoon, something was up. "I don't have much time. I've got to get this done. I've got a carburetor job at two," Dan said—then, sensing Ray's disappointment—"but I've got a couple of cold ones in the house, and I guess I could spare a few minutes."

Beers in hand, Dan returned. "What's on your mind, Ray? Kids acting up? Shirley giving you a hard time again? Money problems?" "No, the kids are fine. So's Shirley," Ray said, "and I've always got money problems. It's just, well ... I've got to talk to somebody I can trust about something really big. I mean this could be big-time shit, Dan, and I've got to talk to someone I can trust about it." Ray took a few gulps of his beer, waiting for his friend to speak. "What the hell is it?" Dan asked straightforwardly.

Ray wanted to tell Dan everything, but he kept his words guarded. "I've got this chance to make some big cash, but I think it might involve something illegal," he confided. "Hey, man, I know things are pretty tough, but do you really want to go screwing up your life with shit like that?" Dan shot back. "If you go getting yourself in trouble, what are your kids going to think?"

"Hell, it's for the kids that I'm even thinking about doing it," Ray replied.

"What's it all about? What've you got to do?" Dan asked.

"Not much. Take some cargo from one place to another. And I ain't really supposed to be talking about this. If they ever found out I was here talking to you, they'd be pissed, and I'd be in deep shit."

"Damn it, man. You talking about hauling drugs?" Dan demanded. Ray didn't respond. "Man, if you get caught, it's game over. If you think you had trouble before, it's nothing like you'd have then. Cops don't mess around with drug dealers. Think about that."

"I ain't saying this is drugs," Ray snapped defensively. "And I didn't say I was going to do it. I just said that I had this chance at a good deal, and I got to at least think about it."

"Yeah, well, it sounds to me like you've already got your mind made up. And if it ain't drugs, what the hell is it?" Dan pressed.

"I don't know," Ray shrugged. "But they're talking about big money if I do what they want. God knows I could use the money."

43

"That's what they're counting on. They're always talking big money. But what if something goes wrong? Whose neck is in the noose then? We can all use the extra cash, but this ain't the way to get it." Dan continued. "It's your ass they're gonna fry if you get caught."

"I ain't got a whole hell of a lot to lose," Ray fired back. He had wanted Dan's advice, but he didn't like it much, now that he was getting it. Dan softened his approach. "Listen, I ain't telling you to do it, and I ain't telling you not to. You gotta make up your own mind. Do what you think's right. All's I'm saying is that you better think this through before you jump too quick. Don't forget that you've got three kids to think about. They don't live with you, but they still need you."

Both men finished their beers. Dan spoke up again: "Remember up Shelburne way a few months ago? Remember what happened to those guys? They thought they could truck the stuff out and make a killing, but the cops got them instead. There's a lot of drug activity around here right now. The cops are everywhere. They're really watching. You better know who you're dealing with."

Ray thanked his friend for the beer and left, assuring Dan he wouldn't rush into anything foolish. He headed for the wharves; maybe he could pick up some tips on the men who had pitched to him. There wasn't much in the way of information, so he headed home to wait for Larry's call.

Days after that call, remembering all the agonized self-questioning he had undergone in the twenty-four hours between their meeting and Larry's fateful question—"You in or out?"—he still couldn't understand exactly what had finally prompted his answer: "Yeah, I'm in."

*   *   *

Almost three weeks passed before Larry called with specific instructions about where he wanted Ray to go, and when. There were still some details to discuss, he said, and they had to meet as soon as possible. More talkative than usual, Larry repeatedly cautioned Ray about talking to anyone about the deal—or even considering having second thoughts about his decision: they were counting on him because people were used to seeing Ray hauling all kinds of cargo; no one would even notice his increased trucking activity over the next few weeks. Ray was in, Larry repeated for the third time: it was too late to back out. Ray was told to meet Larry at five the next Sunday morning, on a secluded back road about five miles out of town—few people would be up and about that time of day, he said, particularly on the third weekend in May, a holiday weekend. Ray, assuring Larry that they could count on him, promptly agreed.

The Saturday night before the meeting was an especially restless one for Ray; he tossed and turned, thinking about the venture, worrying about possible consequences. He still wasn't absolutely certain what the cargo was, but if it did turn out to be drugs—which it probably was—he could only hope that everything would work out, and that he'd walk away with his huge payoff. He tried not to think about the possibility of getting caught; if that happened, the world as he knew it would come to an abrupt and unhappy end.

At 4:45 A.M. on Sunday, Ray wheeled his half-ton towards Larry's designated meeting place. It had been raining heavily, and the roads, particularly the gravel ones, were messy, and Ray was glad he was driving a truck with high axle clearance. About a mile and a half down the sloppy road, he saw the clearing Larry had described. Although Ray had lived in these parts all his life, he was not much of a woodsman; these back roads were foreign territory to him. He knew the wharves in the region, but when it came to the woods, and the roads cutting through them, forget it. Ray could have easily lost his way in the maze of back roads in the densely wooded countryside, especially in the rain. He wondered how Larry had found the place—but, then again, that didn't matter, since it was ideal for a secret meeting.

Bringing his truck to a stop near the edge of the woods, Ray turned off the ignition just as the rain started up again. "Damn spring weather," he complained to himself. It was almost five; Ray hoped Larry would be on time—he didn't like it here in the woods, in a torrential rainfall. His truck could get mired, and walking home in this weather was not his idea of a good time. He wondered how he could explain what he had been doing in the middle of the woods at this hour if he had to call someone for help. It was such a ridiculous thing to think about, under the circumstances, that he even managed a smile.

In a matter of minutes, he spotted headlights, then the car. Ray jumped down from the cab and splashed through the ankle-deep mud until he could see Larry motioning him to get in the back. As he closed the door, he noticed Paul sitting up front, beside Larry. "What's he doing here? I thought this meeting was just between you and me?" Ray breathed heavily, his tone betraying his anger. But Paul didn't answer, nor did he even acknowledge Ray's presence.

Larry began the conversation with a warning: "It doesn't matter what he's doing here. He's part of the plan. Get used to him. We've got business to discuss. Whatever's got you pissed off at each other, doesn't matter. We don't want any distractions. No trouble from within our

45

operation. You got that? Is it clear?" Paul, still silent, stared blankly through the windshield, as the wipers slapped back and forth in a futile attempt to push aside the steadily falling rain.

"Is that clear?" Larry repeated. "Yeah, I get the message!" Ray snapped. "What the hell's this all about? You didn't get me out here in all this rain to shit over me, did you? If you did, I'm outta here right now. You can find someone else to do your dirty work. I don't take crap. You ain't paying me enough to make me your kicking boy. Now, is that clear?" he said, mockingly.

Larry was silent for a time, then began to explain. The shipment—he still wasn't specifying—was due in a week, and would come ashore not far from town; Ray would be told the exact location later. Again, Larry stressed the importance of discretion. "If anyone finds out what we're doing, we're all in deep shit. You got to understand that. You got to keep your mouth shut. Is that clear?" Although he still had questions about his role in the operation, Ray assured his new partners that he had not, and would not, speak to anyone about his involvement. Recalling his conversations with Dan, he regretted having confided in his friend— even though he was completely confident that Dan wouldn't talk to anyone else. He'd wanted Dan's advice, but he knew it would have been better to have just made up his mind on his own. Well, it didn't matter, really. Ray and Dan had shared a lot over the years; they knew they could trust each other. Dan would not betray him.

Ray snapped back to the present and suggested that Larry and Paul stop worrying; he wasn't the type of guy to tell people about his business. "Well, we're also concerned about the truck," Larry said. "We need to make sure that once things get rolling, you don't break down somewhere with our cargo on back."

"You don't have to worry about my truck," Ray shot back, defensively. "She's not new and she may not look like much, but she can do this job and anything else you want done. She's a good truck; gotten me through a lot. I trust her to haul anything you got. She's had some pretty heavy trips and done all right. She can handle this. I'd bet my life on it."

"Yeah, whatever," Larry responded coldly. "But we can't take any chances." Turning to look over his right shoulder at Ray, Larry handed him a brown, unsealed envelope. "Here. Get the truck fixed up. Make sure it's in good shape. You've got the kind of van we need. Now we gotta make sure it lasts long enough to move our stuff. It's your responsibility to keep it running until this is over. Anything happens to it while you're on the job, and you'll be held responsible. You don't want that to happen."

46

Ray was caught off guard; he hadn't expected any cash this morning. "What is this?" he asked, taking the envelope and flipping through the bills. "It's two thousand dollars. That should get the truck fixed up. If it costs any more, we'll settle up later."

Relief mingled with Ray's surprise; the van could use some work; it had seen better days. The tires he'd bought from Dan a few weeks earlier weren't reliable, the starter was sluggish, and the universal joint needed repair. Ray pocketed the money and said he'd take care of things. Then, Larry explained the next step. "We won't have much warning when things start to move; we'll get about a day's notice. When we know, you'll know; and you got to be ready to go when it's time." Larry turned again to face Ray. "You must be ready," he stressed. "We don't tolerate delays. Everything is on a strict timetable. If somebody screws up, then we're all screwed. Do you understand that, Ray?" Ray nodded, but Larry wasn't satisfied with the non-verbal assent. "You understand, Ray? You understand how important it is that we stick to the schedule, that when we call, you're ready?" he asked, more forcefully. "Yes! I understand! The truck will be ready; I'll be ready. Don't worry about me—you'll get your money's worth. You can count on that."

"This is not a game, Ray," Larry continued. "Maybe you haven't quite figured it all out yet. This is serious stuff; no room for screw-ups. We all got jobs to do in this; you got yours. If you screw up, you let us all down—you let a lot a people down. Our job is to make sure all the arrangements are made before the cargo gets here. Your job is to make sure the cargo gets from Point A to Point B—no interruptions. You've told us you can do that. Now we're counting on you to follow through. Don't let us down. Do you understand, Ray?"

Silence reigned inside the car, and the rain beat steadily against the metal and glass. Minutes passed. Ray barely moved in the back seat; he stared blankly at the backs of the two heads up front, then, finally, he broke the silence. "You guys must think I'm stupid. You think you can blow in here from Christ knows where and fuck around with us dumb fishermen on the coast. But we ain't that dumb. No one's told me yet, but I know we're talking about drugs. I know enough about drugs to know how serious this is. Like I said, you don't have to worry about my end of the bargain. I'll do what I'm supposed to do. You just have the money you promised me. You got nothing to fuckin' worry about on my end. Just make sure you have my money, or you will be screwed."

Larry and Paul exchanged glances, but said nothing. It was almost as if they'd been pulling Ray's strings to get just that reaction; now they

47

seemed content to let the matter drop. "We're done here, Ray." Larry said suddenly. "You'll hear from us within a week. And don't worry about the money."

On his way out, Ray, still charged up, offered a few more heated words of advice. "I just want to tell you guys not to come in here fuckin' around with us like we're some backwoods hicks or something. Don't underestimate the people around these parts. We ain't stupid. We ain't dumb— this kind of shit goes on around here all the time. You ain't the first to come here doing this. People here are wise to your kind. You might be smart, but there's always people around smarter than you, or smarter than you think you are. Don't forget that. Being cocky ain't gonna get you very far down here on the shore." He didn't wait for an answer. Slamming the door for emphasis, Ray sloshed his way back to his truck; by the time he got there, the car was already heading back out the muddy road. "Assholes," he muttered, pulling himself into his truck and heading home to get out of his wet clothes.

The next day, Ray made an appointment at one of the local garages to get the work done on his truck. He wanted to go to Dan's garage because he knew his friend could use the money, but he couldn't; Dan would ask questions. Ray hadn't spoken to his friend much in the past few weeks, and Dan would want to know what he'd decided to do about the deal; he'd also be curious about where Ray had gotten the money. Better to feel guilty than risk answering questions, Ray decided.

It took two days to put the cube van in top mechanical form. She was running smoothly, and Ray was anxious to hear from Larry. He wanted the whole thing over, as soon as possible. If everything went according to plan, he'd be $25,000 richer in a few weeks. If anything went wrong, he'd end up in jail.

Dubious Distinctions

WHEN POLICE SPEAK OF Queens and Shelburne Counties, on Nova Scotia's South Shore, as the epicentre of Canada's drug-smuggling activities, they usually mention two events that seem to define the pattern they have been tracking for more than twenty years. Both involve record seizures of narcotics—dubious distinctions that stand to this day—and both reflect the massive scope of drug trafficking off the province's coast, a reality made all the more disturbing given grim statistics showing that, of every ten shipments that reach Nova Scotia shores, only one will be intercepted by authorities.

Of the smuggling opportunities that have failed over the years, none are as significant as those in the town of Shelburne in February 1994, when two years of police investigation culminated in the seizure of 5,419 kg of cocaine worth $1 billion; and in the village of Ragged Harbour, just outside Liverpool, in May 1990, when police acting on a tip from a local lobster fisherman moved in to confiscate 35 tonnes of hashish valued at more than $400 million.

CANADA'S LARGEST COCAINE SEIZURE: SHELBURNE, NOVA SCOTIA

The smugglers had to work fast. The North Atlantic in midwinter is unpredictable; at any moment, the chains and ropes connecting the two vessels could easily have snapped under stress and frigid temperatures. Powerful waves could have smashed the vessels against one another, demolishing the smaller boat and killing everyone on board.

Although the calendar says February is a short month, for seafaring Maritimers, the month seems the longest of the year. The men on board these particular vessels knew the dangers, but the risks were worth taking for the promise of wealth—provided they could get their precious cargo ashore. Under cover of darkness and in the midst of an extreme cold spell that had gripped the Atlantic provinces for most of the 1993–94 winter season, the fishing vessel *Lady Teri-Anne*, a 12-metre tuna boat, left the port of Shelburne on the morning of February 21. Later that day, she rendezvoused with the mother ship, *Eve Pacifico*, an 85-metre cargo vessel. This clandestine meeting lasted well into the night; it took time to transfer 5,419 kg of cocaine to the smaller vessel. By morning, the *Lady Teri-Anne*'s hold was full. With the cargo safely stowed, the lone occupant of the tuna boat headed full-speed back into Shelburne harbour, arriving at the government wharf on February 22, about 7:30 A.M.

Four hours after the boat's arrival, authorities swung into action. Dressed in black fatigues and brandishing rifles, they burst from their hiding places like gangbusters. It had been a long wait. Police had spent more than two years working towards this moment, and in recent days they had endured bitterly cold temperatures, watching from their strategically located lookout points along the wharf. They were ready for the kill. The arrival of the *Lady Teri-Anne* at the Shelburne wharf that morning set off a takedown that resulted in the single largest cocaine seizure in Canadian history, and the confiscation of $1 billion worth of the drug. (Before the Shelburne bust, the largest seizure of cocaine, 4,323 kg, had occurred at Casey, Quebec, in November 1992.)

The seizure was larger than the police had anticipated; earlier intelligence reports had suggested that 1,000 kg would be in the shipment. The cargo was originally intended for New Brunswick, where authorities had been working on the case for more than two years. But when the *Lady Teri-Anne* docked at Shelburne wharf, Canada's largest cocaine seizure went down on Nova Scotia's South Shore. In an ironic twist of fate, it seemed almost appropriate that such a sensational bust would take place in the area of Atlantic Canada that has seen more than its share of drug-smuggling activities over the past two decades.

The *Lady Teri-Anne* had unknowingly entered a police dragnet, as heavily armed police officers burst forth from their stakeout points and swooped down on the unsuspecting smuggler on board the fishing boat, like vultures moving in on a carcass. It was over quickly: RCMP officers arrested the man and offloaded dozens of 20- to 30-kg sacks of cocaine found stuffed in the vessel's hold. As police were moving in on the *Lady Teri-Anne*, simultaneous raids were being conducted on two Shelburne-area motels, where five other men were arrested.

The two-year investigation originated in the Bathurst, New Brunswick, area; police stumbled across some information that indicated a major drug shipment was being planned, and several organizations collaborated to thwart it, including the RCMP, the Departments of National Defence and Fisheries and Oceans, and the Canadian Coast Guard.

Harold Hart, a reporter with the Shelburne County weekly newspaper, *The Coast Guard*, was working in his Water Street office that morning, a Tuesday, when he was tipped off that something major was happening at the government wharf. What had started out as a routine day became an experience of excitement and intrigue for the town as heavily armed police officers filled the streets. Hart describes the scene at the wharf as a war zone—dozens of police officers, dressed in black fatigues and carrying automatic weapons.

"It wasn't something you'd expect to see in Shelburne, despite the area's long history as a destination for drug smugglers," Hart recalls. "It was like something right out of a movie." The police, he says, were extremely protective of the cargo they had just intercepted. "They wouldn't let anyone get close enough to get a good look at the stuff, not even the press."

According to one local witness, the raid went off "like lightning," and was over in a matter of seconds. "I didn't know what was going on. These fellows had guns and moved fast. I just stood there and looked," the unidentified witness told Hart. No shots were fired as police stormed the vessel and eventually emerged, leading one man in handcuffs.

Earlier that morning, Hart was later told, several men—presumably RCMP officers—were on patrol at the Cox Shipyard, near the wharf, watching the *Lady Teri-Anne* with binoculars. Before the raid, Hart also found out that workers at Shelburne Marine and at two local motels had had brief encounters with the possible drug-runners, and that medical staff at Shelburne's Roseway Hospital had been informed of the impending bust; they were simply told to have their staff on alert because something major was going to happen. "We were put on alert that something was coming down," hospital administrator Jerry Fraser later told Hart in an interview. "We were asked to make sure our ambulance and medical staff were standing by—I guess there was fear there could be gunfire—[and] we were given instructions not to give out any information."

The day before the bust, the *Lady Teri-Anne*, which had been in storage at Shelburne Marine, was put in the water at the request of the owner, a fisherman from the Caraquet, New Brunswick, area. A spokesman for the marina told Hart he was surprised the *Lady Teri-Anne* was going in the water; over the previous two years, the boat had been used only during the summer tuna season.

The provincial daily newspaper, *The Chronicle-Herald*, quoted the owner (never identified) as saying he had rented the vessel to people who had told him they had a government contract to do a dive for a three-week period off Port Mouton, Queens County. No one knew what they were supposedly diving for, but the pretext was a cover for the smuggling operation. Following the seizure, the *Lady Teri-Anne* was towed back to Shelburne Marine on Tuesday night; on Wednesday morning, the vessel was lifted ashore and blocked up in the position it had been before all the excitement started. The owner of the fishing boat was not arrested; Dan Duffy, an officer with the Halifax RCMP Drug Section, said police determined that the New Brunswick man had no involvement in the ill-fated smuggling scheme.

When the raid finally happened, police sprang into action all over town. Two trucks, which were to be used to transport the cocaine after it was offloaded from the *Lady Teri-Anne*, were seized downtown, and there were the arrests at the motels, where suspects had taken rooms the day before. The owner of the Oxbow Motel, Guy Strange, remembers that one of the men arrested had arrived with a rental truck. "He had a U-haul, and I told him to park it out front, not in front of his room," Strange recalls; the man, who seemed to be a perfectly ordinary traveller, complied. "He was a stranger to us, and he looked no different from other people who come into our establishment," the motel owner says. "We certainly never would have guessed he was involved in drug smuggling or anything illegal." After all, the Oxbow is located right on the main highway between Halifax and Yarmouth, and it is not unusual for people to pull in there for a night's rest.

As for the raid on his motel, Strange recalls a police officer arriving at the motel office shortly after 11:00, asking to look at the register. Then, everything happened very fast; the police were in and out of the room in a matter of minutes, and no shots were fired. "We weren't told ahead of time what was going on, but [police] later explained to us that they had to keep the operation secret, as they did not want the suspects to become suspicious and flee the area," Strange says. "That morning, the police, dressed in SWAT-like uniforms, moved in, and took the guy down. We were not allowed anywhere near the area, because the suspects also had guns and the police were afraid that shots could be fired. They were concerned for our safety."

It was the first time Strange had been so close to a drug seizure, but he says accounts of drug activity in Shelburne, or other areas on the South Shore, never come as a shock to him. "There's no question that there is a big drug problem on the South Shore. All you have to do is look at the coastline, and you can see why the drug pushers like this area so much. We've got so many coves and inlets that they can move into those areas without being detected. So I wasn't surprised when this happened.

But I was afraid for the safety of my staff, because we really did not know what was going to happen that day. The police had their guns drawn when they went into that room, and there's no question they meant business. I'm sure they would have used them if the guys they were after would have fired at them. Fortunately, it didn't come to that."

Arrested were five men from New Brunswick, three from Quebec, and one from Italy. Arrested in the Shelburne take down were Quebec resi-

The Lady Teri-Anne *in dry dock after its cargo of cocaine was intercepted in Shelburne in February 1994.* HAROLD HART, THE SHELBURNE *COAST GUARD* PHOTO

dents Pierino Divito, 56; Roberto Sorenti, 29; Mike Divito, 28, from Montreal; New Brunswick residents Eusebe Gauvin, 36; Robert Mallet, 23; Francois Gauvin, 28; Raymond LeBlanc, 52; Pierre Dugay, 34; and from Italy, Alfredo Chierchia, 58. With the successful take down at the government wharf and the raids on the two motels, authorities had ended their stakeout—and completed two years of investigative work. All that remained was finding the mother ship. For two days before the raid, a Canadian Forces ship and Aurora patrol aircraft had been shadowing the *Eve Pacifico*, believed to be the vessel in question, as it moved up the coast towards Nova Scotia. As the raids were being carried out in Shelburne, the *Eve Pacifico* was being chased down by the destroyer HMCS *Terra Nova*; the crew had been trying to flee, after the drugs were transferred to the fishing vessel, but they gave up when the commander of the naval vessel threatened to fire across the ship's bow. An armed RCMP tactical team boarded and commandeered the ship, which was escorted to CFB

Shearwater, docking at about 3:00 P.M. the day after the raid. The fifteen-member crew, captained by a German, included Ukrainians, Dutch, Russians, and one Venezuelan, who claimed to be a stowaway. He told police he expected to land in the United States and was surprised to find himself on Canadian soil, in the middle of an international drug conspiracy.

The captain, Jurgen Kirchoff, 46, of Germany, was charged with conspiracy to import cocaine into Canada. According to a report in *The Chronicle-Herald*, the captain, representing Pacificsun Shipping Inc. of Cyprus, had purchased the *Eve Pacifico*, as it had been officially registered, on December 10, 1993. Reporter Barry Dorey quoted a spokesman for Sea Trade Shipping Essen, the shipping company in Belgium that had managed the *Eve Pacifico*'s operations, as saying that the captain represented Pacificsun during the sale negotiations. The new owner paid in full and renamed the vessel *Pacifico*. The money for the transaction was transferred through a European bank.

The Sea Trade spokesman also said that the captain oversaw some repair work on the ship in a Polish shipyard, then skippered it to Germany and Belgium, where it took on cargo for South America; the RCMP said they believed the cocaine was loaded in Venezuela. Originally, the ship was destined for Wilmington, Delaware, and Houston, Texas, with a cargo of steel—a cover for the drug-smuggling activity.

Following a week-long interrogation, police decided not to press charges against the crew of the *Pacifico*, other than the captain. After weeks of legal wrangling, the twelve men and two women were expelled from Canada and sent back to their own countries; the stowaway was also sent home to Venezuela

Authorities involved in the seizure, overwhelmed by its magnitude, said keeping such a quantity of cocaine off the streets would put a considerable dent in the market—and, considering the financial investment, might even shut down the syndicates, or at least slow them down substantially.

In the wake of the seizure, Bathurst RCMP Sergeant Gary Legresley said that police began their investigation after receiving some information almost three years before, and added that their persistent, concerted efforts were what led to the successful interception of the shipment. But details of the Shelburne investigation would only come to light over the following two years, as those charged went to trial in Bathurst, New Brunswick in 1996.

For his role in the operation, the captain was imprisoned for fourteen years—a reduction from his sentence of eighteen years because of the time he had spent behind bars following his arrest in February 1994. (The two years counted as double.)

According to a report that appeared in the January 9, 1996, issue of the Saint John *Telegraph-Journal*, the captain's trial painted a full picture of the conspiracy that ended with the Shelburne raids. In handing down the sentence, Court of Queen's Bench Judge Roger McIntyre said he considered the captain an integral player in the conspiracy, whose hierarchy he fully described. At the top, the judge said, was a European mastermind. It was this man who came up with the $2 million to buy the *Eve Pacifico*. On the next level down came those in charge of distribution in Canada, including a Montreal "drug lord" who planned and bankrolled the smuggling operation with the European conspirators. He was sentenced to twenty years in prison, less two years for time served while awaiting trial. Also at that level was a man from Shippigan, New Brunswick, who received a fourteen-year prison term in December 1995.

On the bottom rung of the operation were those who worked for these two men, including three men from the Acadian peninsula in New Brunswick. One man from Bouctouche was originally sentenced to eleven years, but he too had his time reduced by two years, since he had spent fifteen months in prison awaiting trial. Another man from Shippigan was imprisoned for eight years, and the third from Lamèque was handed a six-year term. Earlier in 1995, another Quebec resident pleaded guilty to charges for his role in the conspiracy and was sentenced to twelve years in prison, reduced from fourteen years for time served.

In their defence during sentencing in December 1995 by Court of Queen's Bench Judge Alexander Deschenes, the four New Brunswick men admitted they knew illicit narcotics were being imported but claimed they believed the drugs were less harmful than cocaine—marijuana or hashish. All of them, too, used the equally familiar argument that they became involved in the conspiracy because they had financial difficulties.

Besides the prison sentences handed out, the $1 million raised from the sale of the *Pacifico* was ordered forfeited under the Proceeds of Crime legislation to the Crown, as was all other property confiscated in Canada's largest cocaine seizure.

Interestingly, several of those involved in the Shelburne case were also key players in an earlier smuggling conspiracy off the coast of Nova Scotia. On November 15, 1994, a $30-million cache of cocaine from Venezuela, destined for a Hell's Angels clubhouse in Quebec, was hauled ashore from the murky depths of the Atlantic, 16 km off the coast of Nova Scotia, near

Halifax. The estimated 700 kg of cocaine had been dumped into the sea a year earlier, in August 1993, from a vessel south of Sheet Harbour. There the drugs remained, on the ocean floor, until police and divers from the naval ship HMCS *Cormorant* pulled them on board, after an intensive nineteen-day search. The successful effort was dubbed Operation Jaggy.

The smugglers' drastic attempt to save their cargo stemmed from their fear of aircraft hovering nearby; they would come back for the drugs later, they decided. But, as RCMP officers watched from a distance, they were forced to abandon their retrieval mission because of stormy weather. The police tried their own dive, but bad weather turned them back as well. More than a year later, they tried again—and finally came up with the cocaine, which had been carefully stored in plastic bags stuffed into 20-cm plastic sewer pipes corked at both ends. The discovery of the drugs would play a major role in the trials of the seventeen smugglers, who had been arrested in August 1993 and charged with conspiracy to import cocaine—even though the drugs had been ditched. One of the men immediately pleaded guilty and was sentenced to fifteen years in prison. At the time of the arrests in 1993, more than $500,000 were also seized in a series of raids throughout Quebec. And with the retrieval of the cocaine in the fall of 1994, prosecution efforts soared: ten of the men charged in the smuggling operation changed their pleas to guilty during a court appearance in Montreal on November 17 of that year. Trials for the remaining conspirators are still pending.

CANADA'S LARGEST HASHISH SEIZURE:
RAGGED HARBOUR, NOVA SCOTIA

When workers moved in during the winter of 1990 to clear trees and construct an entry road, the buzz around the little seafaring Queens County community of Ragged Harbour was that a new family was moving in. Everyone believed that the strangers were building a home on the rocky shores of the Atlantic. In this friendly and sparsely populated community, everyone knew everyone else on a first-name basis. No one asked questions; why would they?

Nor did there seem to be anything out of the ordinary, one December morning in 1989, when Liverpool real estate agent Walt MacDonald greeted a casually dressed Montreal businessman asking about a 20-acre parcel of property near Ragged Harbour, a small community about fifteen minutes from town. The man, who introduced himself as Andy Kovacs, and would later become known as Andre Kovacs, was just under six feet; he had sandy-coloured hair, was clean-shaven, and wore aviator-style glasses. Offering $2,000 in cash as a deposit on his selected piece of waterfront property, Kovacs told MacDonald that he was in the pharmaceutical business, and that he was looking to get away from city life.

"He seemed right at ease and appeared to be very comfortable with the business he was conducting," MacDonald recalls. "He gave the impression of being very well educated and told us he was looking for a place on the coast where he could build a home. He said he intended to move his family here to get them away from the busy city. He came across as a real family man, and I remember him especially saying he had two children that he thought would like living next to the ocean."

An aerial view of the cove and land near Ragged Harbour where the record hashish seizure occurred. LIGHTHOUSE PUBLISHING PHOTO

There seemed to be nothing unusual in Kovac's interest in a particular property, MacDonald says. "It happens all the time in this business. People see a piece of land they like, so they come to us only wanting to look at that and nothing else. They've looked around and found something they like. There's nothing unusual about it; it's just that some people know exactly what they want." The deal was closed, and Kovacs went on his way; the land was officially sold in January 1990, for $110,000, registered to a Montreal-based company known as 744-5300 Quebec Inc.

But there was something very unusual about the deal, after all. Most land transactions usually end with the construction of a house or some other type of development, but few are destined for a place in Canada's criminal history books. Kovacs' purchase was.

While he was in Queens County, Kovacs kept a low profile, avoiding most of the locals, especially those in the Ragged Harbour area, and most particularly his neighbours. All dealings pertaining to the property were handled for him through a Halifax-based lawyer, and after the sale was completed, Kovacs vanished. MacDonald says he never saw the man again, and residents of Ragged Harbour don't recall even once seeing him around his property.

Four months later, though, on the Saturday night of May 26, 1990, there was more going on at that secluded property than the local residents had ever contemplated. And early the next morning, the community of twenty-odd houses was swarming with law-enforcement officers from all over the province. The eyes of the nation turned to Ragged Harbour, Nova Scotia, as word of a major police operation began to spread. Local residents were left bewildered. Never, in their wildest imaginations, had the people of Ragged Harbour and other nearby villages—East and West Berlin, Eagle Head or Port Medway—dreamed their sleepy community would be the site of the largest hashish seizure in Canadian criminal history, a record that still holds today. Sunday, May 27, 1990, dawned sunny and warm, a welcome respite from the months of cold weather that had gripped Nova Scotia since early January. The rising temperatures made it an inviting day for a Queens County lobster fisherman to check the traps before the season wrapped up in a week's time. At about 8:00 A.M., the man (who, for protection, remains unnamed) guided his small vessel around the shoals protecting the rich fishing grounds in the secluded coves of Ragged Harbour. The villagers in the area depend largely upon the sea for their livelihood; lobstering is one of their mainstays.

The water was calm and the sun shone brightly. Even the breeze blowing in from the open sea was warm, in stark contrast to the previous day's harsh weather—a major storm had swept up the Eastern Seaboard, wreaking havoc on lobster traps; thousands of dollars' worth of equipment had been lost, and this fisherman was out to check his traps and survey the damage.

In one secluded cove, he found more than his lobster traps: as he entered the inlet, he was startled by a flurry of activity on the rocky beach. From his vantage point, about 100 m offshore, he saw a rubber Zodiac and a raft up on the rocks; there were men—he could not tell how many—unloading a bulky cargo onto a series of conveyor belts extending up the shore to a small saltwater lake on the other side of a natural breakwater. He couldn't tell what the cargo was or make out the men's faces, but the fisherman knew he'd stumbled onto something extraordinary, and decided to radio the RCMP in Yarmouth. Then, fearful, he turned his vessel around and gunned it towards the safety of the open sea.

The men on shore heard the boat's engines and realized their cover was blown; jumping into their vehicles, they fled, abandoning cargo, equipment, and vessels. The exact number of offloaders has never been determined, nor have they ever been identified.

Within minutes of receiving the fisherman's call, the Yarmouth dispatch centre had Liverpool RCMP rolling, but by the time the first officer arrived, about fifteen minutes later, the smugglers were gone; no one had even been left behind to guard the supplies or the cargo—about 35 tonnes of hashish with an estimated street value of more than $400 million. It was the largest hashish seizure in Canadian criminal history. The smugglers had also abandoned thousands of dollars' worth of equipment, including three motorized Zodiacs and a small camping trailer, most likely the base for their operations.

The smuggled hashish was loaded onto rubber rafts that had been intercepted near Ragged Harbour. VERNON OICKLE PHOTO

RCMP officers discovered a quantity of hashish that had already been unloaded from the Zodiacs and stashed on shore; they also found the trailer of a transport truck, positioned to receive the cargo and remove it from the area. The Zodiacs had evidently been used to tow ashore a large rubber raft filled with hashish; the drugs had been unloaded the previous night from a ship anchored off the coast.

RCMP officers take moulds of tire tracks believed to have been made by suspected smuggling vehicles. VERNON OICKLE PHOTO

At the height of activity that day, more than fifty RCMP officers from Liverpool, Bridgewater, Yarmouth, and Halifax had converged on the secluded beach, some of them leading police dogs in the hopes of tracking down any smugglers who might have lingered to protect their stash. Considering the quantity of drugs that had been abandoned, authorities had to consider the possibility that the smugglers might return: strict precautions were imperative to secure the crime scene, protect the officers working on the investigation, and there was particular concern for the safety of nearby residents. The police were helped on land by the Department of Defence, at sea by the Canadian Coast Guard, and in the air by Greenwood-based Canadian Forces Aurora surveillance planes, whose crews were searching for a mother ship from which the drugs had been offloaded. A Department of Fisheries and Oceans helicopter was also called in to search the coastline and neighbouring islands for any clues to what would prove to be among the greatest mysteries in Canada's escalating drug war. For the following four days, all motor vehicles and boats entering the bust zone were checked for possible connections to the smuggling operation; curious locals were turned back at roadblocks manned by heavily armed police officers; and members of the media were not allowed on the scene until mid-afternoon.

The first journalists to arrive were a film crew from CBC Halifax— and, as it turned out, myself. (At the time, I was editor of the *Liverpool Advance*, the local weekly newspaper in Queens County). Upon entering the bust zone, we were told to keep our heads down, literally, as police had not completed their sweep of the area, and there remained the possibility that some of the offloaders could still be nearby—and armed. We were on the scene at our own risk, the officers said—but, while the warning was intimidating, no reporter would miss the chance to record the offloading of Canada's largest hashish seizure. Our access, however, was limited. We couldn't take pictures of the police officers without asking first—many of them were regional undercover drug operatives whose cover would be blown if their faces were seen on TV or in the papers. We could only walk in designated areas, under escort; and although we were permitted to photograph the hashish being unloaded, we had to stay at a distance. The whole experience was impressive to a small-town newspaper reporter used to covering council meetings and social events—all the equipment and cargo the smugglers had left behind in their haste; the large, bricklike packages with brown and black wrappings: it looked for all the world like a scene from a TV crime show, or a movie.

As we talked with the officers, the details slowly began to emerge. This had been an elaborate, if not particularly well-planned, scheme: the Zodiacs had brought the contraband ashore, onto a rocky beach; from there, it was to have been shuttled across a small saltwater lake behind a natural dyke; and on the other side of the lake, the drugs were to have been packed onto a series of conveyor belts and deposited in a transport truck. That was the plan, but it was abandoned as the offloaders fled. From there, the cargo was supposed to go to Ontario and Quebec for distribution. Although early estimates by the RCMP suggested the seizure was significant, it was not until the next morning, Monday, that its full extent became clear—after police discovered more hashish hidden in the pontoons of the raft they had unloaded. It was then that authorities, faced with enough drugs to fill a small house, realized they were dealing with more than a significant shipment, and it didn't take much longer to determine that the seizure was of record proportions.

Yet, despite all the excitement, no arrests had been made. Immediately after arriving to find the hashish, authorities had issued a province-wide all-points bulletin for four vehicles that had been spotted in the area and were suspected to be linked to the smuggling effort—a navy-blue cube van, a royal blue Volvo station wagon, a large white diesel semi-trailer, and a brown recreational vehicle. They were never found.

The RCMP intensified their efforts to track down those involved, but there wasn't much to go on. They knew the hashish originated in Afghanistan or Pakistan because of the markings on the packages, but that wasn't going to take them far—the only real lead they had was the name of the man who had purchased the Ragged Harbour property in January. Police began searching for Andre Kovacs in Montreal—Jim Carter, then staff sergeant at the Liverpool RCMP, had told me Kovacs

was clearly part of the scheme, and that the land had probably been purchased for the drug offload. "Of course this individual would be a
suspect," he said. "We discovered the drugs on this land," he said, referring to the property Kovacs had acquired.

It took the RCMP until 7:30 Monday evening to complete their work at
the scene; the drugs were then taken to Yarmouth and kept under tight
security. On May 31, all but a small portion, needed for evidence in any
court proceedings that might follow, was transported to a Hansport
paper plant and burned.

There were many questions to be answered after the record-breaking
drug bust. Why didn't the smugglers wait one more week, until the end
of the lobster season, when there would have been less chance of discovery? And what was the significance of the distress call received by
search-and-rescue officials in Halifax, just two days before the drugs
were found? That call, authorities acknowledged later, may have been
connected to the shipment. But only maybe: neither the RCMP nor the
air-search officials could ever make a definitive connection between the
two incidents.

The duty watch officer operating the emergency radio system at the
air-search-and-rescue base in Halifax on Friday evening, May 25, 1990,
said the message came in at about 7:00 P.M. "When I got the distress call,
I thought right away that things just didn't seem right." But, he added,
considering there were only two hours of daylight remaining to check out
what could have been a real emergency, rescue crews—including three
aircraft and two cutters—were sent to the SOS coordinates in question.

His concern, the officer explained, arose when the person issuing the
Mayday, who seemed to know proper Maritime emergency procedures, was
also, apparently, providing deliberately misleading information. "There is
a standard procedure that all vessels follow in any emergency," he said.
"A caller will either identify the ship or themselves, and they will give
their location." In this case, although the call came as a distress signal,
"it was very ambiguous." Despite his repeated attempts to get more
information, the caller would only give the watch officer a vague description of the vessel alleged to be in trouble, and was even imprecise about
the number of crew members—between two and seven people. "There
was no way of knowing what the emergency could have been from the
information the caller gave." But when the person issuing the Mayday
gave two possible positions where the troubled vessel was located, "I
knew something was not right."

"An experienced seaman would not do that, unless they deliberately wanted to send us in all directions." It's true, he said, that people in a real emergency can become confused, but the Mayday procedure easily allows a caller to give his or her location by using a series of numbers.

Although rescue crews, assisted by fishing boats in both areas, searched for hours, the watch officer reported that no signs of a troubled vessel were ever found. "The crews of the fishing boats working in both areas that day confirmed they had not witnessed anything unusual," he said, adding that he remains convinced that the call, far from being a true emergency, didn't even fit the parameters of a false alarm—and search-and-rescue workers receive up to one hundred faked calls a year. "Whoever made that call knew what they were doing," he said. "They made the distress call seem close enough to a real emergency that we had to respond. And they knew enough to send us in all directions. Most times you can tell right off when a call is fake, but this case was different; there was just something about it to make it stand out from all the rest."

Because the call came so soon before the Ragged Harbour drug seizure, the question of a possible connection naturally arose. "When a major drug shipment like this is coming in, you don't rule out anything, however remote it may seem," the watch officer said. But, he added, "if the false alarm was connected, what purpose would it serve?" Why would smugglers want to cause several ships and aircraft to converge in the very area where the drugs would be passing—unless someone believed the mother ship could get lost in the extra traffic. The watch officer was at a loss to explain. "To me, it wouldn't really make sense to bring all that attention to the area," he added. "But when you're dealing with something like that, I guess you just never know." While the RCMP considered the possibility of a link between the false alarm and the drug seizure, they had no hard information to go on. The mystery of the false alarm was never solved.

As word of the record-breaking drug bust spread, more questions surfaced about the elaborate operation—and along with the questions came the rumours. RCMP Sergeant Gary Grant, drug awareness coordinator for the province at the time, said police authorities always anticipate rumours in such extreme situations as a major drug seizure, and that, no matter how far-fetched they may seem, all leads must be investigated. RCMP officers at the Liverpool detachment confirmed that, in the weeks following the seizure, they heard many theories from the public on the smuggling scheme. One popular notion was that the Ragged Harbour shipment was a decoy to attract the RCMP's attention while a larger quantity of drugs was being brought into another part of Nova Scotia.

Liverpool RCMP's Jim Carter rejects that idea. "They could have used a much smaller shipment and attracted as much attention, if that was their intention," he said. "There really isn't much evidence to support such a suggestion." Another popular theory alleged that RCMP had blown the incident out of proportion—and that police had not found 35 tonnes of hashish, but stuck to the figure even after learning it was inaccurate, supposedly to protect their image. Carter said this was just not a reasonable suggestion: police would have nothing to gain from such devious action, and besides, it just didn't happen that way. "You couldn't fit the shipment into one truck because it was so large," he said. "It took us almost two whole days to unload it." Indeed, it took several days to destroy all of the drugs, he added.

While RCMP worked hard to dispel the rumours, they continued to surface. It was natural enough: people were overwhelmed, frightened that such large-scale criminal activity could take place right in their own backyards, without somehow being noticed earlier. "You usually only hear about this type of thing happening in other places, like the big cities," said one woman, who lived near the site. "It really scares me that people like this can come into our community and do this without being detected. I just think about what might have happened if one of the local kids—or anyone, for that matter—had walked down there and stumbled onto those guys. God only knows what they might have done to them."

Another local resident agreed that the size of the drug operation should stand as a warning to people everywhere that crime does not occur only in large cities. "I've lived here all my life and I had never seen anything like this before. When they moved in and put that road down to the water, no one ever suspected it was for anything like this. When you see that sort of thing going on, you just automatically assume someone's building a house, but I guess you just never know. But what I'd like to know is how they got the drugs into the shore without being detected in the first place."

There was no lack of theorizing on that question. One person suggested the shipment was offloaded several days before the seizure, allowing the mother ship enough time to get out to sea and avoid detection. Police confirmed that authorities had considered that possibility, Carter said, "but based on our investigation, we found no evidence to support the theory."

And what about Andre Kovacs? Who was this mysterious stranger who blew into town and purchased the land on which the drugs were discovered? The public had their own ideas; many believed Kovacs was working for someone in the community who had been backing the illegal

smuggling operation. Although police said they had ruled out any connection to Queens County other than the offload site itself, they were
never willing to discuss their investigation of Kovacs. He was a mystery
in 1990, and he remains a mystery to this day.

Indeed, police remained closed-mouthed about most of their investigation for a long time. They would say only that their efforts were not
confined to Nova Scotia, or Canada. However, almost seventeen months
after the world's second-largest seizure of hashish, on the shores of
Ragged Harbour, there was finally some news: the RCMP revealed
details of an international investigation closely tied to the Netherlands.

*Abandoned equipment, including rubber Zodiacs, left behind by
the smugglers when they fled the scene.* VERNON OICKLE PHOTO

In October 1991, RCMP spokesman Gary Grant confirmed that five
people who were responsible for importing the illegal contraband to
Canada had been arrested and successfully convicted in Amsterdam. A
sixth man was still at large, but was being pursued. Their ship, the
Coral Sea II, had been seized by Dutch authorities, Grant said, explaining that the RCMP had been involved in an international investigation,
working in cooperation with Interpol and many other international police
forces. The team effort was making progress as early as December 1990,
when Dutch police made a similar seizure of narcotics, in Amsterdam.
The connection to the Canadian case was the offshore supply ship, the
Panamanian-registered *Coral Sea II*, also seized by the Dutch. Because
the RCMP had issued an international call for assistance to solve the

Ragged Harbour case, the Dutch knew about it; Grant explained that the ship's logs and charts revealed that the captain and some crew members were involved with the hashish shipment to Queens County and that the contraband had been transported to Canadian waters on board the *Coral Sea II*. The RCMP were quickly notified and, in March 1991, an officer from the Yarmouth RCMP Drug Section went to the Netherlands to question the suspects.

That investigation provided the Dutch with evidence relating to the hashish seizure in Queens County. This, along with the evidence compiled in the Netherlands, allowed Dutch authorities to charge and prosecute the five individuals, and issue an arrest warrant for a sixth suspect for importation of hashish into Holland. Dutch law also provided for the suspects to be charged for the importation of $400 million worth of drugs seized in Queens County, Grant said. The captain and four crew members were charged and convicted in the Netherlands for illegally importing hashish into that country as well as into Canada. Jeremias Tonga, 39, from Indonesia and captain of the *Coral Sea II* at the time of the Ragged Harbour seizure, was sentenced to three years in prison. He was also fined 17,000 gilders (approximately $9,980 Canadian). Jochem Pieter Bosscher, aged 39 and a citizen of the Netherlands was sentenced to three and one-half years in jail as well as being fined 100,000 gilders (approximately $58,700 Canadian). In addition he was required to forfeit 1.2 million gilders (approximately $704,400 Canadian) seized by Dutch authorities. Pieter Schellevis, 49, from the Netherlands, was imprisoned for twelve months. Hermanus Hebbo Schriebeek, 46, from the Netherlands was sentenced to fifteen months in prison while Albert Schriebeek, also 46 and a citzen of the Netherlands, was sentenced to a fifteen-month jail term.

The *Coral Sea II* was eventually sold. But the case would remain open, Grant said; no Canadians had been charged for the illegal smuggling of drugs into this country. "We are not through yet," he said. "The RCMP will continue to coordinate the file and move the investigation forward in this country." Police have never specified what leads they were pursuing in Canada, but Grant said they were confident that arrests would eventually be made. That hasn't happened.

"There was a substantial Canadian side to this investigation as well," Grant said in 1991, "but we are reluctant to reveal any of our investigation. We can say with some certainty, though, there were no Queens County people involved. We feel confident that eventually this case will be fully solved."

The investigation, according to the Yarmouth RCMP Drug Division, is on hold pending any new information. New cases have taken priority, and the file is now ranked "inactive."

In April 1994, RCMP requested the court to have the 8-hectare property in Ragged Harbour—the land bought by Kovacs—forfeited to the Crown under the new Proceeds of Crime legislation. In the past, only cars, trucks, ships, and equipment had been seized under that law. According to Sergeant Lloyd Melbourne, the head of the RCMP's Proceeds of Crime section, authorities hoped to show the drug rings that they are serious about their efforts to stop the flow of contraband into Canada.

Unloading the hashish at Ragged Harbour.
VERNON OICKLE PHOTO

In September 1994, the Nova Scotia Supreme Court ruled in favour of that action; no representative of the owner defended the charges of importation and possession of hashish, and having property knowing it was obtained by crime. In his decision, Justice Felix Cacchione concluded that the Queens County property had been purchased with money provided by organized crime, and that the company was obviously a cover to buy property on which to offload drugs. As for Andre Kovacs, he has never surfaced.

What has been determined about the mysterious Kovacs is that he laundered money for the land purchase through a foreign exchange service in Montreal; U.S. funds were converted into a Canadian money order and a certified cheque eventually deposited with a Halifax law firm. Court proceedings revealed that even Kovacs' lawyer had to rely upon scribbled notes and phone messages from his client regarding the disbursement of funds for the land purchase and building the access road.

The Queens County Challenge

LIVERPOOL, NOVA SCOTIA, settled in 1759, is a picturesque town steeped in history. Its economy is based largely on the rich forests and once-bountiful Atlantic Ocean. Natural beauty; good people with pride and enthusiasm in their community; a rich heritage of hard work, good and bad times: these are the qualities characteristic of Liverpool and many other communities throughout Queens County.

A rural area, Queens County is located in the southwestern region of Nova Scotia—small in geographical size and population, but resplendently beautiful in landscape and, especially, seascape. There are more than 100 km of coastline, a tourist's paradise and, unfortunately, a drug smuggler's as well.

For hundreds of years, residents of the many quaint communities nestled in the coves and inlets along the coast have profited from the rich treasures of the Atlantic. Places such as Port Medway, East and West Berlin, Western Head, Moose Harbour, Hunts Point, Port Mouton, and Liverpool have relied on the ocean for their livelihood. Today, while fishing is still an important part of the local economy, residents and visitors alike have focused on the recreational and aesthetic qualities of the Atlantic as it laps against the shores of some of the most spectacular and picturesque beaches in Nova Scotia.

The town of Liverpool has a colourful and diverse history. On May 12, 1604, de Monts and Champlain landed at a site now known at Fort Point; more than 150 years later, Liverpool was founded on the same site by New Englanders of Pilgrim stock who discovered the richness of this natural and undisturbed wilderness. The town developed as a port, shipping dried fish and lumber to the West Indies; ships returned laden with molasses, rum, and tropical fruits. The town's exporting traditions continue today: the county's largest exporter. Bowater Mersey Paper Company, exports an estimated $150 million in high quality newsprint, from trees harvested largely in southwestern Nova Scotia, to ports around the world. Established in 1929, Bowater now employs about seven hundred people directly and more than twenty-one hundred through its woodlands and forestry operations.

In many ways, the history of Liverpool is distinctive among Nova Scotian communities of its size; in particular, it shares only with much-larger Halifax a heritage of privateering. From 1760 until the War of 1812, privateers, commissioned out of Liverpool with the King's Letter of Marque, roamed the waters of the North Atlantic in search of bounty. Some called it piracy; others defined it as patriotism as the United States fought for independence. Signs of that privateering era can still be seen in the historic town, on the banks of the beautiful Mersey River. Homes, street names, and landmarks all tell of this heritage.

Over two hundred years, the people of Queens County have met many economic challenges, as people do who live in communities that depend upon natural resources. The 1970s and early 1990s were difficult times for most small communities, but particularly for those whose fortunes rise and fall by the vagaries of land and sea. They have also seen times of trouble because of the return of privateering in its twentieth-century incarnation of drug smuggling: the syndicates and the opportunistic individuals who thrive on this illegal activity discovered in Queens County the same qualities that made the area so attractive to their historical counterparts—easy access from the sea into dozens of protected inlets; and ready transportation of the illegal goods along little-travelled roads. For a number of years, residents—including police—were unaware of the activity, and would have been ill-prepared to deal with the tidal wave of drugs coming ashore in Queens County, even had they known about it. The RCMP drug section responsible for the entire region between Halifax and Yarmouth consisted of two officers, with few resources at their disposal. Even today, Halifax and Yarmouth, at either end of the South Shore, with their own drug sections staffed by dozens of officers cannot put a dent in the multibillion-dollar drug trade.

In 1969, when RCMP Corporal Bob Brogan arrived in Liverpool, the detachment consisted of fewer than ten officers, responsible only for the rural communities of Queens County; the town had its own police force. In those days, officers commanding rural attachments were assigned the rank of corporal, but when the RCMP took over policing of the town in the early 1970s, that rank was upgraded to sergeant. Not until years later was the rank of staff sergeant used at the Liverpool detachment, which today has a contingent of thirteen members.

Brogan, a tall, burly, friendly man with a pleasant disposition, arrived in Liverpool in July, after a posting in Baddeck. When he assumed command, he made two observations: He liked the area because of its natural beauty and friendly people; and he observed that there was an overabundance of drugs available in town. Coming from Baddeck, a community about the same size as Liverpool, Brogan recalls that he was alarmed, overwhelmed, and amazed by the quantity of drugs available, compared to what he'd been used to. Liverpool, he said, was a town under siege by the drug trade.

Now retired from the RCMP, Brogan, high sheriff of Queens and Lunenburg Counties, has many memories of the early drug trade in Liverpool. From his arrival in 1969, he commanded the Liverpool detachment until July 1977. He was then transferred to Yarmouth, where he remained until his retirement in April 1985, returning to Queens County in January 1987 to take the sheriff's job.

"It was a whole different world back then," Brogan recalls of those first days in Liverpool. "In the early 1970s we witnessed a new era arrive in this part of the province—the era of drugs that forever changed this community and many others. It came by the boatload and the truckload. And with it came all the problems you would expect to associate with a drug trade, including an increased crime rate and higher level of violence."

"When I first arrived in Liverpool, I couldn't get over how much drugs were available here. There just seemed to be much more in this town than anywhere else in the province, and it created a challenge for the police. I'm not saying that drugs were blatantly visible on the town streets, but I am saying that if you wanted drugs in this town, they were easy to get. This wasn't the case in most other towns in Nova Scotia in those times. Of course, today, you can get whatever you want, wherever you want, but twenty years ago Liverpool really stuck out, because of the ease with which you could get drugs." In the schools, in the bars, the drugs, especially marijuana and hashish, just kept coming, bringing new surprises as dealers, ever-resourceful and heartened by the ease with which they could carry on their illegal trade, tried out every imaginable method to enhance their booming business. Brogan recalls one incident in which a local man was found bringing drugs into the community through the mail and then selling it to drug suppliers from other provinces. "There were dozens of stories to tell as people found new ways to get their drugs into the community."

*　　*　　*

The men took their time. It didn't matter to them that they might be seen by people from nearby homes in the small fishing villages dotting the coast. The spring breeze blew in off the ocean as the strangers casually

70

loaded their goods into the back of the camper, then sped away. It was a different era—a time when people didn't pay much attention to activity along the province's coastline, and the operation went off without a hitch. Although no one can say for certain, many other shipments of drugs had probably come into Nova Scotia before. But this one was special because it had a date with destiny in Canada's criminal records; it marked the beginning of the drug war in Nova Scotia.

This first recorded major drug importation into Nova Scotia occurred in Queens County in the early 1970s; sketchy police records mark the arrival sometime in 1971 or 1972. Members of the Liverpool RCMP detachment were dispatched to the sleepy fishing village of Port L'Hebert to check out some bizarre activity, and stumbled unwittingly into the netherworld of the drug trade.

Straddling the Queens and Shelburne County lines, Port L'Hebert is a close-knit community: people are observant of what goes on around them, but avoid getting involved in others' business. Neighbours watch out for each other, but have little interest in the activities of strangers, unless a local person is affected. That's how it was and, for the most part, how it is today in many small Nova Scotian communities.

It was a typical Maritime spring day, and life in Queens County was laid-back, as usual. Then, two officers from Liverpool were called to check out some suspicious activity reported in the Port L'Hebert area. To the constables, it was a routine patrol. That changed, however, when Grant and his partner responded to the call. "It was probably one of the more bizarre cases that I had ever seen," Grant recalls. "I saw a lot of strange stuff in my years with the force, but this was just bizarre."

When the two Liverpool RCMP officers arrived at the end of a narrow dirt road that stopped right on the rugged, rocky shore, they found what Grant describes as "some pretty unusual stuff." Strewn throughout the woods near the water's edge, and hidden in the underbrush, were the bits and pieces of a camper truck's interior. "We found everything from inside a camper—like someone had stripped it down on the inside to leave only the frame and outside walls. We found the wall panelling, mattresses, a sink, dishes, and anything else that you can think of that would be in a camper. There it was, spread throughout the woods. Someone had just put it there under the evergreens and left it there. We had no idea how long it had been in the woods, but it was obvious it had been there awhile, as the wind had gotten a hold of it and tossed it all over the place."

Grant says police estimated that the material had been there for several weeks, and that it was only when high winds started blowing it around that someone noticed and phoned the RCMP. He also offers the opinion that the caller was more concerned about garbage littering up the shore than they were about drug smugglers. Either way, however, the RCMP had been called to the scene of the first documented drug importation site in the province.

"When we arrived there, even we weren't really thinking about drugs or smugglers," Grant says, acknowledging that public apathy about drugs probably affected the authorities to some extent. "But after we got there and saw all of this stuff strewn throughout the woods, we began asking ourselves why anyone would put this mess out there. You could tell that whoever had done this had really torn that camper apart, and we questioned the motive for such activity." These were pertinent questions, and Grant says it was the type of thinking that finally put the RCMP on the trail of drug smugglers.

In their subsequent investigation, the RCMP learned that, weeks earlier, local fishermen had observed a small vessel—a 1 metre pleasure craft, they guessed—land on the rocks where the road met the shore, and meet a camper truck. Then, the onlookers saw the crew of the boat transfer their cargo to the waiting vehicle. A few hours later, they watched the boat head back out, making for open sea, while the camper truck left the area. No one found the activity peculiar or suspicious, so the incident was not reported to authorities.

"We just couldn't get over it," Grant recalls. "Here we had these people who actually saw what happened, but no one thought about contacting the police, because they didn't think it was important enough. If they had called us, we might have caught those guys in the act—or at least with the goods in their possession—and been able to press charges. As it was, by the time we were called the trail was cold. We never did catch whoever it was that was involved."

Based upon the size of the boat and camper, Grant estimates that the smugglers could have transported up to 2 tonnes of drugs, which would have been stashed tightly in the back of the stripped-down truck. He speculates that the shipment was hashish, since witnesses described the cargo as being small, square bundles, wrapped in brown packaging. As the investigation into the offload progressed, Grant says the RCMP grew more and more frustrated with the realization that, had they been notified earlier, there would have been a good chance of intercepting the smugglers. "We understood that everyone minded their own business in places like Port L'Hebert; that was tradition. But we could've had those guys; that's what bugged me then, and it still bugs me today to think that someone got away when they could have been stopped if people would have taken it upon themselves to get involved." The police found out that the camper truck was from Ontario—one witness paid particular attention to that detail, but didn't get the licence plate number. The frustration was heightened when Grant and his partner began to think about the implications: "We wondered that, if this shipment got through, how much more was getting by us?"

No one was ever arrested in the Port L'Hebert operation, but Grant says it wasn't for lack of trying. In fact, he adds, a few weeks after the call to Port L'Hebert, investigators thought they were making progress when a sailboat that matched the description of the vessel in Port L'Hebert was seen in Lunenburg. "I'm convinced that it was the same boat that brought the drugs to Port L'Hebert, but we could never prove it. By the time we got there, they had enough time to clean it and remove any trace of the drugs—or anything, for that matter." After that, the investigation went cold and the file was never successfully closed.

In the 1970s, Grant was at the height of his focus on drug enforcement efforts, and he stresses that the case was a particular disappointment. "It really bugged me when we came up empty-handed. I hated to lose a case, but I also appreciated and understood the reality that we could not be everywhere."

With this new attitude, RCMP set out to crack the known rings operating in Liverpool at the time. There were many, but Brogan says the one place that seemed to attract more drug activity than almost anywhere else was the Mersey Tavern, at the rear of the historic Mersey Hotel in downtown Liverpool. Long since closed down, the tavern had a reputation for black-market activity, including drug trafficking, and for underage drinking.

"It was a bad place," Brogan recalls. "You could pretty well get anything you wanted in there, including drugs. But we had to be careful how we approached the tavern. If you sent in an officer and the guys in there knew he was a cop, he could get into a whole lot of trouble. We had an unwritten policy that no officer ever went in there alone, unless there was absolutely no other alternative. We usually went in there by teams so that an officer could always have someone to watch their back—that sort of thing. We never really had any serious incidents, but we were lucky. I can recall that we had many close calls that could have exploded into a major confrontation."

For the police, going into the Mersey Tavern was like walking into a hornet's nest, but late in September 1975, they did exactly that. It was a move that put the Mersey Tavern—and many local drug traffickers—out of business. Friday evening, September 19, the local RCMP, assisted by the recently formed Halifax Drug Squad, staged a successful raid on the tavern. As a result, eight people were arrested under the Narcotics Control Act. Nine minors, ranging in age from fifteen to eighteen, were subsequently charged under the Liquor Control Act. There were about sixty people there as the busts went down.

At the time, police felt that shutting the place down was probably the best way to combat the drug trade in Liverpool—a major signal to dealers that the party was over; local authorities were serious about wiping out the scourge that had gripped the once-peaceful community. Seventeen uniformed and plain-clothes RCMP officers participated in one of the province's first-ever drug raids, blocking all the exits and rounding up the suspects. Two Liverpool homes were searched later that evening, resulting in charges of possession of an unregistered revolver and possession of drugs. All were sentenced after being charged.

Brogan says he does not have any delusions that the drug trade was eradicated because of their efforts, but he proudly notes that, following the raids and continued police presence on the drug scene, the market went further underground. "We didn't have any false expectations about the situation. We knew that drugs were still around because we continued to find them long after the old tavern closed down. However, they didn't seem to be as easy to come by. I believe it was the beginning of a policing effort that continues even to this day."

In the years since, Brogan has continued to maintain a close watch on Liverpool—it was a community he cared about and planned to make his home, as he has. However, his observations about today's situation are not encouraging. While the drug trade may not be as open as it was in the 1970s, it has escalated to epidemic proportions, which, he acknowledges, continues to create a serious drug problem in the community, as elsewhere. "There's no way that you'll ever totally get rid of drugs, because there's just too many of them. They're everywhere; you can get whatever you want, whenever you want them."

However, while some people are still alarmed by the availability of drugs in their communities, others have become complacent and accepting. One Liverpool resident, who saw the raid on the Mersey Tavern, says that twenty years ago the availability of drugs was the main issue of the day. Because he no longer associates with the trade, he has agreed to talk only on the condition that he remain anonymous—a reasonable request, he says, considering that he has a family and a job to think about. "It seems like people were talking about them more back then; that they really cared what happened around here. I'm not saying that people don't care any more, it's just that they don't seem to react like they used to. Maybe they're just getting tired of it."

The witness agrees that the raid on the Mersey Tavern was a milestone in the local drug war. "If you had to go back in time and pinpoint an event that sent a strong signal to drug dealers in these parts, I'd say that would have to be it. I remember that before the raid, the guys would deal right there in the open. It was nothing to walk in there and buy a couple of joints any time you wanted them. That kind of stuff happened all the time. But I have to admit, everyone was really surprised and caught off guard when the cops burst in there that night. There was no warning."

Calling his memory of events "a bit cloudy," because they occurred more than twenty years ago, the middle-aged man describes the raid. "I can remember when the cops burst into the tavern. It was like something out of the movies. Actually, it was kind of exciting. Everyone just kind of dropped what they were doing when those cops swarmed through the doors. I remember, too, that no one was allowed to leave. It didn't matter if they suspected you of doing drugs or not; you weren't allowed to go anywhere until they were sure you were clean. It seemed like it took hours."

This Liverpool man, who openly admits he has used drugs over the years, says he was lucky not to get arrested that evening. Another time, he might have been holding a joint or two. "It was one of those things that you had to see for yourself, but it was something I'll remember because it really drove home the point to me that the cops meant business. After that, I never did any amount of drugs, because I really feared going to jail. That night really scared the shit out of me." Today, the Mersey Tavern witness says he believes authorities are doing the best job they can in addressing the drug problem. "Let's face it, there's only so much anyone can do about this kind of stuff. It's not something we want to admit, but drugs are still around here and they are available to just about anyone who wants them." In fact, he adds, drug deals are still going on right on the streets.

"But I don't think that makes Liverpool any different from any other community. I've seen it myself," the man continues. "It happened one Friday evening not too long ago when I was getting ready to go home from work. Out behind the building where I parked my car, there were two young fellows doing their business. It was broad daylight and there they were, right out in the open, buying and selling their drugs. That's when I realized just how serious the drug problem was. When you see something like that, it really leaves an impression."

* * *

Just as the small but determined Liverpool RCMP detachment became a force to be reckoned with in the town's drug netherworld, the officers also began to make considerable progress in coming to terms with the much more formidable challenge of smuggling. Busts such as the record seizure of hashish at Ragged Harbour have shown over the years that if police continue to struggle against the almost insurmountable odds of international narcotics cartels, they have also been giving the smugglers a run for their money, and sometimes win the race.

The *Maybird* is an early example of this kind of significant break-through. The same year Grant and his partner, along with officers from other detachments, successfully ended the Mersey Tavern's legacy of illicit drug and liquor activity, they took on a hashish-smuggling scheme off the coast of Port Mouton, near Liverpool, with altogether different results than those at Port L'Hebert.

In the summer of 1975, an unlikely trio of would-be smugglers, based in Florida, formed a partnership and devised a plan to take drugs into North America. It was supposed to be their ticket to wealth, but in the end, it was their undoing.

By the end of July, the two men and one woman had purchased a moderately sized pleasure yacht and prepared its hold for the illegal cargo they intended to transport. In her better days, the *Maybird* had been a quality-looking, seaworthy vessel that more than likely served as a fine status symbol for some well-to-do yachting enthusiast—until Randy, Phil, and Lisa got hold of her. Before leaving their Florida port, the trio totally stripped the *Maybird*, leaving on board only those items they considered essential to their trip. Every available bit of room was needed for the contraband once it was secured from their source in Morocco.

Months earlier, Phil had flown to Morocco, where he arranged for a supply of hashish from exporters there. Ironically, his contacts ran deep into the Moroccan army, and when the *Maybird* arrived, it was the army, not the drug smugglers or powerful drug lords, that loaded the illegal cargo. Today, this scenario would be unthinkable: the Moroccan government has cracked down hard on drug dealers. But twenty years ago, trade in illicit substances was just emerging as a worldwide phenomenon, and it was not unusual for some factions to condone, even promote, such

76

activity. The full size of the *Maybird*'s cargo remains a mystery; it is known, however, that once the three Americans had completed their transactions in Morocco, they put to sea, heading for Nova Scotia.

It was not an easy voyage. The transatlantic crossing, which was supposed to last less than two weeks, took more than a month. For starters, the smugglers had engine trouble; then the *Maybird*'s battery went dead; eventually they ran out of fresh water, and their food rations were precariously low. They were not even sure if they were headed in the right direction, since none of them had any experience at sea. If the vessel had not been carrying such a potentially harmful cargo, it would have been almost a comedy of errors. But this was no laughing matter: the *Maybird*'s crew wanted to get their precious cargo to Nova Scotia, and ultimately into the hands of users—including children—through the underground market. Their objective was to turn over the drugs and get rich.

It seemed that everything was going wrong for this group of smugglers on their ill-conceived voyage. Indeed, it was miraculous that they managed to survive until help finally arrived—ironically, in the form of a Canadian Coast Guard cutter that intercepted the *Maybird* during its last week at sea. Instead of boarding the vessel, the Coast Guard crew generously replenished the *Maybird*'s water and other supplies, and gave the crew a fresh battery. Then they sent the vessel on its way— complete with its stash of hashish.

Meanwhile, in Nova Scotia, the plan was running even further off-track. The trio was supposed to rendezvous with offloaders near White Point, a quaint village nestled on the coast about five miles south of Liverpool. Famous for its spectacular sandy beaches, picturesque scenery, and many resort facilities, White Point—the smugglers believed —would provide the perfect cover for a drug offload. Indeed, it might have, had the plan come together as they had hoped. The beach front afforded easy access to the water, yet was protected from prying eyes by the rugged rock outcrops and dense forests. But exact timing was essential; any deviation from a rigid schedule could have led to trouble, and despite their efforts, the smugglers encountered problem after problem because of careless planning and poor execution. Their inexperience was painfully obvious.

According to the plan, a recreational vehicle was supposed to be waiting to transport the hashish to Quebec, where the drugs would be sold on the black market at an enormous profit. It sounded so simple. Yet, since even the best-laid plans can go astray, this trio's venture had no hope of succeeding. The yacht and the transport vehicle were to rendezvous in

September, and when October arrived, the offloaders grew restless, worrying that if they remained in the area, someone might get suspicious. With no means of communicating with their co-conspirators, they panicked, packed up, and left the area.

Meanwhile, the *Maybird* edged closer to the southern coast of Nova Scotia, its crew's frustrations mounting. They were a month behind schedule, and their many problems finally led to a confrontation. Just off the tip of Port Mouton, a fishing village about ten miles southwest of White Point, the now-volatile partnership dissolved. One of the men was set adrift in a rubber raft with 227 kg of hashish, which supposedly represented his share of the shipment. He also got to take his guitar, but none of the remaining supplies. The *Maybird*, with the other crew members and the bulk of the cargo still on board, returned to the open sea. The vessel was never intercepted nor was it ever reported to have stopped in any known port. Her fate remains a mystery. The fate of the second man, the woman, and the cargo also remains a mystery.

However, the man who had been set adrift in the rubber raft had a date with destiny. He was one of the first in a long line of smugglers who would soon infiltrate the coastline of Nova Scotia, and among the first of a smaller list of smugglers intercepted by authorities over the following decades.

Randy, a rugged and athletic twenty-five-year-old, was close to the rendezvous point when he decided there was a good chance that his compatriots might no longer be waiting on shore, and recognizing his plight—in a small rubber raft with no supplies, on the unpredictable Atlantic—he opted to take his chances in Port Mouton, nearer than White Point. That choice led to even more trouble. As he approached the shores of Cadden Bay, a rocky and secluded beach near Port Mouton, Randy jettisoned the outboard motor, then rowed to land, hoping to find shelter and get out of his predicament, somehow. He had no way of knowing exactly where he was, or how far from the nearest houses he had landed his raft. His odyssey was getting more intense by the hour.

Once onshore, Randy unloaded the cargo on the rocks and covered the raft with brush. He found a dry, safe place to hide the drugs—under several piles of brush and shrubs—then, with his guitar strapped to his back, headed for civilization. Or such was his hope. Following the rocky beach, Randy believed he would eventually come across a village or, at the very least, a wharf with fishermen who could offer help. He did not realize that the rocky shores of Nova Scotia can run undisturbed for miles. Walking the wet, slippery rocks of the Atlantic coastline is a challenge for even the most fit individual, but for someone who has just spent a month cooped up on a small boat with little exercise and less food and water, the trek is next to impossible.

He hung on for a few hours, but the weak and confused smuggler was beginning to understand the seriousness of his situation—and then it got worse. Randy slipped, and broke the big toe on his left foot. He was in great pain, lost, cold, hungry, and wet. If he went back to the raft, he would have to row around the coast since he had foolishly dumped his motor; and he knew he couldn't make it. If he stopped where he was, stranded on the rocks, he would grow weaker and disoriented. If he continued on, he might be going further away from civilization. It seemed there was no plausible option.

For once, however, luck was on Randy's side. A fisherman spotted him, picked him up off the rocks, and took him to a small motel, the Stonehurst, in Port Mouton. The story might have ended there if the fisherman had not told his friends about the unusual stranger with a broken toe and a guitar strapped to his back whom he'd found stranded on the rocks near Cadden Bay.

The Liverpool RCMP were not directly notified about the incident, but it wasn't long before word spread through the community—and reached Grant. The officer's efforts on developing a network of reliable informants, people who felt they could trust Grant enough to tell him about the drug dealers without fear of prosecution, had paid off. It was through these sources that Grant found out about Randy.

"When you live in a small place like Port Mouton and talk about things, its doesn't take long for word to get around," Grant recalls. "In this case, the fisherman talked about what he had seen, and word got back to us. I'm not really sure what I was up to when I heard about the stranger, or even if I thought about drugs right away. But I knew instantly that something just did not seem right about the whole situation. After all, how often is it that you find a stranger with a broken toe walking on the rocky beach with a guitar strapped on his back? It just didn't add up, and because I'm a naturally curious person, I just felt the situation was worth taking a closer look."

When Grant arrived at the Stonehurst Motel, three days later, he learned that the mysterious man had checked out the previous afternoon. He also discovered that, on his first day in Port Mouton, the stranger had made several calls, and stayed in his motel room until the next day, and was then picked up by a man in a car. The motel operator, an elderly woman with a Scottish accent, could not identify the man or the vehicle;

79

however, she did allow Grant to search the stranger's room. There, Grant remembers, he found clues that eventually led to Randy's undoing. In his haste to leave, Randy had left some papers indisputably linking him to a major drug-smuggling scheme—his passport and some schematic drawings of the *Maybird* that clearly illustrated how the yacht was to be converted into a drug boat. Grant found these items in a plastic bag that had somehow fallen down behind the bed.

"Actually, I couldn't believe my luck," Grant says. "It seems like this guy's luck was getting worse by the day, but mine was just about as good as a policeman could imagine. How often would you expect to walk into a hotel room of a stranger and find papers that would connect him to a drug-smuggling scheme? Not too bloody often!"

With the cooperation of the motel operator, Grant took the man's passport and the drawings to be photocopied. Once that was done, he put the papers back in the plastic bag and returned the package to the motel room with clear instructions that if anyone returned for them, he was to be notified immediately. Weeks passed, and there was no news. Then, the motel operator called Grant to tell him that the stranger had just returned looking for the package; this time he was travelling in an RV with Quebec licence plates. The police also learned that Randy and his companion, a man named Doug, had brought along an aluminum boat and motor, and were headed to Carter's Beach in Southwest Port Mouton. This was a secluded location where the smugglers—or so they thought— were unlikely to be detected. The plan was to get their vehicle close to the water, launch their boat, then go round a rocky point to find the spot where Randy had come ashore almost a month earlier. Of course, they had no idea the police were watching from a distance, ready to move in when they had located the drugs.

Life was not kind to these smugglers. Shortly after they had put the boat in the water, the motor burned out, leaving them stranded on the waves. The two men reluctantly rowed back to the beach to reassess the situation. "This entire case was really bizarre, and a comedy of errors from start to end," Grant points out. "It was a lesson in what drug smugglers shouldn't do. Nothing went right for these guys, but they were persistent, I'll give them that much."

Randy and Doug were determined to get to Cadden Bay, even if it meant walking through the thick woods. As the RCMP watched, out of sight, the smugglers drove to the end of a road in Southwest Port Mouton, which terminates at a cluster of small homes. From there, they would have to walk only a 100 metres or so, locate the hashish, and carry it back to the vehicle. But the little-used path to the waterfront had long since grown over, and the going was difficult. Still, they were driven on by their determination. Hours later, when Randy and Doug returned, each carrying several yellow bags, the police knew they had caught them red-handed, but decided to wait for their next move. "We didn't know what was down there, but we found it hard to believe that these men would go to so much trouble just to get a couple of bags of hash. On the other hand, they fooled us that time, because they didn't return to the woods any more," he explains. "Instead, they got back into the camper and headed back to Liverpool. To be honest, we weren't really sure if there were any more drugs down there or not, so we had to decide if we wanted to take those guys down then, or wait to see if they would return. We decided to take them down before they left Queens County in case there were no more drugs back down there on the beach."

The RCMP followed the vehicle back to Liverpool, stopped in a parking lot, and watched as the two men changed their clothes and then headed out of town, towards Halifax. The police made their move on the outskirts of town. In the subsequent arrests and seizure, the RCMP confiscated about 23 kg of hashish, but, Grant says, they were convinced there was more to the smuggling scheme than that small quantity of drugs; the conspirators had already spent more than the return on such an investment.

"It just didn't click," Grant says. "It wasn't normal for those guys to go through all of that trouble for such a small amount of drugs. We were convinced that there had to be more to it than that." Randy and Doug were charged with possession for the purposes of trafficking, and the officers headed back to check out the beach.

It took an entire day for the RCMP, with the assistance of helicopters and police dogs, to uncover the rest of the drugs. "We found the rubber raft almost right off the bat, but the drugs were not that easy to locate. In fact, I can remember one officer crawling around that beach on his hands and knees looking for the drugs, even though we weren't sure if there was still anything there or not. But you've got to do that sort of stuff sometimes if you want to have any luck stopping these guys. Police work isn't always glamorous; in fact, most of the time it's downright dirty, but someone's got to do it."

After a painstaking search, RCMP found six canvas sailbags containing 227 kg of hashish, worth hundreds of thousands of dollars. With the drugs from the vehicle and now the drugs from the beach where the smugglers had been observed, police had an open-and-shut case. Grant recalls spending a lot of time interrogating Randy. "Back then, things were a whole lot different than they are today," he recalls. "You could talk to your man without having to watch where you stepped. I remember one day taking the guy for a walk on the beach, where he told me everything that happened. That's how we know so much about how this all got started, and about what happened on the *Maybird* and after he made it to the beach on the rubber raft. You couldn't do that today, or they'd have the police in court instead of the criminal."

Randy and Doug both were sentenced to three-year prison terms for illegal importation and trafficking. "Usually, luck will be against the police, but this is one time that it was on the side of the good guys and we made it work for us."

The Shelburne County Connection

IF THERE IS ONE AREA in Nova Scotia that rivals Queens County's status as the province's drug-smuggling capital, it is Shelburne County. Similar to Queens geographically, Shelburne has a population of about twenty thousand. It, too, depends mostly upon the Atlantic Ocean for its livelihood: the fishing industry, particularly lobstering, has been the mainstay of this South Shore region for hundreds of years; Shelburne, settled in the late 1700s, calls itself the lobstering capital of Nova Scotia.

The town of Shelburne was founded by United Empire Loyalists and in 1783 was the fourth-largest city in North America. Although today it is more of a small rural town, the community continues to embrace its proud heritage while striving to build a prosperous future. In recent years, the downturn of the fishery has made this aim a considerable challenge.

Like most people in rural Nova Scotia, the residents of Shelburne take pride in their way of life. They are a hard-working people, toiling mostly on the sea. Since the 1970s, the seas have delivered more than the people had bargained for.

Headlines in the June 4, 1980, issue of the weekly Shelburne *Coast Guard* called a seizure of marijuana at the town's wharf the second-largest in the history of North America. Although the records have since been broken and the names of the vessels changed over the years, this 1980 story could have been written in any month in any community along the South Shore over the past two decades. It was reported that the 19.5-metre vessel *M.V. Patricia*, a converted shrimp boat, was illegally transporting approximately 22 tonnes of marijuana. Packed into the rusted and weather-beaten hulk of the American-registered vessel, this contraband had an estimated street value of more than $50 million. The largest seizure at the time had been in British Columbia—33.5 tonnes— in May 1979.

Although there had been other drug busts in the province, particularly in Queens County, the take down of the *Patricia* is recognized by authorities as the first major drug interception on the seas. The quantity, by today's standards, is insignificant, but this shipment of marijuana heralded a new twist in the story of the war on drug smuggling.

Sergeant Wayne MacNeil, then a sergeant at the Shelburne RCMP detachment, recalls that the U.S. Drug Enforcement Agency (DEA) had been monitoring the boat as it came up the Eastern Seaboard. American authorities first became suspicious when, instead of entering Canadian territorial waters, the boat kept a close parallel to the coast as it travelled northward—an activity known as hovering, which alerted DEA officials to the presence of a possible drug boat bound for a rendezvous with offloaders.

The *Patricia* did finally enter Canadian waters, and U.S. officials notified their counterparts across the border. The fisheries boat *Louisburg*, with five RCMP members aboard, overtook the *Patricia* approximately 65 nautical miles off the coast of Nova Scotia at 11:15 A.M. on May 31. Officials said later there was little trouble during the high-seas confrontation but acknowledged that shots had been fired.

RCMP officers boarded and searched the *Patricia*, which was then escorted under guard into Shelburne Harbour; there, drug authorities and RCMP officers from Halifax, Bridgewater, Liverpool, Shelburne, and Yarmouth watched as the vessel was docked. Eight crew members—all Colombians—and an American captain were taken into custody and given a medical clearance before being escorted to the Shelburne jail for interrogation. At the wharf, twenty officers worked through the night unloading, weighing, and tagging the drugs, which were stored in two tractor-trailers. The boat was moved to the Shelburne Marine Wharf and secured for further investigation.

Gary Grant, by then with the Bridgewater RCMP, was there when the *Patricia* was brought in. He explains that although the ship's destination was never discovered, "It didn't really matter much because here we were, looking at a suspicious wreck of a ship about to enter Canadian waters, probably with a cargo of illegal drugs. At that time, Canadian authorities had little choice but to act." Police later conceded that Canadians had no authority to intercept the vessel—the *Patricia* was in international territory, although at one point the vessel had ventured into Canadian waters. It was a bold move by the RCMP officials, and it could have backfired if the case had gone to court in Canada because Canadian authorities had no jurisdiction.

Armed only with their regulation pistols and rifles, an emergency response team of RCMP officers had boarded the fisheries vessel and headed out to sea for their rendezvous with the *Patricia*. "When you think about it now, you really know and appreciate how dangerous—

maybe even stupid—it was to do that sort of thing. The members weren't really all that well-armed or prepared to take on a suspected drug-smuggling ship. We had no idea how many people were on that vessel, or what kind of weapons those guys had on board with them."

Able to laugh about it now, Grant says it was lucky the suspects did not resist, and even luckier that they had no weapons aboard. As the *Louisburg* pulled alongside the *Patricia*, the suspect vessel was ordered to stop; the captain ignored the Canadian authorities and ordered full

The Patricia *tied at the wharf in Shelburne in June 1980.* RCMP FILES PHOTO

steam ahead. "The boys weren't putting up with any of that foolishness," Grant recalls. "You can't play around when engaged in a take down, because you don't know what the other side is going to do. You're playing with lives, and you don't want to see anyone get hurt or killed."

Shots—he can't remember how many—were fired into the wheelhouse of the *Patricia*, stopping it dead in the water. "I guess they knew we were serious and, when the boys started shooting, that they meant business. You gotta show 'em who's boss if you're gonna deal with these guys."

RCMP boarded the *Patricia*—"a dirty scum of a rust bucket" is Grant's succinct appraisal of the vessel—and arrested the men on board. "This crew was worse than anything we had ever encountered before. As a matter of fact, I don't think I ever encountered anything like it again for the rest of the time I was in drug enforcement. They were filthy, and the ship was a complete mess. It was immediately obvious that they had lived like pigs for weeks; it's a wonder they didn't get some kind of disease, like dysentery or something. We even learned the captain had refused to give his crew fresh water or, for that matter, allowed them to use the bathroom under proper sanitary conditions. It was a pig's pen."

Once the boat and crew were secured, the vessel was towed to Shelburne Harbour, which, Grant explains, opened an entirely new set of difficulties for the police. "We had no idea what we were going to do with these guys," he says. "They're all scum, but these fellows were worse. You couldn't get close to these guys; they were filthy and they stunk like you wouldn't believe. We took them to a local motel and the rooms had to be fumigated after they left—that's how bad they smelled, and they had fleas besides. It was disgusting."

The smugglers were held under tight security at the motel while police attempted to interrogate them. At the same time, Canadian authorities were trying to decide what to do with the Colombians. Like some crews, they were not even aware of their ship's cargo; and because the seizure had been made in Canadian customs waters, beyond the 12-mile nautical limit, only customs law applied, not criminal law. No charges were laid against the crew, who were deported.

However, the American captain didn't get away scot-free. "We knew this guy was the leader of the group and was most likely involved with the plan from the very beginning," he explains. "We also suspected he had contacts somewhere in the United States, probably wherever he was planning to go. The Colombians were just another casualty of the drug trade, but we wanted to get this other guy; we wanted him really bad."

For days, RCMP interviewed the captain, hoping to get information to help them infiltrate the smuggling ring for which the drugs were intended. "We worked hard on that guy, staying with him day and night, trying to get him to talk. It finally worked." Under police pressure, the captain of the *Patricia* finally admitted that the marijuana was, in fact, destined for the United States; specifically, for the Boston area. "He didn't tell us anything that we didn't already suspect, but at least we now had it from his own mouth, and that was good enough for us." Working with American authorities, the RCMP freed the captain, who was quickly deported. "This guy must have though Lady Luck was smiling on him that day. He must have thought we were out in left field or something, because Canadian authorities had decided not to prosecute him in Canada. He was in for a rude awakening."

When the captain stepped off a plane in Boston, federal drug officers arrested him for conspiracy to import drugs. "You see, although we had secured the drugs in our country, the *Patricia* was actually taken down outside Canada's limits so there may have been some question about our authority. And since during our interrogation, the captain had actually confessed to conspiring to take drugs into the United States and not into Canada, it was determined that the United States would have a better claim on him."

At the trial, Canadian authorities, including Grant, described the captain's confession. On the strength of their testimony, the captain was found guilty of drug conspiracy and sentenced to a seven-year prison term.

The incident on board the *Patricia* represents a potential danger in the drug trade, Grant points out. "When you're trying to take down these drug smugglers, you don't have any idea about what kind of weapons they have or to what extremes they'll go to protect their cargo. Some of those guys are crazy, and they might do anything. Working in drug enforcement is dangerous because of its unpredictability. No matter what precautions the police may take, they can't control the human side of the equation. When you're in the middle of a take down, you don't know how these guys will react. It's the kind of situation where dangers unfold without warning, and police officers have to be prepared for all possibilities. Our guys are good, and that's what has probably prevented serious trouble over the years."

Grant has high praise for both Canadian and American drug-enforcement officers, who are the front-line soldiers in the escalating drug war. "We take these guys for granted but, you know, they lay their lives on the line when they're out there in the field. I guess it's a lot like that old saying— it's a dirty job, but someone's got to do it, and we all should be glad there are people out there doing this particular job."

Another good example of collaborative police work involved a shipment of hashish intercepted at Lockeport, south of Shelburne. On April 16, 1985, the vessel *Ernestina* sailed from Tripoli, Lebanon, with a cargo of hashish—not an unusual port of origin, since authorities in North America estimate that more than 70 per cent of the hashish coming into Canada and the United States originates from that war-torn Middle East country. Ships leave the port every day loaded with illegal drugs, the country's main export. The *Ernestina*, with her seven-man crew, had a schedule to keep and a multimillion-dollar cargo to deliver. The captain gave orders to head towards Nova Scotia for a prearranged meeting with another vessel to offload the cargo in Nova Scotia for distribution on the black market. The Nova Scotia vessel was the *Lady Sharell* out of Lockeport.

It would take almost a month for the two ships to sail into the annals of Canadian criminal history as major players in one of the country's largest-

87

ever drug seizures. On Friday, May 24, the two vessels met on the high seas, where the 13.2 tonnes—453 bales—of hashish from the *Ernestina*'s hold were moved to the deck, awaiting transfer to the fishing vessel.

However, a few days earlier, an RCMP response team had moved into position at the government wharf in Lockeport, ready for the *Lady Sharell*'s return to port. They had been planning a trap for more than nineteen months, having gained the cooperation of a Lockeport businessman, Leonard Mitchell, who had been working with the smugglers as an undercover operative for the RCMP. Sixty officers were in the Lockeport area during that week in May, supported by air and land backup from the Department of Defence and the Coast Guard.

It took about an hour for the *Lady Sharell* to take on the cargo: an ocean transfer is a risky business, but this operation went smoothly on the rough Atlantic, five nautical miles off the eastern tip of Sable Island. Around 5:50 A.M., the recently refurbished fishing boat entered Lockeport Harbour, cutting through the early spring morning mist.

As the crew tied her to the wharf, RCMP officers sprung from their hiding places, while two mock explosions created a diversion to confuse the smugglers. The police scrambled into position, a nearby Coast Guard cutter moving in behind the *Lady Sharell*, blocking retreat into the open sea. The operation took minutes; soon the offloaded drugs were secured and the smugglers en route to the lockup, an hour away in Yarmouth. Six men from Florida were arrested and charged with unlawfully importing a narcotic. They were Maurice Scott Germain Jr, 45, Big Pine Key; Anthony Francis Busco, 27, Miami; David Tuthill, 36, Port St. Lucy; John Frederic Cassidy, 50, Marathon Shores; Robert Louis Barnett, 58, Key West; and Roy Paul O'Dare (alias Louis James Atherton), 29, Miami.

As the land drama was unfolding, the Canadian Forces destroyer *Iroquois* began pursuit of the mother ship, the *Ernestina*. About 10:00 A.M., the captain realized it was foolish to attempt a high-seas chase in the thick fog that had moved in, and the *Ernestina* stopped almost immediately. An armed RCMP task force on board the *Iroquois* boarded the vessel, and there was no resistance from the crew. On Monday, May 27, the *Ernestina* sailed into the Canadian Forces Base Shearwater, near Halifax, where the ship was kept under tight security and searched from stem to stern. The seven-man crew were charged with importing narcotics into Nova Scotia.

The drug bust, estimated at more than $38 million, made national and international headlines: the Lockeport interception was reported as the largest seizure in North America at the time, a great payoff for almost two years of investigation involving not only Canadian authorities, but also drug squads from Miami and Boston. The scope of the operation showed how drug smuggling along Nova Scotia's largely unprotected coastline was beginning to escalate; it also showed what cooperative police work can accomplish, even under considerable odds— in that only one in ten shipments is intercepted.

Seven of the RCMP officers involved with the Lockeport operation were from the Liverpool detachment, including Constable Keith Beaver, who explained that police immediately recognized the full scope of the seizure. "Our involvement was not the investigation itself," he recalls. "We were only involved with the take down on the day it actually hap-

Removing the narcotics from the Lady Sharell *required dozens of police officers.* THE SHELBURNE COAST GUARD PHOTO

pened. Mainly, we assisted in the arrests and the removal of the drugs." Beaver's memories of events are focused on the overwhelming quantity of drugs seized. "It was awesome in comparison to the amount of drugs we come across in [places like] Queens County. When you're involved in drug enforcement every day, you get small quantities of the stuff from the streets, but I can't recall ever seeing anything like that."

Unfortunately, in the years since the Lockeport seizure, authorities have seen drug shipments that far surpass that intercepted on the *Lady Sharell*. But in 1985 the Lockeport bust was significant. Beaver remembers it took officers between three and four hours to weigh and remove the drugs that had been brought onto the wharf. "It was a very note-worthy day and [the RCMP] felt everything had gone according to our plan. The men all worked extremely well together—it was a job well done."

RCMP officer Peter Williamson, staff sergeant of the Liverpool detachment at the time of the event, agrees with Beaver's observations. With more than thirty-four years of experience on the force, Williamson spent much of his time on the province's South Shore, first at the Chester detachment, then in Liverpool, between 1978 and 1988; from there he

A number of transport trucks were used to haul the hashish from Lockeport to Yarmouth for disposal. THE SHELBURNE *COAST GUARD* PHOTO

moved back up the coast to Bridgewater, where he served as staff sergeant until his retirement in early 1995. He recalls having witnessed many drug seizures, but none that compared to Lockeport in 1985. "Of course, there have been many since then that were bigger and more sensational than the Lockeport bust, but that was a big one for the 1980s and really the first of any significance," Williamson recalls. "It was a time when Nova Scotia was bracing for the major drug trade about to explode along the coast. If we were intercepting shipments like that, just imagine how many were getting by. For all those that we do manage to get, we also know of shipments that came in right under our noses and we never knew about it. In these cases, we didn't find out about them until long after the fact and the drugs were all gone."

In 1985, when the Lockeport seizure occurred, Williamson remembers that the public was overwhelmed by its scope; so, he says, were the authorities. "Most of the men involved in the actual take down that day didn't know what was happening until just before it took place." For security reasons, such operations are conducted on a need-to-know basis, particularly in this case, which involved a local citizen as an undercover operative. "In these types of situations, the fewer people who know anything, the better it is," Williamson explains. As a high-ranking officer, he knew about the operation in advance, and was in charge of securing the site after the emergency response team made the arrests, and overseeing the collection and cataloguing all exhibits that would be used in subsequent court proceedings.

On the day of the take down, Williamson recalls that he and other Liverpool officers left their detachment shortly before 6:00 A.M., to arrive in Lockeport at a predetermined time that was expected to coincide with the seizure. However, he says, "We could tell from first glance that we were going to be at the wharf for a while. We had been led to believe that this was going to be a big bust, but we had no idea just how major it was. There's no question it was a good bust and certainly worth all the effort that went into the case."

The Lockeport seizure was also noteworthy because it marked the first time that the RCMP had used a civilian in covert operations as a police operative. Canadian authorities had little prior experience of witness protection programs, but the RCMP developed one soon after the Lockeport bust. In the absence of such, the operative was nevertheless paid for his work and given a new identity—but only after lengthy legal battles. "When you're dealing with drug traffickers, you're dealing with people who know what they're doing," says Williamson. "Those guys in Lockeport were professional smugglers. Everyone involved in that operation had a job to do, and they had the backing of some organized crime syndicate. They might have pulled it off if we wouldn't have got lucky and had someone come forward to help us with the case after he had been approached by the smugglers to help him find a boat." In fact, he notes, the smugglers' plan was so well laid, that if police had not been tipped off, the drug traders might have gotten their contraband into Lockeport. "I think that this is one case where the public—one man—made a difference. If we're going to beat this thing, then everyone needs to follow his example."

Big and small, shipments of illicit drugs continued to arrive steadily in Shelburne, bound for the North American drug markets. Despite the high stakes, the smugglers continued to undertake risks, relying on the fact that Nova Scotia authorities were overworked and under-equipped.

They didn't always prove correct in their assessment. During the last week of May 1986, Shelburne airwaves crackled with excitement. Rumours of another major drug offload ran rampant throughout the communities that hug the Atlantic coast in the southwestern region of the province. Residents of small towns and villages dotting Shelburne County were getting used to drug-smuggling activity; the 1980s had seen many major seizures in their communities and drug smuggling was being taken for granted. But the talk was full of anticipation as people speculated about suspicious activity in and around the seafaring hamlet of Cape Negro, a ten-minute drive from Shelburne. Rumours began to circulate when a small pleasure craft, the *Sealayne 60*, docked at the village wharf. Cape Negro is a sparsely populated community, whose residents notice any strange vessel docked at the local wharf, and speculation was fuelled during the week when residents observed unusual goings-on around the boat and the nearby beach. As the rumours spread, authorities were tipped off that something unusual was happening in this relatively isolated, usually peaceful community.

An investigation revealed that the crew off the *Sealayne 60* was engaged in drug-smuggling activity, and authorities planned a raid. They hoped to remove any doubt about possession by intercepting the shipment as it was being transported from the offload point—just to ensure their case was airtight. On Tuesday, June 2, the trap was set; police watched from their vantage points along a stretch of road on the outskirts of Shelburne, in locations they felt would allow a smooth, unobstructed operation.

By mid-morning, the suspects were in a van, heading towards Halifax. It took only minutes to get police vehicles into position, forcing the van to pull over on a section of Highway 103 near the village of Jordan Falls. Part of the *Sealayne 60*'s illegal cargo was found inside, and three men from Caraquet, New Brunswick, were arrested in the take down and charged with possession of the small quantity of marijuana discovered in the vehicle. After the arrests, RCMP launched an aerial search of the beach and areas near the Cape Negro wharf, where the *Sealayne 60* had docked a week earlier; they recovered fourteen bales of Caribbean marijuana weighing 176 kg and worth an estimated half-million dollars. The yacht-type vessel, which police suspected had been used to transport the drugs into Nova Scotia, was registered in Picton, Ontario. The *Sealayne 60* was seized and docked near a wharf not far from Lockeport.

About twenty-five officers from the Shelburne, Barrington, and Yarmouth RCMP detachments joined forces in the raid, initiated by members of the Barrington RCMP. One RCMP boat and a helicopter assisted the ground forces, providing sea and air surveillance. The *Sealayne 60* bust was not as large or sensational as earlier seizures, but police say it showed that smugglers take many risks to get their shipments into Canada—risks that don't always pay off.

One Shelburne County fisherman, who watched the Lockeport take down at a distance, says it was hard to believe another seizure would take place nearby, only about a year later. The man, who was

The Sealayne 60 *intercepted in June 1986 in yet another illegal smuggling scheme in Shelburne County.*
THE SHELBURNE *COAST GUARD* PHOTO

on the highway as the bust occurred, comments: "I guess, by now, you should really expect this kind of stuff to happen around here, but not on the highways, when you're just driving along, heading into town, and minding your own business. Then, all of a sudden, you see all these police cars and flashing lights; it puts a scare in a person. The first thing you think of is that there must have been a fire or a bad accident, and you wonder if someone you know is involved."

That particular morning, he was driving alone in his half-ton truck. As he crested a small hill, he could see a cluster of police cars on the road ahead; some cruisers were pulled off on the shoulder, while others had stopped right in the middle of the highway, blocking the flow of traffic, which was minimal at that time of day. "At first, I though it was an accident and someone must have been hurt really bad to have that many police cars around. But then they made us stop and wait until they took three guys out of this dark-coloured van and put them in the police cars. I couldn't believe this sort of thing was happening—again—in Shelburne, and this time right in the middle of the highway. There were policemen with guns drawn, while others made the arrests and searched the van. You might expect that this sort of thing happens near the water, but you never expect to see it on the roads."

The unidentified man recalls that although the arrests and seizure

93

created quite a stir in the community, the level of excitement was nothing like that created by previous busts. "I think maybe people were getting tired of all this activity."

RCMP Sergeant Bill Parker, Nova Scotia drug coordinator, was with the Yarmouth Drug Squad when the *Sealayne 60* was taken down. In the investigation following the bust, Parker says RCMP figured out that the smugglers had been working for quite some time to offload their shipment. "We really had no idea how much drugs those guys had on that boat, but we figure they had unloaded most of it before we got there. We had enough to make arrests, but we wished we could have gotten there before they had the chance to get any of that stuff out on the market."

In a more recent seizure, a group of smugglers who had jettisoned much of their contraband after being spooked by aircraft—much like the conspirators off Sheet Harbour in the RCMP's successful retrieval of a quantity of cocaine—struggled desperately to offload what was left on the shores of a secluded cove in Shelburne County. On this October night in 1991, however, the law of averages was with the good guys. As the loaded dump trucks sped down Highway 103 past the commuters of Lockeport, Liverpool, and Bridgewater, en route from Shelburne to Halifax, the chase began. With sirens blaring and lights flashing, the RCMP intercepted the trucks near Chester, just before dawn. Nine men were arrested and about seven tonnes of hashish, worth an estimated $75 million, were seized.

Several RCMP detachments were involved in the case, headed by drug sections in Halifax and Yarmouth and resulting from an ongoing investigation by the two drug sections. Police efforts were concentrated in the East Green Harbour and Lockeport areas, where they believed the drugs were brought ashore, but the shipping and offloading methods remain unanswered questions. However, the collection and distribution functions of the drug ring were successfully infiltrated, the result of cooperation between the public and police; in this case, residents reported suspicious activity to the RCMP.

Less than a year later, the Shelburne hash haul surfaced again. It was early June 1992 when the net was pulled on board a foreign fishing trawler anchored near Sable Island. The fishermen had come up with more than they'd bargained for—a bale of hashish valued at between $250,000 and $300,000 and weighing 22.7 kg. This was part of the shipment that had been thrown overboard by the smugglers fearful that their plans had been discovered; the full amount of hashish has never been recovered.

The Slippery Slope

MEANWHILE, ELSEWHERE ON THE SOUTH SHORE, Ray Martin was just beginning his foray into the world of drug smuggling. At midnight, about a week after his previous phone call, a Monday, Larry phoned with new instructions. Ray was to be at an abandoned wharf near an isolated cove about a half-hour from town—a location he'd visited, although not recently. The wharf had been dilapidated then, and he wondered how any boat could get in close enough to use it now. Abandoned at least twenty years before, it had since all but rotted away, due to neglect. Even local fishermen who know the waters in that area avoided the location.

Ray did not discuss his concerns with Larry; after their last discussion, he'd decided to ask no more questions. He would simply follow instructions and treat these guys just as he would any other customers. He would do the job, take their money, and be gone; the less he knew, the better off he'd probably be. He just hoped these smugglers knew what they were doing. They were playing with his life. If they miscalculated or overlooked any details, then he was going to pay.

Larry told him to leave home at 5:30 the next morning and not to talk to anyone or make any stops, but drive directly to the wharf, where he would be told what to do next. Ray would have to travel south along the coast, first on the main road, then over a gravel road—a half-hour total, he figured. There were a few houses along the secondary road, but none close enough to the wharf for anyone to get a look. Ray hoped anyone who noticed his truck that morning would just shrug it off as a local trucker doing business in the area; although people weren't used to seeing vehicles around, since the wharf was abandoned. As he neared the coast, the road became narrower and rougher—another cause for concern. Stupid arrangements, Ray thought. The guys were supposed to be prepared—yeah, sure. For a few seconds, he considered turning around and high-tailing it back home. But it was too late; he was in too deep. His only option was to see the thing through and hope that his activity on this quiet road didn't draw any attention.

Close to the wharf he saw a man on the crest of a hill overlooking the ocean and the road. He couldn't tell if the guy had a gun, but he looked like a guard. Farther along the road, he was waved to a halt by a second man dressed in a black flak jacket and pants, carrying a semi-automatic assault rifle. The man, who spoke with a French accent like Larry's, checked out the truck and Ray, then told him to go on to the wharf but remain in the truck.

Ray obeyed, suddenly impressed with the set-up. From the truck, he watched three men unloading hundreds of brick-sized bundles wrapped in brown packaging from two aluminum motorboats tied to the rotting wharf. He could see a third boat on the water heading out to the mouth of the harbour, where a blue-and-white fishing boat was anchored. He couldn't read the name on the boat.

Off to one side of the wharf on the rocky beach, a brown canvas tent, its flap slightly open, was partly hidden under the spruces and alders. Ray could see Larry and Paul inside, with a third man he didn't know. On a makeshift table inside the tent was a collection of radio equipment and electronic gear, including a police scanner—it looked like the one Dan kept in his garage to listen for accidents and get leads on potential customers.

Ray found the intrigue exciting. The fact that he was now embroiled in a smuggling operation was oddly exhilarating, especially since he knew that at any moment the police could swoop down and throw them all in jail. He willed himself not to think about the police, and just waited in the truck, watching the activity on the wharf. The three offloaders worked steadily, seemingly indifferent to Ray's presence.

After about fifteen minutes, Larry emerged from the tent, walked over to the truck, and told Ray to back up as close as possible to the wharf, then come inside the tent. Ray manoeuvred the 1-ton truck as close as he could, but boulders, placed in front of the wharf when it was declared unsafe, prevented him from getting too close. The offloaders would have to carry the bundles to the covered truck. Inside the tent—Larry and Paul had left—Ray watched the third man monitor the airwaves, paying particular attention to the police frequencies and the scanner. Every fifteen minutes, he broadcast a series of numbers, which had to be some type of code directed to the fishing boat anchored in the harbour; but there was never a reciprocal broadcast.

Hours passed as Ray watched the offloaders stack the brown bundles in his truck—a big job. Increasingly nervous, he yearned to get back on the road, back in the relative safety of his truck.

Around 3:00 P.M., Larry finally returned, bringing coffee; the first load

96

was ready to be moved, but they would wait until 5:00, when traffic would be heaviest. Ray was to drive to a second location, about forty-five miles from the wharf, where the cargo would be unloaded and stored until it could be distributed to dealers. At that point, Ray confirmed that the cargo was hashish, which had left Europe three weeks before, and would be stored at 'the second location, where Ray was headed, until it could be safely moved out of the province to its final, unspecified, destination. Once the first load was off the truck, Larry said, Ray was to make sure the truck was refuelled, then return to the wharf for reloading. They would move the second load well after dark; this was to avoid following a regular pattern in their transporting over the next couple of days. Ray, he said, should get some sleep while the second shipment was being loaded.

Larry then handed Ray a small brown leather case containing the first installment of $10,000; still hoping for more information about the smugglers, he tried to prolong the conversation, asking Larry about the choice of location for the offload. There were other places in the region that would have provided better cover, he said, confiding that he was nervous about the people who lived on the road.

"We've checked this place out. There's no reason for concern," Larry said. "You worry too much about things that don't concern you. We're satisfied with this area. Everything's been taken care of. We've checked out the houses on this road. There's nothing to worry about. One house has been empty for years; the people in another are away. Everything's going okay. Don't get spooked. Stick to the plan and we'll be fine."

Ray took advantage of the opening to ask more questions, and inquired about the man stationed in the tent. "It's been a long time sitting in there with this guy, and I don't even know what in the hell his name is." Turning to Ray and Larry, the man quickly offered, "Nick. That's it. The name's Nick." Then just as abruptly, Nick went back to his radio and electronic gadgets. "Nick's got an important job. Don't disturb him," Larry said. "He's monitoring for anything unusual, anything that might spell trouble. If the cops are on their way, they're not going to come right out and broadcast it. But they will use codes and secret transmissions, thinking we'll be listening. Nick's got to listen to make sure they're not trying to sneak up on us. He can't talk to you and you can't talk to him. No distractions."

Satisfied that he'd caught Larry in a talkative mood, Ray tried one more question. "Whatever happened to Tobias? I haven't seen him since we met in the bar." Larry hesitated. "He's close by, but not in the area.

97

He's doing other things for us, but he knows what's going on." Ray recalled the conversation at the bar more than a month before, and thought again that Tobias must be the head of the operation. But it was obvious that he wasn't going to get any more information out of Larry, so he dropped the subject.

Before leaving the tent, Larry took out a hand-drawn map, pointed out a logging road on the outskirts of town, and gave Ray some final instructions. "At five o'clock, go to your truck. Don't wait for me; just take the truck and drive to this other location. You have fifty minutes to deliver the cargo. If you're not there in fifty minutes, we'll assume something went wrong and we'll leave. If anything happens on the road, don't come back here. If the cops should stop you, don't tell them anything. If they do stop you, you're on your own. If you find out that the cops have hit either location, don't take the truck to either one. Find a safe place, hide it, and get the hell out of there, 'cause they'll be looking for you. If that happens, someone will pick up the stuff later. Once you get to the cabin and unload, you'll have one and a half hours to get back here. That gives you time to do whatever you need to do. Remember, don't be late; fifty minutes. No more."

On the dot of five, Ray went to his truck, where the three offloaders had begun stockpiling the second shipment of brown blocks on the wharf for the next run. Obviously, the smugglers felt the wharf was safe enough to use, despite its condition. Heading out the road, Ray felt jittery, but it was too late to worry, he told himself as he drove along in his truck, loaded with hashish probably worth a couple hundred thousand dollars on the street. Familiar with most of the roads in this region, Ray knew the route to the second location. He also knew that it was a road police usually travelled; he'd have to drive carefully so as not to draw attention to the truck. After all, he reasoned, the police had seen him on the road often enough to think that he was just hauling a load of fish or scrap metal for a local dealer. In fact, Ray knew most of the local officers well enough to wave in recognition when he passed them on the highway. Still he felt nervous, and tried thinking about the money again, and all the things he could do with it.

Turning onto another road near the outskirts of town, and heading inland, Ray figured it would take half an hour to get to the old logging road Larry had described. Going would be slow there, and the cabin where the hashish would be stored was about fifteen minutes off this dirt road. That allowed only five minutes to compensate for unexpected traffic or other delays. Ray now understood why the truck had to be in good repair; he felt the pressure of the tight schedule, but he had to maintain a steady speed if he did not want to draw attention. Once on the dirt road, he breathed a sigh of relief: the most dangerous part of the trip was behind him.

It was 5:47 when he reached the cabin. Ray had made good time, and felt impressed, both with himself and with the drug conspirators for their planning, which had been fine-tuned down to the last detail. Paul, who was waiting for him, began issuing orders to the four offloaders, who would do all the heavy work. The cabin was only an empty shell; its inner walls had been removed, leaving only the main support beams. From the outside, with all the windows boarded over, it looked like the place had been abandoned for years. Once again, Ray was impressed. The cabin was a good location to stash the hash—unless someone stumbled onto it by accident. It was nearly nine when the final blocks were removed from Ray's truck and stashed inside the cabin. Paul reminded Ray of his instructions. He now had ninety minutes to get back to the wharf, and he had to stop along the way and top up his fuel. One more load had to be moved before morning, so Ray had to be on time, which, he crisply informed Paul, would not be a problem.

After leaving the cabin and refuelling his truck, Ray headed for home. He had to put the $10,000 in a safe place—no way was he going to take the money with him. He was risking his life for this money, and he damned well wasn't going to lose it now. At home, he stashed the money behind a false panel he had put in the closet of the master bedroom a few years before, when he was drinking and hiding his liquor from Shirley. He had also put money there over the years, and Shirley had never found it; it was a secure place, he was sure.

He spent about a half-hour at home, recalling the day's events, thinking of the careful attention to detail the smugglers had put into the operation, and recalling Larry's warning that timing was essential to a successful operation. When Ray had first been given the chance to get in on the deal, he hadn't fully understood the scope of the operation. Now he knew it involved big money and was probably backed by a crime syndicate. This made him nervous. He hadn't thought about what might be in store for him after the drugs were moved. If an organized crime syndicate was behind the scheme, would they leave him alone after the drugs were moved, or would they consider him a loose end? Might they consider him a threat because of what he knew? A liability? Even a disposable part of the plan? He would have to be careful. At ten, he left the house and headed back to the wharf.

99

Nick was still in the tent, still listening. Ray wondered how anyone could stay in one place for so long: he must be well paid, Ray thought, backing up the truck to the wharf, where the next load was stacked in neat piles, waiting for him. Larry was also waiting for him. "Everything right on track?" Larry asked, not really needing an answer, since he had already received a report from Paul. "Yeah! Just like clockwork," Ray said. "Good!" Larry said, telling Ray he should try and get a few hours' sleep on the cot in the tent. They were going to load, then wait until 2:30 A.M. to move it out. By then the RCMP in town would be off duty, offering a relatively clear window of opportunity to move the load undetected. The smugglers had done their homework, and knew that in this small rural town, there are a few hours in the early morning when the RCMP is between shifts and there are no regular patrols—just enough time for a safe run.

Ray wasn't sure he could sleep, but he decided to try, and welcomed the chance to rest his eyes, anyway. Tired after the day's activity, he finally dozed off; at 1:45, Larry woke him, offered him a coffee, and told him the truck was ready. The plan was still to move the drugs at 2:30, when the police were off the roads. Reminding Ray once again that he would have fifty minutes from the time he left the wharf to get to the cabin, and should make good time considering the lack of traffic, Larry sent him on his way: it was precisely 2:30 Wednesday morning when he headed towards the cabin for a second time. This run, too, went according to plan; in fact, Ray arrived with almost ten minutes to spare. It was almost three hours before the second shipment was secure inside the cabin, and Paul was giving Ray a new set of instructions. "Tomorrow, we run on a different schedule," he said. "Be at the wharf at ten sharp in the morning. Do not contact anyone. Refuel the truck, and if the phone rings at home, don't answer it. You might be nervous—say too much, especially to someone you know. Just forget about other people until you're done here. It's safer that way."

Ray, still uneasy about the possible connection to organized crime, decided to fish for information. "How many more runs?" he asked Paul. "You'll know soon enough. We're paying you to tie your truck up for a week. Is there a problem with that?" "No, no problem. I just like to be prepared."

Despite the bad chemistry between him and Paul, he felt he'd get a straight answer. Paul hesitated, glaring at Ray, who pressed on. "I like to know what to expect, that's all. You know—to get psyched up." Paul finally answered: "At least three more trips, maybe four. It depends," he said, then sized Ray up as if considering saying more. "Two more later today, one Thursday—maybe two—or sometime Friday. Think you can handle it?"

"Yeah." Ray shot back. "Just one more thing. Who's backing you guys? Organized crime?"

"Shut up!" Paul snapped. "No more questions. Do what you're told and keep your mouth shut. You'll do okay. That goes for after we're gone, too. If you ever tell anyone about this, we'll find out and I can tell you this much, these guys don't take no shit off anyone. Don't fuck with them. Do what you're paid to do and don't ask questions. Don't ever cross these guys. They'll blow your fuckin' brains out. This is big-time shit. Understand?"

"Yeah," Ray grinned nervously. "I got the picture."

"This ain't no joke. These guys play for keeps."

"I wasn't joking," Ray said. "I'm only doing this for the money, not to get myself killed."

Paul became stone-faced and stern. "You'll get the money; just keep your part of the deal."

"Big-time shit, eh?" Ray asked. "Where are these guys from, anyway?"

Paul ended the conversation. "It's late. You better get outta here before the cops get back on the road. Remember, be at the wharf at ten sharp."

Hoping Paul would relay the message to his superiors, Ray said, "Remember, I'm well known in these parts, and if anything happens to me, a lot of people will be asking a lot of questions." Paul didn't answer as Ray climbed into his truck and manoeuvred the vehicle back onto the logging road and out towards the highway; in the rearview mirror, he could still see Paul standing beside the cabin, and hoped he hadn't been too cocky.

In the morning Ray returned to the wharf for the next shipment. Larry was waiting with his next set of instructions and a message. "I understand that you and Paul had an interesting talk this morning. He says you're worried about what happens to you after this." "Yeah, I'm worried. Shouldn't I be?" Their faces were inches apart as Larry spoke: "I'm only going to say this once. The only thing you have to worry about is doing the job you're getting paid to do. But if anything goes wrong and we find out you were behind it, then you'll have something to worry about. We checked you out before we hired you. We thought we could trust you. Now, if that's not the case, then we've got a problem. A big problem. It's too late to back out now, but you've nothing to fear from us unless you screw us. Then you'd better worry big-time. Enjoy your money and keep your mouth shut, that's all you gotta do. Now we've got work to do; we must keep focused on what we're doing so that we don't make any mistakes." Ray didn't answer. He didn't have to. He knew talking was not high on Larry's priority list—he'd already said more than he usually did.

When the next shipment was loaded, Ray was back on the road, at noon. As he drove he thought about Larry's words. These people had a weak spot, after all; they'd responded to his threat. Now he was safe, as long as he kept up his end of the deal—which wouldn't be a worry for them, since he had another $15,000 to collect and wasn't about to jeopardize that. Ray moved one more load of hashish to the cabin later that Wednesday, and the final one at noon on Thursday. In all, he had made five trips from the wharf to the cabin, and everything had gone well.

On Thursday afternoon, Ray collected his $15,000, along with one last set of instructions from Paul at the cabin. He was not to return to the wharf or the cabin; he was to go home, resume his normal routine, and avoid spending large sums of money that could draw curiosity; and he was to clean his truck inside and out, vacuum every inch of the interior, then wash it from top to bottom to dispose of any evidence, such as the vacuum cleaner dust. If Ray followed these instructions, Paul assured him he'd have no trouble, either from the law or from their organization.

When Ray left the cabin that Thursday afternoon, it was the last time he would ever see or hear from Paul. He would, however, be hearing from Larry again.

*   *   *

Not long after Ray Martin had wrapped up his deal with the smugglers, he was surprised to see his experience mirrored in a drug operation elsewhere in the province. Fortunately for Ray, his venture had been more successful.

In September 1982, suspicious activity drew the RCMP to a small community on the province's southwest coast. It was a crisp, cool morning in Digby, the leaves' brilliant colours hinted at cold weather ahead. Digby, a sleepy little community steeped in Acadian heritage, would not seem the natural location for an ambitious undercover sting operation involving hundreds of thousands of dollars in contraband drugs and dozens of international law-enforcement officers. But drug-smuggling operations create unusual circumstances and use out-of-the-way communities; in that sense, then, Digby—specifically, an area outside town called Corberrie—was exactly the right place.

The drug investigation was uncovered by a Digby landowner whose identity has never been revealed by authorities. Oblivious to the

102

undercover activity around him, the man, out for an early walk, happened upon a telephone strung up in the middle of the woods. It was such an unusual sight that he began asking questions, and inadvertently set off a chain of events that could have destroyed the drug operation. There were a few fishing and hunting cabins in the area, but no telephones; the nearest telephone pole was about three miles away, and someone had obviously gone to great lengths to hide the phone, burying it and the cable under brush and leaves.

Amazed, the Digby man used the phone to make calls from the remote location to friends and relatives, who also had questions. What was a phone doing in the woods, three miles from civilization and buried under piles of brush? Who had put it there, and why?

It didn't take long for word of the discovery to spread: Digby is a typical small town, where most people know each other and everyone likes to talk—not a place to easily keep secrets. Eventually, the Digby man called the RCMP to report his find; the police were initially elusive, then told him they had put the phone there as part of a deer-jacking investigation they were conducting. This was part of their surveillance procedure, and they urged him not to talk about his discovery, lest the suspects be tipped off. The man bought the story and agreed to remain silent, to the police's relief. Part of their story was true: the mysterious phone was an integral part of a major undercover surveillance operation, but it wasn't directed at deer jackers; instead, authorities were hot on the trail of drug smugglers they had been watching since earlier in the year.

Sergeant Bill Parker, RCMP drug coordinator for H division in Nova Scotia since September 1994, has more than twenty-five years of experience on the force, much of it in drug enforcement. He was assigned to the Yarmouth Drug Section in September 1982. "When we got that call from that fellow and we found out that he was calling us on our phone out in the woods, we thought we had lost the case because we feared our cover had been blown," Parker recalls. "If these smugglers had overheard that a phone had been concealed in the woods three miles out in the middle of nowhere, they might have put two and two together. They would have surely been spooked and most likely would have left the area."

The RCMP had found out four months earlier that the Digby area was being targeted by American and Canadian smugglers for a major drug importation. In May, the police received information that a group of possible smugglers—Americans—were in Nova Scotia staking out possible locations where a shipment could be received, stored, and eventually sent to the United States. "Like strangers usually do when they're in these small communities asking questions, this group of conspirators drew attention to themselves by purchasing large amounts of supplies and doing things that just don't fit into normal small-town life in rural Nova Scotia," Parker says.

The RCMP launched a surveillance effort to see if the men were engaging in some type of illegal activity, and were able to confirm that the strangers were planning to receive an offload of drugs. "We learned that the drugs would ultimately be distributed in the United States, but like a lot of drug smugglers these days, the guys chose to bring it through Nova Scotia because they thought there would be less chance of getting caught," Parker explains. "Their plan was to have smaller boats meet the mother ship off the coast of Nova Scotia and then bring the drugs into the Digby area where, in turn, the contraband would be stored in a number of hunting cottages that had been purchased and prepared as storage sheds. We didn't know how long they had planned to keep the stuff in those sheds, but we came to find out they would eventually move the drugs to Maine for wider distribution in the United States."

The RCMP learned that the drugs would arrive on a ship from Colombia that would rendezvous with a fishing boat sent from the Digby area. The plan called for a high-risk sea transfer of the drugs, but as Parker points out: "These kinds of guys are used to taking risks. They're willing to take chances if it means they might make big bucks for their trouble." The drugs were to be transported under cover of darkness; once on shore, they would be loaded onto a number of small trailers, then moved to storage sheds located throughout the Digby Neck area.

Throughout the summer of 1982, authorities waited and watched the conspirators, until the drugs finally arrived, in late September. Originally, the arrival had been planned for June, when a ship was reported heading north from Colombia; but the vessel had trouble in a storm and plans were made to try again, about September 30. When the drugs arrived and were transferred according to the offload plan, authorities remained undercover. "We had been watching the wharves and storage sheds since around the first of September," Parker says. "We weren't exactly sure when the drugs were going to arrive. We had a pretty good idea, but we just didn't have an exact timetable."

As for the phone, he says, it was installed in the woods near the sheds, so that police could remain undercover. "We couldn't risk using radios because the smugglers may have been monitoring the airwaves, so the phone became the next best option." As it turned out, it was the phone

104

that almost blew their cover, but, Parker notes, "Luckily for us, it didn't turn out that way. It was one time when we got a break."

Throughout September 1982, an emergency response team remained ready for action once the drugs were delivered, the sheds were secured, and "the entire offload area was cordoned off under strict police control," Parker says. "We had set this trap for the smugglers through some good police work, and all we had to do was wait for them to walk into it. It seemed like the waiting would never end, but we finally got them."

Police had learned that two Americans had moved into the Digby area to spearhead the offloading plans, while two other Americans—brothers —remained in Florida. Although the brothers were suspected of being the chief organizers, they never entered Canada, so they were never arrested in connection with the operation. Besides the Americans, at least three Canadians from the Digby area, who were to offload and store the drugs, were also under suspicion.

Once the drugs were safely stored in the sheds, the police sprung their trap: the take down involved about one hundred police officers stationed at four different sites around the Digby area, and 8.2 tonnes of marijuana was confiscated. Parker says police encountered very little resistance from the smugglers, who were charged with conspiracy to import drugs; prison terms ranged from three to eight years.

Parker describes the Corberrie experience as a typical seizure in which smugglers move into a small community and try to fit in while arranging their criminal activity. "These Americans did that, but other people in the community recognized that something was not right and notified the police. Here, being strangers from outside the community eventually went against these guys. To some people, these strangers stuck out and attracted attention to themselves. Sometimes, smaller communities are not necessarily the best place for this kind of opera-tion—certainly not in this instance. It doesn't always work out that way."

In the years since his successful drug run, Ray Martin has often thought that it was simply a matter of luck that the operation was not infiltrated by authorities. At any given time in the weeks leading up to the offload, or during the transportation of the drugs, they could have been stopped. But if anyone in the community noticed anything suspi-cious, they didn't report it; and Ray believes his involvement most likely deflected any suspicions locals might have had, since he was well known in the area. Tobias and the others had been smart to get a local involved.

In the weeks following the drug offload, Ray experienced frequent bouts of nervous tension. He feared police would catch up to him, or, worse yet, he feared being chased by the smugglers themselves. Despite all their reassurances, Ray wasn't convinced that he was safe from the mob. He knew too much. He was afraid they would come after him to keep him from talking.

He never talked about the operation. Even when pressured by his friend Dan, he refused to say whether or not he had taken the offer. Ray believes Dan may have suspected he did, but accepted his friend's explanation that he had found other jobs that paid well, so he didn't need to get involved in anything illegal. In the months following the drug operation, Ray found himself growing apart from Dan. He didn't know who was responsible for that, but their friendship cooled to the point that the two men barely saw each other. When they did meet, their discussions were always cordial but brief. Ray believes Dan may have suspected him of becoming involved in drug smuggling and didn't want to be connected in case the police ever became suspicious. For his part, Ray backed away from Dan, fearing he might inadvertently drag his friend into the operation. Pulling away from friends and family became a familiar pattern for Ray: the drug deal left him a lonely man. He waited two months before spending any of the money he had earned, and even then shelled out only small amounts. Eventually, though, he cleared up his debts—the reason he had agreed to become involved in the illegal activity in the first place—and bought special gifts for his children. That, more than anything, made all the risks worth taking. If he couldn't see his children, he could at least give them some of the things they wanted.

Almost four months after the operation Ray got a call from Larry. He was surprised; he never thought he'd hear from them again. It was early October, and he'd just returned from a late-afternoon run to Yarmouth when the phone rang. "How are things, Ray?" Larry sounded pleasant. Fear washed over Ray. What did they want now? Surely not to use him to run more drugs: that would almost be like inviting the police to come calling.

Ray responded to Larry's questioning courteously, still apprehensive about a connection with organized crime. "Everything's fine, I guess. How's things with you guys? I didn't think I'd ever hear from you again. Everything okay? I ain't been back to the wharf or the cabin. I guess you got the stuff out okay. I never heard anything and around here I would have heard about it if something had happened."

"Everything's okay. We got it out about a week later. No problem. Like I told you, Ray, plan carefully and things always work out." Larry spoke with confidence.

"So whaddya want now? I don't know if I can handle anything like that again." Ray felt he should be up front with Larry and not string him on. Larry laughed. "Ray, you underestimate yourself. You did a fine job for us down there. I have to tell you we were all very impressed with how you handled yourself. The first time's hard. It gets easier. And the money gets better, too. That's what it's all about. Money. Everyone wants as much as they can get. You ain't no different than anyone else. Times are tough, and you gotta do what you gotta do to make ends meet. Right?"

"Don't bullshit me," Ray shot back. He wasn't going to be suckered into anything again with talk of big money. "What's it this time? Doesn't really matter; I told you I'm not interested. It's too risky."

Larry hesitated, then said: "That's what I like about you, Ray. Straight to the point. You don't screw around; you want to get right down to business. Well, all right then. We do have another proposition for you, but nothing like the last time. We'd like for you to be a front man."

Ray paused. "What in hell's a front man? I'm doing just fine without you guys. I like things the way they are."

"Come on, Ray. You like the money. I remember the way you were always worrying about getting your $25,000. Money's important to you. And this is easy money—real easy money. All you got to do is drive. We arrange for you to pick up some of our stuff with your truck at certain designated places, and you deliver it to our people around the province. It's real easy. You get two thousand dollars for every pickup and delivery. Easy money. Two or three times a month. Think about it. That's a lot of cash. I know you could use it."

Ray was speechless. It was good money, but he had thought his involvement in the drug trade was behind him. Now here was an offer for doing practically nothing. There was a risk, of course, but it sounded too easy for him to refuse. Finally he spoke. "I don't know, Larry. It sounds risky. Every time I put that shit on my truck, I risk getting caught. I don't know if I want that again. I don't think I can handle it. It won't be you; I'd be the one they'd catch with this shit on his hands."

"Yeah, but every time you put that stuff on your truck, you're also putting money into your pocket. Don't forget about the money. You won't get another offer like this anytime soon."

"When do you need an answer? I need time to think."

"You think too much," Larry chided. "Tell you what. We've got a load that we'll need moved from the city down to your part of the province next week. I'll call in two days. I'll have to know then."

"One more thing, Larry. Why do you guys want me to do this? How do you know you can trust me?"

"I think you proved the last time that we could trust you, Ray. That's the reason we want you now. I know you're desperate for money and when this came up, I suggested you. You made an impression the last time, and it didn't take much for me to sell you to the others. But they'll want to know as soon as possible."

Ray's internal alarms were ringing again. He wasn't anxious to offend anyone connected with organized crime. "Will they be pissed if I say no?"

"I don't think so, Ray. They'll be disappointed, but don't worry about pissing them off. Fucking up a deal's one thing, but turning down a job is no big deal."

"I don't know what to say, Larry. I'd like the money, that's for sure. But I don't like the risks."

"There's risks in any business. The money makes up for them. You should know from the last time that we're careful. But you're right, though. There's no guarantees."

"Well, give me two days and I'll think about it. Call me Thursday night around ten, I'll be home, okay?"

Ray was left pondering his future once again. He'd thought all this was behind him. Besides, now his finances were in order, even if his personal life wasn't. He wanted to put his problems behind him; now everything was complicated again. Still, the money would mean financial security even when his trucking business was slow. On the other hand, Ray didn't want to become a drug dealer. Although technically he wouldn't be dealing directly on the streets, he would be supplying the pushers who fed the users, and his past involvement hadn't directly exposed him to the scum feeding off other people's hardships. Deep inside, he wanted to keep it that way.

There was a lot to think about. Would his conscience win over the money? There was no easy answer. He had read about drug dealers and addicts; he knew some first-hand. But the money was good. Greed is a powerful master, and it won out.

* * *

It was a dingy, cold night in the winter of 1988 when the young woman approached Ray Martin's truck, parked on the corner of Maynard Street. He was there to meet his contact and make a delivery, but he welcomed the brief diversion. As Ray wound down the window, he noticed her engaging smile and bright green eyes. She asked him to call her Tanya—obviously an alias, but he agreed. An icy wind whipped her long blonde hair, as she attempted to make small talk, asking what Ray was doing out alone so late on such a cold night. He knew she wanted more than conversation, but he wasn't interested; he had business to attend to. He should have sent her on her way, but he was touched by the deceiving innocence of her youth; he felt an urge to help her, but he knew he couldn't get involved.

"I could ask you the same thing," he replied, suggesting that if she was cold, she was welcome to sit in the cab—but that was all, he made clear. "I'm waiting for someone, so you can't stay long. He's gonna be here in about twenty minutes." Without hesitation, she darted around the front of the truck and jumped in the passenger side, next to Ray. "Don't you ever take time to check the guys out before you get in and go running off with them?" he asked. "I could have been a serial killer or something. You never know what kind of creep you're gonna run into around these streets at this time of night. You gotta be more careful or you'll get yourself hurt."

"You're telling me? I live around here. But I knew you were okay," she said, grinning. "It's kind of a strange gift that I have, like some kind of extra sense or something. I can spot the weird ones a mile off. I knew right off I could trust you. You got this kinda look that says you're okay. I trust my intuition. Most of the time, I can tell when something's not right."

"Yeah, well I think young girls like you gotta get a lot smarter or they're gonna be picking a lot more of you out of the ditches," Ray lectured. "Looks can fool you and even get you hurt. It's a crazy world out there, and you don't know who you can trust, even if he looks nice. A guy might seem all right on the surface, but he could be dangerous." They exchanged understanding glances and let the matter drop: Ray had made his point. He turned up the heater, realizing how ridiculous he must have sounded scolding a young woman who obviously had more street sense than he, even though she was half his age, or less. Still, he couldn't help noticing how much she resembled his elder daughter, and shuddered to think that the two girls were probably about the same age. He wanted to reach out to the young woman sitting beside him, put his arms around her, like a father. But that couldn't happen.

"So, Tanya, why aren't you at home where it's warm and safe?" It was a stupid question, but he had to make conversation and didn't know what else to say. She laughed. "You know. Gotta work to survive. Besides, it's not much warmer where I live, anyway, so I might as well be here where I can at least earn a few bucks. It's not really all that bad when you're out there. You just kinda get used to it; make the most of it, I guess." Pitying the young woman, he wondered what could have gone wrong to send her to the streets, fighting to survive. "It can't be that bad, can it?" It was a sincere attempt to understand Tanya's world. "Mister, you don't know the half of it." She paused, pushing her bare hands towards the dashboard heater in search of extra warmth. "But you got better things to do than to sit around here listening to my hard-luck story."

"No, I'd really like to hear it. 'Course it ain't none of my business, so you don't have to tell me nothing that you don't want to. It's really up to you." She hesitated, studying Ray's ageing face, hauntingly illuminated by the lights from the dashboard, as if trying to decide whether she wanted to bare her soul. "There ain't really all that much to tell," she finally said. "My life's been the shits from the start, and that's the good part. You heard of bad luck and tough breaks? Well, I've had them all. Guess I've had more than my share."

Tanya described the streets as a ghetto of crime, hate, and corruption—a place where no one is your friend. "It's a real hell-hole, a sewer filled with scum-sucking rats. Like I tell people who question what I'm doing, don't judge me until you've walked a mile in my shoes. That shuts 'em up real fast. There's a lot of drugs around here, and that's bad. I do drugs, you know. Guess you've already figured that out. I ain't on much right now, but I might as well get that out in the open right up front."

She took a brief pause to collect her thoughts, "Anyway, who in the hell doesn't do drugs these days? Hell, how do you think a person could survive in this shit if you didn't have something to help you get by? Some days that's the only way I could get through my stinking life." Turning to Ray for a reaction, she saw he was listening intently, so she went on. It had been a while since she'd opened up to anyone, but for some reason Tanya felt she could tell Ray just about anything without being judged. "I gotta work to get by, and I need the drugs to help me get through the work. You ain't stupid. You know the drill—what a girl has got to do to make it. But if you knew what that was really like, you'd know why I do drugs. If you were in the same kind of crap as me—up to your ass every day in all this shit—you'd do drugs too. Life on the streets ain't no picnic. It's rough. Tough bastards out there. Nobody cares who they hurt or how they do it. You just learn not to get in their way—you fuck up with some of these guys and it's game over.

"It's sad, but that's how it is. Life kinda stinks that way. I don't apologize for anything I have to do to get by. I survive. That's all that matters to me. There's a lot more than me out there doing it, and some that are doing a lot worse than me. I ain't the worst one you could have bumped into tonight. Some of them are real dogs. Losers work the streets. You got lucky when you got me."

Ray sat speechless, listening to the intimate details of Tanya's life. The young woman, maybe twenty, explained that she gave up years ago trying to figure out how she became trapped in a life on the streets or why she couldn't get away. "There's no easy answers. It's not something that I like to think about. In fact, I work hard at trying to forget. It's easier when you forget.

"I left home when I was really young because of all the crap I had to take there. I thought I could go out in the world and make it big, but I just kinda ended up here in this hell. Now I have to live with all this shit and abuse. We don't deserve the bad rap, you know. We get the bad name but these guys, the customers who use us, they're the real scum and they walk away with a fucking smile on their face. But hey, they help pay the bills. You gotta remember that no matter how tough it gets out there, grin and bear it, you know what I mean?"

Ray shook his head, acknowledging her question. But he couldn't really understand her predicament. In her world, survival of the fittest was the reality. "You have to be tough to survive. You gotta do what you gotta do. That's the name of the game. You gotta stop worrying about what you've become and get on with doing your thing or you'll die out there. Sure, I'd like to get away from all this shit, but what am I going to do, become a brain surgeon or something?"

Dressed in a thigh-length brown leather coat (fake, she admitted with a light chuckle) and skin-tight jeans, she said she now had few options. "I never finished school, I'm working the streets, and I do drugs. Who would give me a job? That would make a pretty interesting résumé, wouldn't it?" Tanya's attempt to make light of her predicament failed. It was no laughing matter, and Ray wondered how she could joke about such a lifestyle, but kept his opinion to himself. Sensing his concern, she took a more serious tone, admitting to her fear that street life would kill her, but insisting she was always careful. "Each time I hear of some young girl being killed or getting hurt out there, it makes me sick. It makes me want to throw up. It could be me. I know it's dangerous, but I have no choice. I think about it every night when I go out."

Tanya described many times when she came face-to-face with drug dealers she knew would have turned violent if she hadn't had their money. "These guys don't fool around; they'll beat the shit out of you if you try to cross them, or if you owe them a few lousy dollars." In the crack cocaine community, indeed, dealers do resort to violence—there's a lot of money involved. "Violence is second nature to these guys. They don't care if they hurt you or kill other people just as long as they get their cash," Tanya said. "I've seen some of these guys do things that would make you sick, like punching girls in the face or the stomach, kicking them in the guts or teeth, slamming other guys' hands in car doors, beating the shit out of the other guys, throwing people down stairs, breaking bones and stuff like that. I ain't seen nobody get killed yet, but I know they'd do it. These guys mean business."

After dark, mostly between midnight and 6:00 A.M., is when drug dealers do their business almost anywhere they please, Tanya explained. "They're not careless, though, but they'll do it just about wherever they can make a deal." Crack houses are common throughout the city, she pointed out—places where deals are made and drugs are used. Gesturing with her arms in a sweeping motion, she said, "There's a lot of them around here and in places where you just wouldn't expect to find them—nice neighbourhoods. I've been to some; they're pretty disgusting places; real dumps where the low-life hangs out." With that, Tanya announced that she had to leave before someone saw her talking with a stranger who wasn't a customer. "If you talk too long to a stranger around here and don't make a deal, then people get suspicious and that's not healthy. They might think you're a cop or something, and that won't be good for me. I've stayed too long as it is," she adds, reaching down to open the truck door. "If you're not buying, then I gotta go—that's business."

Ray shrugged off the comment but encouraged her to stay. "No rush. My friend won't be here for awhile yet. You can stay a few more minutes. I don't think anyone will notice."

"You don't know who will notice what," she responded sharply. "I'd like to stay longer. You're nice. Maybe I'll see you again when you've got more time. Maybe next time you'll want to do more than just talk. That'd be okay with me."

"I don't get out around here much," Ray explained. "I doubt if you'll ever see me again, but thanks. I just wish I could help you. Here, take this," he said, pushing a twenty into the tiny hands of the young woman he had met only moments earlier. "It ain't much, but it might help a little. You gotta find some way to get out of this place before it's too late."

"There isn't much anyone can do for me now, and I don't want your money, mister. I didn't earn it."

"Take it. I want you to have it. That way no one can say we weren't doing business."

"Well, okay, thanks." With that, the young woman disappeared into the night just as mysteriously as she had appeared by the truck fifteen minutes before. Ray's stomach knotted as he thought of the reality of her world, thankful his daughter had a better road to follow.

It was getting late. With Tanya gone, Ray went back to thinking about business. Where was Frank? He had to be on time; there could be no delays. Nervously tapping the steering wheel, Ray scanned the street corner, fearful that the police might show up. This was Ray's fifth delivery for Larry. No one—not his children, not Shirley, not even his friend Dan—suspected Ray had become a drug runner. If people had questions about where Ray got his extra money, they kept it to themselves.

When he agreed to run drugs for Larry's organization, he knew what the job entailed. In recent months, he had delivered drug shipments to various drop-off points throughout the province, but this was his first delivery to Halifax, and Ray was nervous about the increased chances of being seen. He didn't like being in a neighbourhood where the criminal activity drew regular police patrols. His other deliveries had been to secluded places, not the middle of a densely populated area of the city. That was the way Frank wanted it, though; he felt the police would never expect a drug drop to go down right under their noses, and Ray could only hope he was right.

He had met Frank only once before, on his second delivery. He didn't even know Frank's last name but, for some reason, Ray felt he could trust him. A small-featured man in his mid-thirties, Frank lived somewhere in the Halifax area and was one of the organization's best pushers. Frank had worked for the organization for almost five years, Larry told Ray, and they had never had any trouble—always on time with his payments, always reliable to move the goods. These were the kinds of people the organization wanted, Larry said. Tonight, Ray hoped Frank would live up to his reputation for being reliable and prompt. It was getting late, and Ray still faced a couple hour's drive back to the South Shore.

At exactly 4:30 A.M., Ray spotted Frank emerging from the shadows, wearing a dark-green bomber jacket with the collar tight around his chin to keep out the cold. Opening the passenger door, Frank slid inside the warm cab and greeted Ray with a smile. "How's things tonight, Ray?" "Cold." Ray replied. Frank was quick to pick up on Ray's uneasiness. "Don't worry, Ray. I'm sure we're all right out here tonight. It's late and it's too cold for the cops. They're all back at the station, keeping warm. This is a good cover, 'cause they would never expect for us to do this right out here in the open, especially around these parts. They don't know about us. Stop worrying."

"I hope you're right, 'cause we're both in this if we get caught tonight.

113

Think we should do this right here, then, or do you want to go some-where else? It's both our asses if the cops show up."

"I think we're okay right here, but if you'd feel better going somewhere else, then let's go."

Ray hesitated, clenching his hands tightly around the steering wheel, thinking about his options. Then finally he replied, "What the fuck! If they're going to catch us, they may as well catch us now and get it over with." He climbed down from the cab and went to the back of the cube van. He'd devised what he thought was an ingenious hiding place for the pre-cious cargo he was transporting: atop the inside walls and the floor of the truck's large cargo compartment, he had built a second layer with sheet metal, creating a storage space in between, no more than eight centime-tres wide—just big enough to store the small chucks of hashish he was moving. Big enough to hide thousands of dollar's worth of drugs. He felt the truck would have passed the inspection of a highway patrol cop if he were ever stopped, although he was in no hurry to test that theory.

Pulling himself up inside the truck, Ray removed a small floor panel and retrieved a dozen chunks of black hash, each about the size of a box of regular staples. Stashing them in a brown paper grocery bag, Ray paused, knowing the police could be waiting outside. But it was too late. If they were out there, they already had him and Frank red-handed. Taking a deep breath, he threw open the door and jumped down onto the cold, empty street. There were no cops. In fact, there was no one around; the neighbourhood was deathly quiet. He joined Frank in the cab, thank-ful for his good luck. "I got to tell you, Frank, this stuff's a little hard on the head. I don't know how you can go on doing this and keep it all together. I think I'd go crazy." Frank peeked inside the bag. "Yeah, that's why they pay you the big bucks." Both men laughed. This night was theirs.

According to Larry's plan, Ray was to deliver the goods to Frank, but no money would change hands. Ray figured the hash was worth about $20,000, maybe $30,000 on the street, but Frank would have to meet another courier at another location to make the payment. Ray did not know the other courier, where the second meeting would take place, or when the payment was to happen. That way, if he were caught, he couldn't tell the police about the rest of the operation: the organization wouldn't lose both the drugs and the cash—a precaution they took with all their operations, Larry had assured Ray.

"So what will you do for the rest of the night, Frank?" Ray asked. "Got no real plans," Frank replied. "I got a delivery to make; the guy's waiting right now. When I'm done there, I think I'll head home to get some sleep. Got a few rough, busy days coming up. Gotta move this stuff and get the money back on time, or Larry will be pissed." Ray understood. He knew how meticulous Larry was about running a tight schedule.

"Move much of this stuff?" Ray casually asked as Frank opened the door to leave. He didn't want to seem nosy, but he was always curious about the people he dealt with. "Couple hundred thousand dollars' worth a year. Money might be tight, but not for this shit. Listen, I'd like to stay and chat, but let's not push our luck."

"You're right." Ray agreed. "Be careful. I'll see you in a few more trips, unless something happens."

"Now what do you think's gonna happen, Ray? Larry says you worry too much and he's right. I like you, Ray, but worrying could make you careless. Think of the money when you get uptight, and find something else to worry about." Ray grinned sheepishly. "Maybe you're right. See ya later." Frank nodded, jumped to the pavement, and slammed the door.

Ray watched him disappear around the corner of a nearby building, then started the truck and headed out of the city towards the South Shore. Passing derelict, run-down buildings where street people were huddled, he thought about Tanya and shivered, wondering what she was doing that moment. He thought about the drugs he had just helped to deliver into the hands of the pushers—maybe even into her hands. That was the part of the job he disliked. He wasn't a proponent of drugs, but he tried to forget about that. Instead, he focused on his children and planned what to give them with his next payment. But no matter how hard he tried, he couldn't forget Tanya, or Frank's job and its dangers. They had been lucky tonight. Someday, Ray realized, the luck would run out.

Dangerous Days and Dirty Laundry

CRIME, VIOLENCE, AND DEATH: these words are synonymous with the drug trade. As the drugs arrive in Canada and make their way through the sophisticated and highly elaborate underground market, they have but one destination—through the streets and into the hands of the users. At this point, there is more than an enforcement problem; there is a plague—a social disease infecting almost everyone in every community across the country.

Authorities throughout Nova Scotia are faced with the same dilemma: trafficking is such a massive endeavour, which involves so many people, that it is impossible to keep it under control. The Halifax area seems particularly vulnerable, according to the city's police department. The drug trade in the metro area is growing at alarming rates, and authorities are finding it difficult to keep up with the explosion of new and increasingly dangerous drugs.

The 1990s have witnessed the arrival of cocaine, and with it came crack, the most powerful and addictive drug available on the underground market; some medical professionals believe that a person can become hooked on it after only one or two tries. Crack, which is made by cooking up cocaine with other chemicals, first surfaced in the Halifax area in 1988 and since then has spread throughout Nova Scotia, gradually becoming the drug of choice for many users.

Halifax police officers say that in the years since crack and other hard drugs arrived in the city, there has been an increase in the rates of violence, assault, theft, and robbery. But they single out crack as most prevalent on the city's streets, adding that it also presents them with more of a challenge.

While other forms of drugs can become addictive, there are more casual users of marijuana and hashish than of crack—and less demand. Crack cocaine, on the other hand, is so popular that it can be purchased anywhere in the city, even on street corners; and law enforcement is more difficult because its higher numbers of users are more prone to violence, particularly because of their desperation to feed their habit, and suppliers' intolerance of an addict's inability to pay for goods purchased.

"It's hard to get a handle on the situation when dealers are making the transactions right on the street corners," as one police officer expresses the drug's popularity. "It happens all the time in Halifax, in many different locations throughout the city. It's like the drug dealers think they're immune to the police or something; like they're flaunting their illegal activity and just daring us to come after them."

In December 1994, Halifax police took the dare. They made the largest-ever drug bust in the city's history, arresting fifty people on a range of 109 different charges. "Before that raid, the crack problem was getting out of hand. You literally could go down to the street and buy whatever you wanted. It improved for a while after the raid, but eventually the dealers will work their way back to the top by finding different locations to work their trade."

Police can monitor the supply of drugs that are available on the streets by its selling price. When the price is high, they know the supply is low, just as low prices mean a high supply. "It's the law of supply and demand. In recent years we've seen the prices go down steadily, so that tells us that the supply is growing." The same amount of crack that sold for forty dollars last year is selling for about twenty dollars this year, he says. "That means there's a lot of the stuff out there on the streets. It's a constant supply, and it seems like that no matter how hard we work at trying to clean it up, there's always more of it coming in."

Police believe they are doing the best job they can from a street-level enforcement perspective. "But you're dealing with a fairly big problem when you've got crack houses throughout the city, and drug transactions taking place right on the street corners. We investigate all leads, no matter how insignificant they may seem. And whenever we have new information about a possible deal, we go after it. We are quite active in the city, but it's a difficult task."

While police in other parts of Nova Scotia recognize they have a drug problem, they acknowledge their situation doesn't compare with that of Halifax. Still, rural areas are touched by the drug trade, and most authorities say their difficulties, too, are growing with the passing of each year. Everett Densmore, former victims' services and crime prevention officer at the Liverpool RCMP detachment, points out: "It's nothing like they have in Halifax or other larger areas. [But] drugs are there, no matter how small the community seems. The drug trade is just so big that you can't get away from it."

Although the volume may be smaller, the types of drugs are the same, Densmore explains. "It doesn't matter what you want; you can get it. Hash and marijuana are still very popular in places like Liverpool, but you can get the harsher drugs like crack cocaine, if that's what you want. Let's put it this way, anything that's available in the city is available here. If you want it, you can get it."

There was a time, a few years back, that drugs could also be purchased right on the streets of downtown Liverpool, but Densmore says a major enforcement effort, spearheaded by the raid on the Mersey Tavern, has eradicated much of that activity. "However, we don't fool ourselves. We know the drugs are still here; they're just better hidden. But if you know where to go, you're never that far from the action."

There is one difference between rural and urban drug trades, Densmore says; in smaller communities, dealers usually do business on their own, while in the cities, dealers are part of a much larger organization. As well, rural areas aren't quite as prone to crimes such as break-and-entry and theft, associated with the urban drug trade along with assault and other violent crimes. "It's probably because of the population differences, but the small-town drug trade just does not seem to bring that type of action with it. I believe that's because in small towns, everybody knows who the dealers are, and if they were to do anything that serious, then they'd be more likely to get caught. In the city, it's easier for the perpetrators to get lost, as they have a better chance to remain anonymous."

In Lunenburg County, where drug trafficking also constitutes a major problem, authorities say the substances are available if the buyer knows where to look. Although rural communities may not have crack houses, they do have organized drug rings, which can blanket most neighbourhoods. Lunenburg County authorities face another problem—their proximity to the metro area. Police point out that dealers in their community can get to Halifax, purchase drugs, and be back to their customers within three hours. Indeed, most of the drugs sold in Lunenburg County come from the Halifax area.

As the drug trade continues to grow, geography is becoming less of a barrier for drug dealers as high profit margins fuel the trade. In Yarmouth in February 1996, RCMP arrested a local woman as she stepped from a bus, and charged her with possession for the purposes of trafficking after they recovered a quantity of crack cocaine. In January 1996, a Halifax cocaine dealer was imprisoned for seven years after pleading guilty to possession of almost 2 kg of uncut cocaine for the purpose of trafficking. Police said that the $300,000 cache of cocaine most likely came directly from Colombia. Also in January, a North Sydney woman who used her home as a stash house for cocaine dealers was imprisoned for three and a half years after pleading guilty to two counts of possession for the purpose of trafficking and one count of conspiracy to traffic cocaine. She was one of thirteen people charged a year earlier following a seven-month RCMP investigation. In December 1995, Cape Breton Regional Police arrested twenty-four people and seized $10,000 worth of hashish, cocaine, and LSD after a two-month undercover operation. Those arrested were charged with a total of forty-nine offences, mostly drug trafficking. The same month, Sydney RCMP arrested two men from Moncton and seized 10 kg of hashish. And earlier in December, Sydney RCMP arrested twelve people on thirty-five narcotics charges, after a four-month investigation. A Lunenburg County man was charged with trafficking cocaine in December 1995, after a raid by Bridgewater RCMP that was the culmination of a two-year investigation.

Nova Scotia has seen its fair share of homegrown marijuana operations bent on producing dangerously powerful versions of the drug. For example, the RCMP accidentally stumbled across a hydroponic marijuana-growing operation on May 6, 1996, when firefighters were called to a blaze at a mobile home in Cole Harbour on Lawrencetown Road. Police seized seventy-eight marijuana plants and a variety of paraphernalia used in these illegal cultivation operations. Windsor and New Minas RCMP arrested four men on April 19, 1996, after busting a major marijuana-growing operation in Centre Burlington, about 16 km northeast of Windsor. Police raided two homes and charged the four with a variety of drug-related offences, including cultivation of a narcotic, possession for the purposes of trafficking, and conspiracy to commit an indictable offence. More than six hundred marijuana plants were seized, as well as hydroponic growing equipment, an undisclosed quantity of cocaine, and some cash. This bust followed another take down in Hants County a week earlier; in the April 12 raid, the RCMP charged four men and one woman; three of the men were Mexican and were alleged to be in Canada illegally. Police confiscated six hundred marijuana plants and a variety of hydroponic equipment in a house and barn in Bishopville, a small community on the border of Kings and Hants Counties.

And it goes on and on. In late January 1996, police arrested four people in the Truro area and charged them with possession and trafficking. Confiscated in the raids was a quantity of cash, cocaine, hashish, marijuana, LSD, and a variety of drug paraphernalia. Also that month, two men were jailed for their role in the largest marijuana-growing operation uncovered in the province in the past two years: that same month, seven people were charged after Truro RCMP raided hydroponic operations in Burnside, Colchester County, and Admiral Rock, Hants County. Police seized fifty-five hundred plants and 230 kg of dried marijuana at the indoor operation. Eight people were charged on fifty-two different counts in early December 1995, after police raided three basements in homes in Jeddore, Lawrencetown, and Lake Echo, where they discovered marijuana-growing laboratories. In October 1995, Parrsboro RCMP seized more than $83,000 worth of marijuana in a local home; two men and one woman were charged with possession for the purposes of trafficking, cultivation of a narcotic substance, and unsafe storage of firearms. In March 1996, five men and one woman were arrested when RCMP seized $50,000 worth of drugs after a two-month undercover investigation in the Amherst area. Police also seized two vehicles and other assets in an operation involving RCMP from Truro, Amherst, Stellarton, and Halifax along with officers from the Truro and Amherst police departments. A month earlier, police in Sydney arrested and charged seven men for conspiracy to traffic in narcotics. The busts were made after a joint effort by the RCMP and the Cape Breton Regional Police task force led to the seizure of 10 kg of hashish from a car in North Sydney in December 1995. Also in February that year, two Kings County men were charged with trafficking after police seized a quantity of drugs at a Wolfville house. Confiscated in the search were 39 tablets of LSD, 17.5 g of hashish, and 4 g of mescaline.

On December 17, 1996, at approximately 10:30 A.M., Chester RCMP responded to a possible house fire in Gold River, a small coastal community along Nova Scotia's South Shore between Chester and Mahone Bay. Neighbours had reported what they thought was smoke pouring out of the small bungalow. RCMP noted a strong marijuana odour coming from a vent in the attic. After searching for injured people, the vacant house was secured and a search warrant was obtained.

When Chester RCMP and two members of the Bridgewater Drug Squad entered the house through the dead-bolted basement door, they found 506 marijuana plants in 3 different stages of growth in the basement. The basement contained fourteen 1,000-watt light bulbs on individual ballasts connected to a timing device. The suspect or suspects had tapped into the power grid. Bridgewater Drug Squad member Corporal John Oster said at a January 3, 1997, press conference that the power was being stolen. The power was coming into the building, he said, without going through the metre. The timer provided a day and night setting for the plants.

Following a closer search, police found that the entire basement had been insulated with styrofoam and a vapour barrier. An intricate ventilation system had been set up to exhaust the moist air from inside and bring in fresh air. Also inside were large quantities of peat moss and starter pots that indicated a long-term, year-round operation had been planned. Corporal Oster noted there were also piles of soil, extra pots, a mixing barrel for fertilizer as well as plants inside the 600-square-foot space. "They were planned at two different times so that when one crop was finished, the other crop was already on its way." There were also small plants on the floor which Corporal Oster said were either clones or seed plants. "This growth can go on and on and on, one crop after another."

Lead investigator, Chester RCMP Constable Hank Pollard, estimated the annual street value of the marijuana would have surpassed $1.7 million. Acknowledging this was a "minimum" estimation he said it would have increased annually as the operation grew. RCMP said they believed this was the largest indoor growing operation ever infiltrated in Nova Scotia because of the complexity and expertise involved as well as the large number of plants. The house where the bust was made had been rented in October 1996 but police said they believed no marijuana made it to the streets from this particular operation before the raid. At the time, Chester RCMP Sergeant Rod Douthwright told Bridgewater *Bulletin* reporter Mark Roberts that he believed the market could have been anywhere in Nova Scotia, perhaps even outside the province.

Residents in the small village were overwhelmed that such a massive illegal drug operation could be happening in their midst without being detected. One witness said he often saw two young men in their early to mid-twenties going from the house into the local corner store to buy sandwiches and use the phone. The resident said one of the men claimed he was an electrician settling in the area to wait for a job he expected to get in Bridgewater. The two men did not drive an expensive car and they were dressed the same as other young people. Another resident said he did not suspect drugs were being cultivated in the house. The neighbour said the occupants of the house had unusual hours but besides the hours and the lights, area residents were not overly suspicious of the activity. "I was surprised, yet not surprised, because there are a lot of drugs around, but I was surprised at the amount and the value."

Sergeant Douthwright said these types of rural operations could be a trend because criminals may feel that sparsely populated rural areas are safer from police scrutiny than urban regions. Constable Pollard said small amounts of traffic, covered windows, irregular visiting times and large amounts of material going in and out of the house are signs to look for in a cultivation operation of this type. Both officers agreed this bust was unique to the detachment. Constable Pollard said, "We were very surprised to find what we found there. I was overwhelmed because it was my first indoor operation of this size and I think the other members involved were surprised as well." Sergeant Douthwright added, "We can attribute this [bust] to good luck but we can also attribute this to good work by the people involved—the fire people and the investigators."

On January 30, 1997, police caught the twenty-nine-year-old man they believed was responsible for the large marijuana-growing operation. The suspect was arrested in Dartmouth after allegedly robbing a jewellery store. He had been wanted on a Canada-wide warrant in connection with the Gold River bust. In addition to charges of robbery and possessing a weapon, the man faced charges connected with the marijuana operation, including cultivation. In a unique twist of circumstances, the man's thirty-one-year-old brother was arrested the same day and charged in connection with a similar operation in Glen Margaret. The brother was charged with cultivating marijuana and stealing electricity after police raided a rented home at St. Margarets Bay on January 30.

On March 4, 1997, in Dartmouth Provincial Court, the man charged in the Gold River raid was sentenced to thirty-three months in prison. He had been charged with possession of marijuana for the purpose of trafficking, cultivation of marijuana, and theft of electricity. He also received additional time on unrelated charges, which gave him a total of four years in prison.

Sometimes, simple headlines tell it all: Pair arrested after marijuana seized. Drug charges draw not guilty plea. Tobacco, cash, and marijuana seized. Drug charges laid after raid. Drug seizure nets large haul of marijuana, hydroponic gear. Drug charges laid against six. Thirty-five nabbed in tri-county drug raid. Men sentenced on drug charges. Police seize booze, drugs from car. Cops nab three in crack bust. Cape Breton drug bust nabs seven people. Marijuana plants seized near Truro. Cops crack down on drug dealers. Drug round-up largest ever in Halifax. Drug bust made in Sheet Harbour. Undercover drug operation results in eleven charges. Drug charges laid against thirteen people in sting operation. Forty-three ensnared in Bridgewater-Dartmouth drug dragnet. RCMP charge man after seizing cocaine.

* * *

Beyond the sheer proliferation and variety of drugs making their way across the province is the story of huge profits being made by large-scale traffickers—the Tobiases, Pauls, and Larrys of the world. The RCMP explain that to benefit from the proceeds of crime, drug traffickers must conceal the origin and ownership of funds while retaining control over them. Proceeds of crime must be legitimized and integrated into the mainstream economy, and traffickers use a variety of money-laundering techniques to mount operations of varying size and complexity, their diversity limited only by their ability to use financial resources and exploit legal opportunities.

By examining money-laundering, the RCMP have identified several common characteristics, including the increase of international transactions; the capacity to adapt to a changing legal environment; and the continued expansion of laundering operations to all sectors of the Canadian economy. In recent years, the international component of money laundering has come to play a dominant role. As crime syndicates grow and solidify in Asia, Europe, and the Americas, they develop the capacity to transfer illicit funds in and out of several countries simultaneously. Driven by a need for anonymity, they use all available financial tools to intensify international transactions and hamper criminal investigations.

In 1993, RCMP say, Canadian laundering operations commonly spanned several continents. Illicit funds generated in Canada were channelled by legitimate transactions to South America via Europe, the United States, and Central America. Drug money obtained in the United States by Southwest Asian heroin traffickers was sent back to source countries via Canada. South and Central American routes used to channel illicit funds out of North America were also used to move suspected drug money in and out of Eastern Europe. Authorities note that the variety of money-laundering routes into Canada is countless and Canada often represents only one link in a chain of transactions.

The same year, RCMP identified a new concern. Free trade zones, in which countries are exempt from customs rules and regulations, can also be used for money-laundering operations. "Intelligence indicates that, in the past year, South American drug-trafficking organizations have reviewed the trade options created by the North American Free Trade Agreement, which came into force on January 1, 1994. Authorities admit, however, they are still not sure what kind of impact the trade deal will have on money laundering, but they are sure enforcement will be made more difficult as a result as money will become more difficult to trace.

The drug traffickers today are moving away from the practice of depositing large sums of cash in banks; in Canada, they make extensive use of currency exchange businesses to launder drug money. Nor do they restrict their transactions to the financial industry. All sectors of the economy are being used: a variety of consumer goods such as real estate are bought and sold in Canada and abroad to secure the movement of drug money; and import and export contracts involving various commodities are negotiated to facilitate the flow of funds. Brokers, lawyers, and accountants are hired by trafficking organizations to provide expertise, knowledge of the markets, and business practices essential to the establishment of efficient money-laundering operations. The legitimacy of these established professions adds another layer of anonymity.

One informer, who must remain anonymous for fear of retaliation from the drug traders for whom he worked, claims he was personally involved in transactions worth millions of dollars. Louie said, in a phone call from an undisclosed location in North America, that because authorities have engaged in an all-out effort to shut down the drug trade in Canada, buyers and sellers now devise ways of fronting their illegal operations with legitimate businesses. Such people hide themselves behind mountains of paperwork and layers of people, making it virtually impossible to see to the top.

"I don't think we're necessarily talking about high-priced bankers in three-piece suits on Wall Street or anything like that," he said. "They certainly weren't in the cases I worked with. But we are talking about smart people who know what the cops are up to and how to avoid blowing their covers," he said, with a certain amount of reluctance to go into hard detail, but with obvious knowledge of the subject. "The people you hear about who get caught selling the drugs on the streets, or are arrested when the police make those big busts, are not the brains behind the operation. The head guys never get caught, because there's no way to get at them. They've hidden themselves so well in their organizations that the cops can't touch them. Really, if they want to stop this kind of stuff from happening, they're going to have to get to these guys—the bosses, I mean. These people pull all the strings, put up all the money, and make all the decisions. The guys taken down in the busts are at the bottom of the heap, and it doesn't matter to the organizations whether the police get them or not—they're dispensable. The only way to stop the drug activity is to get those guys at the top, and that's never going to be an easy thing to do."

This perception resonates in a disturbing echo of Dan's warning to his friend Ray Martin, as does Louie's further views of the top echelons of the trade. He insists that in Canada, the kingpins move about with great ease, believing that the police cannot touch them. "They're quite arrogant, you know. They really believe that they're above the law, and when you look at it from their perspective, I guess you could say they really are. Money does buy protection and if you have enough of it, you can get protection from just about anything—even the police." Louie says he would fear for his life if anyone ever found out he talked about what he knows. "These guys don't fool around; if you screw with them, you're in deep shit. They wouldn't hesitate coming after someone they thought betrayed them. We're talking about people with connections, and if you don't think this kind of shit happens in this country, then you're sadly mistaken. It happens every day. I've seen them do things and I know they'll come after you if you piss them off. Yeah, some of them might even try to kill you if you cross the right one."

Despite his fears, Louie talked about some of his experiences because he had been out of the business for some time now and wanted to see some of these drug dealers "get what they deserve. "Some of these guys are real bastards, and I'd like to see them all stopped. I'm sure it will never come to that, but at least by having my say, I sort of feel like I'm doing my share. I'll never go to the police and tell them what I know, because that would mean I'd have to go to court or jail or something like that. I'm just not prepared to put my life on the line." Without being specific, Louie recalled several transactions where drug money was used to purchase real estate. "We did that a lot," he explains. "That's a common practice, you know. A lot of the guys do it—they buy land with the money they made from selling drugs under the name of some fake company, keep it for a certain period of time, and then unload it for a real good profit. They deposit the drug money they made into banks and then buy property with cheques or money orders and put it in somebody else's name. That way, the money is swallowed up and lost in the regular economy.

"It works: I remember one time when I bought us a piece of land near the ocean for less than $92,000, and then three years later we resold it for almost $200,000," he recalled. "That's what you call making a good return on your investment. To the rest of the world it looks like these guys make a lot of money being smart real-estate dealers. But it's not really all that impressive when you think about it. In a lot of cases, it's good timing and good luck—good timing to buy the property when it's cheap, and good luck that it can be sold for a hefty profit. I guess maybe that's good business, after all."

Anyone, he pointed out, can purchase land for the right price. If the transaction is done properly, there is no need for authorities or banks to become involved, thus eliminating the risk of detection. In such deals,

Louie explained, there are no financial checks and no investigation. "It's not really all that impressive, but it does work and it has resulted in some people making a whole lot of money. If you walk into a real-estate company with a couple of hundred thousand dollars to buy a prime piece of land, are they going to turn you down? I don't think so!" Millions of dollars worth of land is purchased every year in Canada with funds obtained through the drug trade, he said. "But you would be hard-pressed to prove it, considering how well these guys are hidden. I don't think the police would ever be able to touch the guys at the top."

There are some differences in laundering techniques in Canada, some necessitated by the comparative scope of resources here in comparison to those of richly financed international cartels. Small drug traffickers, for example, lack the resources and connections for sophisticated operations, so they often resort to using the names of friends and relatives to register vehicles or conceal ownership of real estate. However, as law enforcement pressures mount, the larger Canadian-based organizations have begun to engage in increasingly complex laundering operations, following their foreign counterparts in using legal and financial advisers to avoid enforcement countermeasures. Bank accounts are opened in tax havens, and companies established to facilitate the integration of illicit funds, which could amount to billions of dollars—the rough estimate determined by calculating the value of seizures and factoring in the suggested value of drugs that safely reach Canadian shores, and streets.

Smaller traders have to work alone, but larger syndicates have worldwide connections; trafficking profits generated in Canada and recouped by parent organizations in source countries are mostly laundered through complex international transactions initiated here. RCMP say this is especially true of Colombian cocaine-trafficking organizations operating in Canada, which use financial institutions other than banks to convert Canadian cash into U.S. currency. The converted funds are then either wire-transferred out of the country or used to purchase goods that are sent abroad. Police know that large quantities of illegally acquired funds are moved annually from the United States to Canada. In one incident in 1990, American authorities seized just under $500,000 (U.S.) in cash from traffickers en route to Canada. The money, believed to be part of a large laundering operation, was to have been deposited in a Canadian bank account. In another incident, more than $100,000 (U.S.) in cash was found concealed in a vehicle entering Ontario. And in 1991, authorities say proceeds were transferred to bank accounts in Europe, South America, and the United States. This is not uncommon practice.

To avoid creating any paper trail, some traffickers, such as the Colombians, directly smuggle bulk shipments of hard currency abroad.

The transfer of funds for laundering or investment purposes is also accomplished through Canadian banking transactions that are part of a complex web of worldwide financial operations, enabling organizations to take advantage of Canada's sophisticated financial system to quickly and efficiently move illicit funds. For instance, police know that in 1991, many foreign-based trafficking organizations used Canadian bank accounts in a multilayer process, moving drug money from one country to another. In one such case, they say that more than $50 million (U.S.) was involved.

Conversely, police say, foreign-based traffickers also invest in Canada, as major political changes abroad affect the international flow of drug money and impact on investment decisions. The Eastern European countries and the newly created states of the former Soviet Union could prove attractive and provide easily accessed points to international money markets. As well, Hong Kong's integration with the People's Republic of China in 1997 is prompting criminal organizations to relocate funds abroad. It is known that in 1991, laundered drug profits were moved from Hong Kong to Canada and other countries, often to purchase real estate and invest in companies.

Despite what authorities know—or believe they know—they have had little success infiltrating drug-related money laundering. Steps have been taken to address the issue, but authorities admit they only scratch the surface of the underground market. As Louie is quick to point out, "The police really have no idea just how big this thing is. And when they are lucky enough to catch someone, there's always somebody else with a better system and more contacts just ready to step in to take that position in the marketplace. It's a big problem, there's no doubt about that; big enough that it would scare the hell out of people if they ever really saw the entire picture. It's too big really to do anything about it."

And it just keeps getting bigger. In September 1994, the Canadian Press reported that drug dealers had found a way of getting around Canadian law in order to launder hundreds of millions of dollars through banks and brokerage firms. Federal regulations require such financial institutions to keep records of cash deposits of $10,000 or more, including the name and occupation of the depositor, which must be kept on file for five years. But the same is not required of large cheques, more than $10,000 money orders, or money-wired accounts, although Canadian banks have now voluntarily agreed to track large transfers and cheques.

Quoting an investigator with the RCMP in Toronto, the Canadian Press said in 1994 wire-transfers of drug money are "being done all the time." Cash is usually smuggled out of the U.S. to countries that have lax reporting regulations; the money is then wired back to Canadian or U.S. banks and investment dealers. The process is called "layering," because it obscures the money trail.

Brokerage firms are often targeted because wire transactions are common, the Toronto RCMP investigator said. "We know for a fact that stock brokerages, not all by any stretch of the imagination, are engaged in the business," adding that certain of these firms have helped in several investigations of individual brokers, but few charges have been laid. Police must prove the broker knew the client earned the money from an illegal activity.

In the United States in September 1994, several Wall Street brokerages dismissed a report that said they were under investigation on suspicion that some of their brokers were laundering illegal drug profits. Meanwhile, U.S. Treasury officials drafted regulations to include wire transfers within current reporting rules. However, the Canadian Bankers Association in Montreal said similar rules are not necessary in Canada because its members claim the problem does not exist here. Furthermore, they said, including wire transactions in reporting rules could be difficult because of the sheer numbers of such transfers that financial institutions receive every day. The focus of Canada's money-laundering law is on cash—the first step in the process, but as the problem grows increasingly complex and unmanageable, legislation could toughen accordingly.

The South Shore and Beyond

ALTHOUGH THE SOUTH SHORE, particularly Queens and Shelburne Counties, remains the destination of choice for drug smugglers, the abundant coastline of other areas of Nova Scotia—and of Newfoundland—also exerts a powerful attraction for these illegal importers.

CAPE BRETON

Two months after the record-breaking drug seizure at Ragged Harbour in May 1990, the police made another multimillion-dollar bust in Nova Scotia. The RCMP dismissed similarities in the two seizures, but the back-to-back busts were proof of a serious drug-smuggling problem in the province.

On Tuesday, July 31, police completed a six-month investigation by seizing 27 tonnes of hashish valued at about $325 million, and arresting 18 individuals in a sting operation stretching from Newfoundland through Nova Scotia to Quebec. The contraband was intercepted by the RCMP, with the assistance of the Coast Guard and the Canadian Armed Forces. The operation was intercepted as the drugs were being unloaded from 2 boats and packed into rental trucks at the federal wharf in Baleine, a small Cape Breton fishing village near Louisbourg. RCMP recovered more drugs in a tractor-trailer rig near Joliet, Quebec.

The men arrested, from Nova Scotia, Newfoundland, New Brunswick, and Quebec, were all charged with conspiracy to traffic in a narcotic. Also seized were the tractor-trailer, 2 rented 5-ton trucks, a 10.5 metre fishing boat, a 19.5 metre fishing boat, and numerous cars and trucks. Although RCMP agreed that there were many similarities between the seizures, authorities were convinced they were not related.

"The only connection with the two incidents is that both groups of smugglers chose Nova Scotia as the landing point for their drugs, illustrating the role the province plays on the world stage as far as the drug trade is concerned," said Sergeant Gary Grant, then the province's drug awareness coordinator. Smugglers tend to use similar methods—boats and trailer trucks—to deliver to the black market; and the Quebec connection "is not that unusual," Grant said. "Most of the drugs we find on the streets in Nova Scotia have entered this province through the Montreal market. It's no surprise that the drugs in both cases were likely destined for Quebec."

Although mainland Nova Scotia is a prime destination, Cape Breton is also a desirable setting for illegal activity. Since the early 1970s, the island, as well as the North Shore of the province, have had their fair share of drug busts. "You can expect this kind of activity to happen anywhere in

Photo of the 19.5 metre fishing vessel Scotian Maid *taken by surveillance aircraft.*
RCMP FILES PHOTO

Nova Scotia," Grant said after the Baleine seizure. "No one has any claim to being the sole target in this province, though the South Shore, because of its geography, seems to be the prime destination. Other areas of the province are just as susceptible as smugglers seek new destinations."

The illegal smuggling scheme at Baleine began unfolding in late May 1990, in Newfoundland. Sergeant Bill Parker, now the province's drug awareness coordinator, says RCMP in Newfoundland began investigating several suspects in a potential drug-smuggling operation. "It came to our attention that the fishing vessel *Scotian Maid*, out of Cape Breton, might be involved in some type of illegal activity. So we began a surveillance effort to see what we could learn." As police watched, the suspected smugglers went about their business, and by mid-June had moved from Newfoundland to Sydney, Cape Breton. "We still didn't have a great deal of information about the operation, but we knew we were on to something big, so our investigators went to Sydney along with the suspects, watching them from a distance of course," Parker said. Eventually, RCMP learned that the suspected smugglers planned to bring a shipment of hashish into the province through Baleine, near Sydney; then move it on to Quebec. RCMP formulated a plan to intercept the shipment, which turned out to be bigger than authorities had initially anticipated.

The operation began on July 16 when the *Scotian Maid*, purchased from a Cape Breton fisherman for $200,000, left port and subsequently met a mother ship somewhere off the coast of Nova Scotia. During that rendezvous, the contraband was transferred to the *Scotian Maid*. Because the fishing vessel was too big to enter Baleine Harbour, a smaller vessel, the *False Bay*, was secured to take the drugs from the *Scotian Maid* to the wharf at Baleine.

Under cover of darkness on July 30, smugglers began transferring the cargo to the *False Bay*: it would take two nights to bring the shipment ashore. Meanwhile, law enforcement officers were laying in wait near the Baleine wharf. On the first night, they watched the *False Bay* dock, but allowed the smugglers to unload the cargo onto a semi-trailer truck, which left uninterrupted. On the second night, they waited until the smugglers had removed part of the shipment from the *False Bay*—then dozens of camouflaged police officers, brandishing automatic shotguns, burst onto the scene, jolting the fifteen residents of Baleine from their sleep around 1:00 A.M. to wonder at the sight of smugglers being arrested and a huge drug shipment being seized by police. Some residents reported hearing gunshots, but this was a series of small, diversionary explosions set to confuse the smugglers; no weapons were fired.

Tracking dogs were used to find two suspects hiding in nearby bushes, and at least one man was pulled from the water after jumping off the wharf. Shortly after 6:00 A.M., authorities intercepted the *Scotian Maid* farther off the coast, but the mother ship was never located. Sixteen people were arrested at the scene; the 2 boats and 2 rented 5-ton trucks were seized; and a tractor-trailer loaded with hashish was seized in Quebec. Parker explains that the 18-wheeler had left Cape Breton for Quebec, but was tracked by RCMP and intercepted near Joliet, and two conspirators were arrested.

The suspects were charged with conspiracy to traffic a narcotic and possession for the purpose of trafficking. Among those immediately charged were three men from Cape Breton—Daniel Michael Oakey, 36; Wallace Barter, 40; and Raymond Phillip Mills, 42; four men from Quebec—Aris Belzile, 40; Andre DuMont, 35; Florient Despres, 36; Marc

Nadeau, 29; two men from New Brunswick—Jacques Martin, 33, and Emery Martin, 30; and one man from Newfoundland—Melvin Joseph Kenny, 36. Others eventually arrested in connection with the seizure included David Michael Howell from Newfoundland.

All were tried in Nova Scotia courts. Eight pleaded guilty and were sentenced to prison terms ranging from four to eight years, the highest going to a Newfoundland captain. Trials were held for those who pleaded not guilty but, eight months into the proceedings, a mistrial was declared on the issue of language related to the Canadian Charter of Rights and Freedoms. Those still awaiting trial were divided into two groups—four Anglophones went to court in Cape Breton, and six Francophones were tried in Quebec, where, as recently as April 1996, the French proceedings were still dragging on.

One of the Quebec residents on trial in his home province for his alleged involvement in the drug conspiracy, was arrested in March 1996 when he debarked from a plane in the Bahamas. The man had been given permission to vacation outside the country during a break in the court proceedings, but Canadian authorities were unaware that the U.S. was also seeking his arrest in connection with a major cocaine seizure in Buffalo between January 1991 and December 1993.

According to Mike Burke, special agent in charge of the United States Drug Enforcement Agency office in Buffalo, the Quebec resident had been indicted in New York for conspiracy to possess cocaine with intent to distribute and was considered a force behind a shipment of 50 kg of cocaine seized in 1994. Four people, including 2 Colombians, were convicted of drug charges. Besides the outstanding American warrant and his Quebec trial, the man also faced a preliminary hearing in Newfoundland in connection with the seizure of more than 20 tonnes of hashish in that province.

When American authorities learned that he was going to be in the Bahamas, the federal Drug Enforcement Agency got a provisional warrant and arranged for the Royal Bahamian Police to arrest the Canadian as he got off the plane. The DEA planned to extradite the Quebec resident to the United States for trial there; his fate is still in the hands of the courts.

Two of the men tried in Cape Breton in June 1994 drew particularly lengthy terms: one was handed a fourteen-year sentence, the other a twelve-year term. During sentence proceedings, in August 1994, Supreme Court Justice Frank Edwards described the first man as a key local organizer of the smuggling plan, who played a central role in the conspiracy. According to evidence presented at the trial by federal prose-cutor Marian Fortune-Stone, he paid $200,000 in cash to buy the *Scotian Maid* in July 1990. "He was trusted and given a trusted role," said Fortune-Stone, adding that he knew the risks of getting involved in such an operation, but chose to ignore them because of the promise of big money.

In his defence, the man claimed he became involved in the smuggling scheme at a time when he needed money desperately. In his presentence report, he said that he'd been approached to join the conspiracy with the promise that he could earn up to $1 million for just 2 days' work. On July 31, 1990, the Cape Bretoner was seen leaving Louisburg Harbour on board his vessel, the *False Bay*; several hours later he was arrested in the take down and his vessel, full of hashish, was seized.

The second man, who helped recruit the Newfoundland captain of the *Scotian Maid*, was described by prosecutors as a man who masterfully talked a law-abiding skipper into becoming involved in a multimillion-dollar drug-smuggling conspiracy during a crucial period in the planning stages. When the conspirators faced postponement or even cancellation of their scheme for lack of a skipper for the *Scotian Maid*, he "used his considerable powers of persuasion" to lure a fellow Newfoundlander into the ring on the promise of good, fast money. As for the captain, he was sentenced to eight years because of the vital role any captain plays in moving drugs during smuggling operations.

Parker says the Baleine take down was an example of how good police work can produce results, no matter how large the operation. "If we wouldn't have worked on the lead that we had gotten in Newfoundland, chances are we never would have made this bust." The operation lasted more than two months and involved RCMP officers from a number of provinces, as well as officials from the Department of Defence and the Coast Guard. Aurora aircraft from CFB Greenwood, the Halifax-based destroyer HMCS *Nipigon*, and the Coast Guard cutter CCGS *Mary Hitchins* also took part in the take down.

One resident of Baleine recalls the take down as spectacular. "I've lived around here all my life and I have never seen anything like that happen," he says, insisting that his identity not be revealed. "It was something you never expect to see, living in a place like Baleine. Not too much happens around here, but they tell me this stuff goes on all the time across Nova Scotia. Until you've actually seen it for yourself, though, it's really hard to picture it.

"It was obvious the cops knew what they were doing and the bad guys

133

knew when their number was up because they didn't really resist," he says. "A few guys tried to make a break for it, but it really was a feeble attempt. Where were they going to go? Here were all these cops swarming onto the wharf and all this confusion going on. The smugglers didn't really have any choice but to surrender."

A pile of hashish confiscated in the Baleine take down. RCMP FILES PHOTO

Law enforcement officers consider the Baleine seizure one of their most successful efforts in the drug wars of the past two decades. Parker calls it a good example of the success that can be achieved with hard work and cooperation between various enforcement agencies. "There's no question, this wouldn't have happened without the dedication of our investigators. It's reassuring that while we know a lot of these shipments are getting through, we are also getting some—this is the ultimate payoff for us."

Despite the successful conclusion of the Baleine file, Cape Breton's role in the continuing drug saga is far from over. In fact, like many places in Nova Scotia, Cape Breton continues to attract drug conspirators. In September 1995, 3.6 tonnes of hashish valued at an estimated $72 million was discovered floating in an abandoned rubber raft, drifting off the coast of Louisburg. The Coast Guard discovered the contraband after being notified early Wednesday morning, September 14, that a life raft had been spotted about 40 km off the coast.

Two days later, the Coast Guard found what authorities believed was the mother ship of the hashish recovered in the rubber raft. Authorities confirmed they had discovered the 40-metre ship aground and abandoned on a remote piece of Cape Breton coastline known as Capelin Cove, in Richmond County, during an aerial search of the coast. Initially, RCMP said their investigation revealed that the ship, the *Chiloli*, could have been registered in Panama, because that name had been painted below that of the ship. While police had no lead on its owners, they believed the ship had been in the isolated cove for about two days before the aerial discovery.

A week later, authorities found a second rubber raft, this one containing 3.5 tonnes of hashish valued at an estimated $60,000. The Coast Guard made the discovery approximately 15 nautical miles southeast of Scatterie Island. Finally, authorities also recovered another 45.4 kg of hashish during a search of the mother ship, a 484-tonne platform supply vessel used mostly with oil rigs. Police said that the discovery of the 2 rafts suggested the smugglers had removed a quantity of drugs from the *Chiloli* before bad weather pushed the vessel sideways onto the secluded beach. From there, offloaders used all-terrain vehicles to remove an unknown quantity of hashish to waiting vehicles, which then took the goods away from the coast. Considering the quantity of drugs left floating on the Atlantic Ocean, they believe the shipment was a large one.

Although no arrests have been made in the Capelin Cove case, the RCMP confirmed in October 1995 that they had identified the owner and origin of the mother ship. The name *Chiloli* proved to be fake, as did the Panama "registration" painted below it; the ship was the *Viking Ruby*, registered in the United Arab Emirates. The owner had given it to a shipping company to manage, and the company subsequently leased it. But to whom? Authorities have not yet found out.

THE HALIFAX AREA

It was a typical early-summer storm on the Atlantic coast. Rough weather had arrived with little warning that day, bringing a swell that rose almost 10 metres and sent walls of water crashing against the rocky shore. In such weather the breakers at Peggys Cove, a world-famous tourist destination located 32 km outside Halifax, are particularly spectacular. But the swells can also be deadly; gigantic waves have snatched a number of unsuspecting sightseers off the granite boulders near the lighthouse.

Anyone at sea during this July 1980 storm had been advised to get to shore as quickly as possible—a particular challenge for the four-member crew of the *Sea Tern*, a 14.4 metre ketch registered in New Bedford, Connecticut. The vessel had encountered engine trouble off Peggys Cove, and the winds had pushed it precariously close to the craggy rocks along the rugged coastline. With the ship's engine down, the 4-member crew radioed for help, then prayed for a miracle.

The emergency crews monitoring the Coast Guard radio station at Chebucto Head were watching out for Mayday calls that day, and expected a lot of action. But the distress call from the *Sea Tern* was unusual; instead of asking for help to get ashore, the captain, known as Salvador, a thirty-four-year-old American, wanted directions out of the cove.

The radio operator, realizing the *Sea Tern*'s proximity to a rocky shoal, asked if the vessel required a tow or on-site assistance from the Coast Guard. Salvador was insistent: such help was not required; the crew could get out of the cove on their own, given proper directions. The radio operator became suspicious and insisted that the Coast Guard provide assistance, knowing that anyone in legitimate trouble in such weather would welcome assistance—unless, of course, they had something to hide. Again, the *Sea Tern* refused help; at which point the operator notified the Halifax National Crime Intelligence Section and Canada Customs.

Investigators sprang into action: shortly after receiving the call, the Coast Guard dispatched a 13.2 metre rescue vessel from Sambro, a nearby fishing village, to the *Sea Tern*'s last reported location. On board were the vessel's 3 crew members and 2 RCMP officers; the sea spray was heavy, the winds fierce, and visibility very poor. When the rescuers reached their destination, there was no sign of the *Sea Tern*. Authorities first thought the vessel had capsized, but when no debris was found, the Coast Guard cutter circled several small islands and found it sheltered behind Shut-In Island, near Peggys Cove.

The Coast Guard managed to secure a line to the *Sea Tern* and tow it into St. Margarets Bay, where customs officials were waiting to board. This proved to be an even more difficult exercise—as RCMP officers boarded the vessel, the captain set fire to 19 L of fuel stored on board. While police and crew members scrambled for safety, 3 successive explosions rocked the vessel, sending flames, smoke, and debris in all directions. The third blast blew the captain out of the companionway and across the deck. When the danger had passed, authorities returned to the scorched *Sea Tern* and initiated a search that subsequently revealed the *Sea Tern* had, indeed, been carrying drugs—hashish.

RCMP files reveal that 4 people—3 Americans and 1 Portuguese—were charged under the Narcotic Control Act for attempting to import 4.5 tonnes of hashish into Canada on board the *Sea Tern*. In 1980, that quantity of hashish would have fetched more than $22 million on the open market—a substantial seizure for those days.

When the four eventually went to trial, they argued in their defence that they had not intended to import the drugs into Canada, but were targeting the United States; an engine breakdown and heavy seas had put them in Canadian waters. Because they had not planned to bring their cargo into Canada, they had broken no Canadian laws, they argued. But the defence proved futile. They were each sentenced to seven years in prison. The court accepted prosecution arguments that because Salvador had three years earlier spent some time in Nova Scotia and, in fact, owned property in the province, in all likelihood the drugs were intended for this country.

The scorched interior of the Sea Tern *after being set afire by drug smugglers. In the foreground are bales of hashish.* RCMP FILES PHOTO

During their investigation, Canadian authorities discovered that the *Sea Tern* had been built in 1948 as a racing yacht for Scandinavian royalty. About thirty years later, the vessel was sold in New England and refitted with a large diesel engine to make it better able to haul large cargoes. The crew also revealed that the hashish had been grown in Lebanon and was loaded onto the vessel from a deserted stretch of beach on the Atlantic coast of Morocco. From there, the vessel sailed to North America.

Off the coast of Nova Scotia, the ship ran into engine trouble. One RCMP officer who was at the scene recalls: "It seems the new diesel engine had performed so well that the old propeller shaft, which had not been replaced, snapped, leaving the vessel powerless. This in itself would not have been disastrous, because the *Sea Tern* was still designed as an ocean-going yacht; but the storms that blow off the coast of Nova Scotia can be fierce. It seems the *Sea Tern* got caught in one of them and was blown into shore, causing the skipper to call the Coast Guard to request directions."

The four men were sent to the Springhill Medium Security Penitentiary, where they became model prisoners. While this should have closed the file on the *Sea Tern*, a year after the sentencing the case took an even more bizarre turn. Salvador, the *Sea Tern*'s captain, had become part of a program through which inmates are taken into schools to speak to students about crime and about the value of getting a good education. These lectures always took place under guard, and for the most part, proved successful, as prisoners used themselves as examples in their sombre and, hopefully, powerful messages. At the end of one of these lectures, Salvador asked if he could be excused to go to the washroom, then slipped out of the school—and out of the country. He was not seen again for almost three years, when he turned himself in to the Cape Cod Anti-Smuggling Task Force, upon hearing that his father was seriously ill. He was convinced authorities would be waiting for him when he visited his father; in fact, his decision proved a lucky break for authorities, who had not been expecting him. After extradition proceedings, Salvador was returned to Springhill to finish his time.

Brent Crowhurst recalls the *Sea Tern* and acknowledges that luck played a big part in the take down. "These guys may have gotten away with what they were doing if they had only replaced the propeller when the ship was being refurbished. Basically, there was no great investigative effort on the part of the police. It was just one of these cases where things go our way. But even at that, it was a major drug bust for the 1980s and it confirmed for us that drugs were coming into the province. We were just beginning to see the beginnings of a major criminal trend, and it hasn't stopped growing."

In another Halifax-area case, an offer of hospitality led to the seizure of a quantity of hashish. The 3 fishermen thought they were just being friendly when they approached the 2 men on board a 17 metre luxury cabin cruiser anchored off the south coast of Nova Scotia. They wanted to show the Quebecers some down-home hospitality by making them feel welcome and offering any assistance they needed. It was a cool Sunday afternoon in May 1991 when the three clambered onto the deck of the Quebec boat, offering their hands in friendship. But the two strangers remained aloof and nervous. They avoided conversation, although it is customary at sea to return overtures of hospitality. The Nova Scotians felt rejected by the ungracious attitude and angry because they were not welcome on board. Well, it was obvious the Quebec men did not want company, so the fishermen beat a hasty retreat.

The next thing they heard was a report that the mysterious boat had blown up—hours after they had been on board—leaving only debris and many questions. The men had vanished. It was later learned that they went ashore in a rubber dinghy near Prospect Bay after the fishermen had left. A subsequent RCMP investigation revealed that the yacht was the Montreal-registered *Paganel*, a suspected drug-running vessel. A day later, the RCMP recovered 1.5 tonnes of black Asian hashish, wrapped in plastic, at a wharf where the *Paganel* had briefly docked earlier. Fishermen had brought the contraband ashore with their regular catch.

What really happened to the *Paganel* in the few hours after the fishermen left remains a mystery. Although the media suggested the *Paganel* had been blown up in an attempt to destroy evidence, it has not been confirmed that there was indeed an explosion. While authorities acknowledge that the *Paganel* is under water near Peggys Cove, not far from Halifax, they have never suggested why or how it was scuttled, nor does the debris suggest there was an explosion. In fact, few details have ever been released by the RCMP. According to their files, the *Paganel* incident is still under active investigation; details will only be made public when the file is closed, lest suspects discover what authorities have learned in their investigations.

Constable Wayne Williams, who has more than five years of experience in the RCMP's drug division, was on the scene during the initial investigation. He says there wasn't much to see. "All I can say is that a lot of debris was found on the water, but that does not mean the ship was blown up," he says. "The investigation into what may or may not have happened to the *Paganel* is ongoing so that means there's not much we can talk about, especially since no arrests have ever been made in the case."

He does confirm that before the vessel sank, authorities had received calls about a suspicious vessel in the area, near Sambro and Prospect. "We hear from people a lot, and when you get these types of calls, you take them seriously, so we naturally suspected the vessel may have been involved in some type of drug-running operation, and indeed, it appears it was."

As for details of the smuggling operation, Constable Williams says that aspect of the investigation is still being pursued. "This is an active investigation, and we're still learning more about it as we go. That's about all we're prepared to say until we get a good break in this case."

LUNENBURG COUNTY

Chester was the scene of Canada's largest drug seizure of the day when, on the morning of Saturday, May 28, 1977, RCMP seized 5.85 tonnes of cannabis, with an estimated street value of $14 million.

Two days earlier, after the RCMP had asked local residents to take note of any strange ships in the waters off the coast of Nova Scotia, an area fisherman reported a 21 metre ketch on the Blandford coast, between Aspotogan and Colemans Cove. The *Delia*, registered in Glasgow, Scotland, was reported to be exploring the coast in an unusual and suspicious manner. The Chester detachment of the RCMP investigated and, in the woods, they found a rubber dinghy and vehicles with American licence plates. "We picked up two individuals who were carrying a small amount of marijuana—enough for us to hold them for questioning. Then members in plain clothes continued surveillance until the *Delia* returned," said Peter Williamson, who was a corporal at the Chester RCMP at this time.

The two men did not resist arrest although, according to Williamson, they did possess firearms. As well as the ship, the dinghy, a half-ton truck, a motorcycle, and a pleasure craft were seized in the raid. A third man was arrested that night, and the RCMP arrested a fourth man on board the *Delia* when they discovered the holds were full of marijuana and hashish. Sergeant Bill Smith, of the RCMP, described the cannabis as high-quality—Colombian green, gold, and red marijuana; and hashish in liquid and solid form. The RCMP had not yet identified the smugglers' contacts, but were investigating local and international connections.

With the importations of drugs emerging as a major challenge for law enforcement officials in Nova Scotia by 1977, RCMP had a special three-man drug squad in Bridgewater to conduct the investigation after the seizure of the *Delia*. "We had to put the men in place because we have so many drugs imported along the South Shore," Williamson explained. "Although there are not many major seizures like this, there is a heavy traffic of drugs circulating at the local level in small lots of a pound or so." RCMP cruisers and Coast Guard vessels patrol the coast, but they cannot board a boat unless there are signs of suspicious activities. Constant road checks are carried out by patrol cars along the highways, in hopes of seizing some of the drugs. "They try to get in as close to the main highway going to Quebec and Ontario as they can," he said. "Then they head north by inconspicuous means to Montreal or Toronto, where the drugs are distributed on the street."

Bench warrants were issued after two of the *Delia* suspects, who had been freed on bail, failed to show up for their Supreme Court trial, in Bridgewater. Meanwhile, the Supreme Court trial for two other men, was underway in a Bridgewater courthouse.

One of the first witnesses to take the stand was an RCMP evidence man, Constable Jeffrey Wells, who explained that after RCMP had been alerted to a strange vessel on the morning of May 27, they set up surveillance of a cottage in Colemans Cove, which was raided that evening; two men were arrested. The RCMP then continued their surveillance and early the next morning they saw a yacht at the mouth of the cove. There, they arrested a man on the yacht and another on the beach. Constable Wells testified that when RCMP unloaded the yacht at the government wharf in Chester, two trucks were needed to transport the cargo to Halifax. Unloading the trucks at RCMP headquarters in Halifax was interrupted by the discovery of cockroaches "the size of rats," Wells testified—"thousands" of them—necessitating fumigation of the cargo.

RCMP Corporal Richard Cameron, head of the Bridgewater drug squad at the time, testified that one of the men who was arrested on the yacht, had been asleep in the cabin and caught unaware. The odour of marijuana was so strong that it could be smelled more than 20 metres from the vessel, into which bales of drugs had been crammed below deck, throughout the rear, the cabin, the washroom, the forward cabin, and the forecastle. Other RCMP witnesses testified that the *Delia* had left the Island of Marguerite, off the coast of Colombia, with its illegal cargo, on April 13. It took 44 days to complete its 2,400 nautical mile journey to Nova Scotia's South Shore.

As the trial of the remaining two suspects entered its second week, on November 1, the accused failed to appear in court. They had been staying at a Bridgewater inn, but when police investigated their absence they found the men had paid their bill and left town the previous night. It is not clear why they were on bail when the other two had skipped. Crown Prosecutor Joe Kennedy (now a Surpreme Court Judge), said the two men "saw the handwriting on the wall and took off," and Mr. Justice Vincent Morrison promptly ordered bench warrants issued, but said it was in the best interests of justice to complete the trial, which ended with both Americans being found guilty on four charges connected with the smuggling conspiracy. The jury deliberated for three and a half hours before reaching a verdict after the two-week trial. Justice Morrison handed down the minimum sentence for importation—seven years. The only problem, of course, was a crucial one—the whereabouts of the men.

Almost eighteen years later, one of the two men, James Joseph Farrelly, then living in suburban Philadelphia, Pennsylvania, was arrested by the FBI, on July 27, 1995. He was denied bail at a hearing on August 3. After fleeing Bridgewater, he had returned to the area where he'd grown up; he had been married and divorced, was now remarried, with a daughter; and he owned property and held a valid driver's licence. Farrelly had made no effort to hide his identity, and was described as a quiet family man, a good neighbour, and a kind father. He worked as an electrical contractor.

Officers in Pennsylvania said Canadian authorities found out about Farrelly's movements in 1989 but legal wrangling over extradition delayed the arrest. The federal prosecutor handling the case would say only that the discovery was made through the course of investigations. Following his arrest, Farrelly waived his right to an extradition hearing, and two RCMP officers flew to Pennsylvania in late August 1995 to bring him back to Halifax. He is now serving his outstanding time at an undisclosed federal prison. Federal prosecutor James Martin said Farrelly agreed to return to Nova Scotia if he were not charged with his 1977 escape. He was brought quickly back to the place of his crime to serve time. Authorities have never confirmed whether they are still looking for the remaining three men. The file, in any case, remains open.

NEWFOUNDLAND
In November 1994, final arrests were made in a drug-smuggling conspiracy that had begun two years before. On November 14, 1992, authorities began tracking a 24 metre fishing vessel about 160 km southwest of Cape Race, Newfoundland. The Spanish-registered *Luciana* failed to return radio transmissions when authorities attempted to make contact, and contrary to Maritime law, the vessel was not flying any flag to identify itself.

When a U.S. Coast Guard cutter attempted to approach the *Luciana*, a high-seas pursuit ensued, lasting for several hours on stormy seas, and ending when the *Luciana*'s crew took to life rafts. The vessel sank suddenly and quickly, and now rests on the bottom of the Atlantic—along with its stash of cocaine. The 3-tonne cargo of drugs would now fetch about $20 million on the open market, but it remains out of reach, and authorities say they will not attempt to recover the illegal cargo because of the depths.

While the *Luciana* and its cargo remain at the bottom of the murky ocean, twenty-two men were charged in the importation conspiracy, thirteen from Nova Scotia. Many cases are still in the courts.

Three years earlier, on April 21, 1991, the drug ship *Marine Transport* hit ice and sank 110 km south of St. John's, Newfoundland. The vessel carried 1,500 kg of cocaine, but divers recovered only 35 kg of a shipment valued at $1 billion. Following the sinking, authorities arrested and charged twenty-one people in connection with the operation, ending two years of investigative work involving the RCMP, the U.S. Drug Enforcement Agency, and police in Quebec, Newfoundland, Nova Scotia, and Florida. Two men from Digby County were among those charged in the conspiracy.

Off the High Seas

WITH THE WING- AND TAIL-FLAPS in position, the pilot of a single-engine aircraft prepared for descent to a remote airfield at Greenfield, about fifteen minutes north of Liverpool. The cargo: an unknown quantity of contraband drugs, most likely hashish.

In the early 1970s, the Queens Municipal Airport, now known as the South Shore Regional Airport, was nothing more than a black-topped runway with one small hanger and a sparsely equipped control tower. At least a ten-minute drive from the nearest house, the airport was an ideal location for an air-drop of illegal drugs from the south, destined for markets in North America. With good access roads and a dense forest to block the view from the nearest roads, authorities suspect the facility has been used for many drug drops, particularly when the public and the police were not yet aware of the immensity of the drug problem.

On this fall day in 1974, conditions were ideal: no ground or air traffic around the airport, the weather perfect for a quick drop. The importers were professionals, touching down as quickly as possible in case their flight path was being tracked by radar. Their plan was to unload the cargo to co-conspirators waiting on the ground and take off again in a matter of minutes. The pilot's colleagues met him at the Greenfield airport with their four-wheel-drive Suburban to load the drugs and take them to a storage area for subsequent sale to drug dealers.

Unbeknownst to the smugglers, they were being observed at a distance by a bemused onlooker as they transferred several packages from the plane to the vehicle. The concerned citizen notified the Liverpool RCMP. "After we received such a tip, we immediately assumed that drugs were involved," says now-retired RCMP officer, Gary Grant. "When this caller described what they had seen, we knew right away that we were dealing with a drug shipment—we just had no idea what it was, how much it was, who we were dealing with, where they came from, or where they went." For years RCMP had suspected that Greenfield, like other remote airports of a similar size in Nova Scotia, was a prime target for drug importation. "But how do you prove it?" asks Grant. "That was our problem. This tip finally gave us the information we had been looking for."

According to the tipster, the smugglers had been observed unloading a quantity of small bales from the plane into a four-wheel-drive vehicle that had been seen in the area about ten minutes before the aircraft landed. Although the informant could identify the make and colour of the vehicle, he was unable to provide a licence-plate number. However, police did learn that when the vehicle left the Greenfield airport, it headed inland, towards a group of small communities hugging the Queens-Lunenburg County line. Armed with only the description, officers fanned out over these communities, checking every vehicle they came across and carefully looking through each community, as they believed the smugglers would probably be based near the airport.

The approach proved successful. "Sometimes, good old legwork is the best way to solve a case. It was this time." RCMP investigators traced the suspects to a single-family home near the outskirts of South Brookfield, a small Queens County village about a fifteen-minute drive from the Greenfield airport. Secondary roads led to their hideaway, which, Grant points out, would never be a suspected base of operations for an international drug-smuggling ring. "We were never able to determine just what was in those particular bales, or if it was drugs at all— which we were sure it was—or how much there was," Grant says. But the RCMP was able to track down the smugglers. "If we had gone in there right at the time, we might have caught them with a quantity of drugs, but we felt that if we waited, we might get them with more."

RCMP learned that a few months before the Greenfield drop, a mysterious man from the United States, whom residents knew only as Tony, had moved into the community and rented a home. From there, apparently, he was masterminding the operations. "It soon became apparent that this guy was bringing in the drugs through the airport and then selling them around Nova Scotia and into Maine. Our information also told us that another major drug shipment was due at the Greenfield airport in the not-too-distant future. We might have been able to get him for possession or trafficking, but we felt if we waited, we might get something even bigger. So we waited."

The waiting paid off. Within weeks of the Greenfield drop, the Nova Scotia RCMP was notified that a small, single-engine aircraft had been rented in Maine and was heading towards the province: American authorities thought that a major drug shipment was on its way. Police waited and watched from a distance as the suspect plane came into view and landed at the Greenfield airport. There, the contraband was unloaded into waiting vehicles that immediately left the scene. When the RCMP finally moved in, they found seven conspirators in possession of a major amount of hashish. All were charged with illegal importation and a variety of drug-related offences, and all were imprisoned.

"We learned many things about the drug trade from that bust," Grant explains. "We learned that if you do your homework and wait for the right timing, you can sometimes catch the bigger fish. Timing is everything in good police work. We also learned that drug dealers can be working right under your noses without anyone—not even the police—ever suspecting that something unusual is going on. That's certainly what was happening in this particular case."

Although not as popular as sea shipments, air drops are a common method used by drug smugglers, and happen regularly in the densely wooded interior of the province, with its numerous small, isolated airstrips. Smugglers know the police can't keep an eye on all of them, just as they can't monitor the entire coastline. Besides, the illegal importers can travel from South America to Nova Scotia in only twelve hours. The police, says Grant, "have not yet keyed in on airfields, because hashish importation via the ocean has taken the brunt of the limelight. Watching every strip is impossible—you can't baby-sit them—so our best deterrent is the eyes and ears of the public."

The province is a smuggler's paradise for air operations: the airfields are not only small and numerous, but infrequently used, and then usually for pleasure or business trips, or aerial forest spraying. Landing lights at many airports can be flicked on using certain radio frequencies; so smugglers can fly in at night, land, and unload their cargoes without detection. Although many airstrips are isolated, they are accessible by road, allowing trucks to wait for the drop. Once the first fly-by is complete, the waiting conspirators load the cargo and are on their way. Like their counterparts at sea, air smugglers are becoming educated about enforcement efforts. It may be dangerous to skirt radar by flying low and refuelling in the air, but smugglers are used to risks. They are also known to drop their shipments from the planes to be recovered by accomplices on the ground, eliminating the need to land as well as the opportunity for interception. What's more, Grant says, time and technological progress are on their side. "The planes are getting bigger and faster, so their success rate will be higher as the years go by, and they'll be willing to take even greater chances."

In midsummer 1990, the RCMP began investigating a drug-smuggling group thought to be operating in several areas of the province, mostly in the Digby area. Citizens responding to the RCMP's request to report suspicious activities were instrumental in the early stages of this effort, which culminated in the interception of a major cocaine shipment bound for Nova Scotia and the North American market. By late summer, RCMP and Halifax drug officers, assisted by Canada Customs, suspected that a quantity of drugs was on its way from Colombia.

On September 21, 1990, mechanical problems forced a DC-3 aircraft to land without lights—and without contacting the control tower—at the international airport in Allentown, Pennsylvania. A task force coordinated by U.S. Drug Enforcement Administration agents searched and seized

The DC-3 plane originally destined for Digby, Nova Scotia, was forced to land in Allentown, Pennsylvania due to mechanical problems. It was carrying more than 1,300 kg of cocaine.
RCMP FILES PHOTO

the aircraft and found more than 1,300 kg of cocaine on board, but no crew or passengers. It was subsequently discovered that this shipment was the one expected by the RCMP in Nova Scotia.

Following that interception, an intensive, continent-wide search was launched for the conspirators. Almost seven months after the seizure, a Canadian man was arrested near the Pennsylvania airport; police eventually established the identity of the group responsible for the smuggling venture, a syndicate of United States nationals and Canadians from Ontario.

In February and March 1991, fifteen Americans and three Canadians were indicted on charges of conspiring to possess cocaine with intent to distribute. Acting on the indictment, on March 11, 1991, Toronto RCMP coordinated the arrests of two other Canadians wanted in this drug conspiracy. Simultaneously, throughout the United States, arrests were taking place involving American citizens also indicted in the conspiracy.

Michael Baylson, United States Attorney for the Eastern Division of

Pennsylvania, said that the seizure of 1,349 kg of cocaine represented the largest ever in the district. According to authorities, the syndicate had planned to bring the cocaine into Nova Scotia from Colombia, then transport it to the United States.

Much capital, supplies, equipment, and manpower had been invested in the operation, whose organizers had been expecting a large return. Aside from those who came up with the money, other conspirators concentrated on soliciting investors, negotiating with Colombian traffickers, setting up the pickup site in Colombia, coordinating the refurbishment of the aircraft, obtaining duffel bags and parachutes for air-dropping the cocaine, recruiting people to go to Nova Scotia in teams to receive the cocaine, and establishing the camps and drop sites. A McDonnell-Douglas DC-3 airplane was fitted out to fly to Colombia, pick up the cocaine, and fly it to Nova Scotia, and in mid-September 1990, the aircraft left Florida for Colombia with four men aboard. One man remained in South America, tendering himself as human collateral for the cocaine, and was to be set free on delivery of the drugs in Nova Scotia. (He was later released.) The other three left Colombia with the drugs, bound for Nova Scotia; but they were forced down in Pennsylvania instead.

Meanwhile, throughout August and early September, seven men established a communications base in Nova Scotia and prepared for the arrival of the plane—the cocaine was to be air-dropped, then stored in specially prepared sites before being distributed.

"When leads pointed to Canada, the [RCMP] stepped in and contributed significant resources and intelligence data which they had already gathered," Baylson commented. "In fact, they already had some leads on members of this ring before the plane landed at the airport. Those leads fit in with the information collected by DEA in Florida and other sections of the United States just like a tight-fitting jigsaw puzzle."

The American indictment brought together the key players in the conspiracy—except the Colombians, the actual exporters of the cocaine in North America. That investigation continued, but was never successfully concluded. American authorities say the conspirators were moving the cocaine for the Cali Cartel in Colombia for a $5 million fee, and that the operation was believed to have been only the beginning of a much larger smuggling expedition. All eighteen men named in the indictment faced a maximum penalty of life imprisonment, a $4 million fine, and a $50 special victim assessment. Successful government proceedings followed.

Following release of the information in March 1991, Nova Scotia RCMP not only confirmed their involvement in the investigation, but also verified that Digby was the location of the suspected drug drop site. A rural area where illegal activities would not have been discovered, its proximity to the U.S. border also made it a suitable location for importation. Ten members of the RCMP's drug section, the Bridgewater detachment, and the Halifax drug squad were involved in the investigation. The confiscated drugs would have been cut before being sold on the street, but had an estimated retail [street] value of $250 million (U.S.). If they had reached Nova Scotia, the drugs would have represented Canada's largest cocaine bust at that time. Instead, the distinction belonged to Pennsylvania.

In November 1992, Nova Scotia authorities were involved in yet another massive air shipment of cocaine, this time destined for Quebec. The RCMP in Nova Scotia and New Brunswick, and provincial police in Quebec had been notified that a shipment of cocaine was expected to pass through the region, and military aircraft had been tracking a plane carrying 3,000 kg of cocaine almost from the time it left Colombia. Coastal Watch contacts were put on the alert, and on Wednesday, November 18, the plane was intercepted. The $1 billion bust, at the time, was the largest cocaine seizure in Canadian history.

CF-18 jet fighters and military helicopters were used in the day-long operation, as the aircraft carrying the drugs tried to sneak into Canadian airspace to reach its landing field. Fishermen along Nova Scotia's southern coast and people throughout the province reported seeing an aircraft early in the day that fit the description. It was flying low over the ocean and hugging the coast, obviously trying to avoid radar detection. The search ended late in the day when the propeller-driven plane, a fifty-passenger Convair modified to carry the drugs and extra fuel, was spotted on a remote airstrip 450 km north of Montreal. Four suspects—a Canadian and three Colombians—were arrested near the aircraft; two others were later arrested driving north towards the airstrip. The six were arraigned in La Tuque, Quebec, the following day.

The police effort began in the morning, when the Halifax RCMP's drug section got word that a suspicious aircraft was heading north, touching off an operation that included Canadian and American police, customs, coast guard, and military agencies. The plane might have slipped through unnoticed five years before; as Constable Dan Duffy, a member of Halifax RCMP's drug section, said, "We wouldn't have had a hope." But increased public awareness and improved policing efforts had changed that scenario. Around 5:30 A.M., members of the Florida-based U.S. Coast Guard-Customs joint drug task force notified Halifax RCMP that a suspicious plane would soon enter Canadian airspace. "They told us if it continued heading north, it would soon cross Nova Scotia," Duffy said, "so we put our contingency plan into effect."

NORAD was contacted and two CF-18 fighters took off to intercept. A command centre was set up by Sackville RCMP to open lines of communication between American and Canadian agencies. An emergency response team was mobilized by Cole Harbour RCMP, and Canada Customs officials were prepared. The plan was to order the plane to land at CFB Shearwater, but the Convair's pilot crossed the western end of the province and the Bay of Fundy, refusing an order to land at Fredericton; then officials lost track of the aircraft over northern New Brunswick. Military helicopters from Quebec began scouring airfields and, within two hours, the plane was spotted. "We were pretty pleased with the way things went," Duffy said. "All the agencies came together, because there was a plan and they all knew their roles. It's quite a task getting all those people in place."

The six suspects were eventually convicted on charges of conspiracy and illegal importation.

In their efforts to make use of every available means of transportation for the shipment of illegal drugs, across international borders or within Canada, smugglers don't limit themselves to the sea and the air. Sometimes, they use the land as well—the highways, secondary roads, and arterial routes can provide just as effective a means of getting their illicit cargo to its destination.

The mountains of Cape Breton are breathtakingly beautiful, laced with a network of roads that curve through peaks and valleys. It is the very lineaments of these roads that is credited with police infiltration of a major drug smuggling conspiracy in 1986. The winding, rolling highways are a navigational challenge even for the most seasoned driver, let alone the driver of a loaded transport truck; at any moment the cargo can shift, causing the driver to lose control. Surprisingly few mishaps are reported on the mountainous highways of Cape Breton, a testimony to the experienced and conscientious drivers who operate the rigs. However, accidents do occasionally happen, and sometimes they bring surprises with them.

Sergeant Bill Parker recalls an accident near Chéticamp that led authorities to a drug operation spanning at least two years. "When the police received the call in October 1986 to help at an accident involving a transport truck, they obviously thought they were responding to a normal motor-vehicle mishap," he says. "They had no way of knowing that they were actually walking right into the middle of an illegal drug-smuggling ring that had been operating out of Cape Breton for a couple of years. As it turns out, this operation was going on right under our noses for quite awhile, and we were no more the wiser."

When police in Chéticamp responded to a call that a five-ton truck had left the road, they found more than the vehicle abandoned on the side of the highway—there was also a cargo of hashish. "Obviously the police were surprised with their find and immediately launched an investigation in an attempt to determine the truck's origin and destination," Parker says. The truck was traced to an isolated fishing wharf near Chéticamp, and police also found out that the abandoned vehicle was one of three identical transport trucks seen leaving the wharf, all on the same day.

Armed with this information, Nova Scotia RCMP launched an all-points bulletin for the other two trucks—not really holding out much hope that the vehicles would be found, since the conspirators had probably heard about the accident. But within a day, a second transport truck with another shipment of hashish was intercepted in New Brunswick; a few days later, the third vehicle was found abandoned—but empty—in Quebec. Authorities were pleased with their efforts. They had infiltrated a smuggling ring, if an unknown one, and confiscated a total of 17.4 tonnes of hashish. "How lucky can you get but to have one of the trucks leave the road and just sit there waiting for police to come along? Again, this was one of those cases where luck was a friend instead of an enemy," Parker says.

During the investigation, Parker says, the RCMP learned that the 1986 shipment was not the first to pass through Chéticamp. "Our information revealed that many shipments had come through that point over the preceding year on their way to markets in Quebec." There was enough evidence to lay conspiracy charges against the smugglers from Quebec although they did not have the substance itself to use as evidence except the 17.4 tonnes they seized in the later shipment. Where police have reasonable proof to lay charges, but no physical evidence, Parker says charges referring to a "dry" conspiracy can be laid, as they were in this case. "In this particular instance, we had sufficient evidence to prove that some sort of contraband—although we did not know what quantity—had passed through Chéticamp since 1985," he explains. "We successfully wrapped up this investigation by laying conspiracy charges against the smugglers dating to 1985, and we won the case. We proved that in actuality the smugglers had been using this location since at least 1985, and maybe longer, to pipe their drugs into the country. It was happening right in front of us, and no one suspected a thing. That illustrates just how far-reaching this drug problem actually is."

* * *

There have been many bizarre incidents during the past three decades illustrating the lengths to which smugglers will go to get their goods onto the street. Here are just a few of them:

On March 14, 1994, RCMP and Canada Customs officers seized 753 kg of cocaine, worth $158 million, from a shipment of hollowed-out sliced pineapples from Colombia. Officials from the Halifax RCMP drug section said the seizure of the drugs, from a container at Halterm Container Terminal, proves smugglers spare no ingenuity in getting their goods to the American market.

Halifax's waterfront is a major importation point for drugs on the Eastern Seaboard, an entry point for all of North America—and the pineapples were not the first example of goods fronting for an illegal cache. In 1992, authorities made two major hashish seizures on the waterfront, the first found behind false walls in a shipment of industrial-strength yarn, the second concealed in peanut roasters.

Smugglers in the 1994 incident bored 5-cm holes in stacks of sliced pineapple and inserted cylindrical packets of cocaine, then packed the fruit in glass jars labelled "Candu" with the slogan "The Delightful Flavour of Nature." The jars were vacuum-sealed and professionally labelled. "This is one of the most sophisticated schemes we have ever seen. This was not a fly-by-night operation, by any means," RCMP Corporal Dan Duffy said in news reports.

Nova Scotia authorities were led to the illegal cargo by a tip from the Montreal RCMP drug section: they seized the container after X-ray machines and a drug dog located the cocaine, then removed the drugs, repacked the fruit, and sent it on to Montreal. The container was picked up and taken to a Montreal warehouse, where two vehicles transported its contents to a business and a home. RCMP searched three addresses in Montreal, Laval, and Châteauguay, questioning several men, who were later released.

Despite the sophistication of the scheme, the conspirators invited scrutiny with one detail—the labels said the product had been packaged in Cali, Colombia, home of the most influential cocaine cartel in today's drug market. Otherwise they might have gotten away with it. "They apparently hoped the glass jars, which revealed nothing until the plastic seal was broken, would pass the initial inspection," Duffy said. "It's possible they also hoped the smell of pineapple would mask the drugs and fool the drug-sniffing dogs." As well, only 425 of the 1,250 cases of 12 jars contained cocaine. "If inspectors had opened the case, they only had a one-in-three chance of finding the cocaine," Duffy said.

But Canada Customs regional manager John Fagan explained that the glass jars also aroused the curiosity of the inspectors; most pineapple is packaged in tins. "Their imagination is incredible," he said.

Importing drugs through legal channels is popular with dealers hoping to avoid problems with the more traditional forms of smuggling. "The whole idea is to put [the drugs] through in a normal, businesslike fashion," Duffy explained. Smugglers have stashed dope in furniture, food, hollowed-out lumber and behind false walls in containers.

*   *   *

Large shipments account for the greater portion of illegal drugs, but another side of the importation effort often goes unnoticed. Smugglers enter Canada every day, concealing illicit drugs on their bodies or in their belongings. Their cargoes may not have a big impact on the black market, but they make a contribution.

Unlike conspirators involved with large shipments, individual couriers take more personal risks. They do not have the protection of the syndicates; they often use conventional routes to bring drugs into the country and, statistically, more often get caught than those involved in smuggling rings. In the spring of 1994, Nova Scotia authorities intercepted two independent drug shipments in less than two months.

The first incident involved a twenty-two-year-old Ontario labourer who was caught with 18 kg of marijuana, worth $200,000. En route to Toronto on a charter flight from Montego Bay, Jamaica, he was arrested when the plane stopped in Halifax at 6:00 A.M., pleaded guilty the following day to importing drugs, and was imprisoned for three and a half years.

Customs officers had decided to search his luggage because, according to the *Daily News*, he appeared "quite nervous and apprehensive." The suspicions were confirmed when they found eight tape-wrapped packages containing the marijuana. Investigators later learned that the Scarborough man had a record for petty crimes in Ontario and was to be paid $4,000 on delivery of the drugs.

In June, a former Halifax resident was sentenced to three years for importing drugs and illegal weapons into Canada via the Yarmouth-Maine ferry. The Yarmouth *Vanguard* reported that a 27-year-old former resident of Halifax and his 20-year-old companion from Jacksonville, North Carolina, were arrested after a 9-mm pistol, ammunition and drugs worth about $35,000 were found by Canada Customs officers.

Searching a bronze-coloured Corvette, authorities discovered about 79 g of cocaine, worth an estimated $16,000, along with some marijuana and crack cocaine. The search also turned up a nickel-plated Smith and Weston 9-mm pistol; inside the gun's 15-round clip RCMP found full-metal-jacket hollow-point ammunition, illegal in Canada but not in the United States.

The ammunition found in the gun had a metal jacket with a serrated, hollow point. Inside, a slender pin or post extended from the tip of the bullet. In an impressive piece of journalism, reporter Brian Medal found out from a New York City gun dealer that this ammunition is often the choice of people who shoot other people on a regular basis. "It's supposed to go in you, open up and stay in you," reporter Brian Medal of the *Herald* said, quoting the gun dealer. "It'll do more damage, because as it opens up it cuts a bigger hole." In addition to the bullets in the pistol, an extra clip with 15 rounds of standard 9-mm ammunition was also seized.

During court testimony, RCMP Constable Claude Aubin was quoted as saying the fifteen rounds of illegal hollow-point ammunition found in the pistol are called "cop killers," because the ammunition penetrates body armour worn by law enforcement officers, and that the ammunition carried in the fifteen-shot spare clip was military issue. Constable Aubin also showed police exhibits that described the smuggling scheme. The cocaine was carried inside compact-disc cases, and the man and his companion had only $43 on them when arrested; in his opinion, they intended to finance their stay in Nova Scotia by selling the cocaine. The defence rejected the argument, pointing that the accused had access to cheques and was carrying valid credit cards.

The woman, a U.S. citizen, pleaded guilty before a justice of the peace in Yarmouth Provincial Court to two charges of possessing illegal drugs, and was fined $800. She was subsequently released from jail and deported to the United States. In a court appearance on June 6, the smuggler was sentenced to three years in prison after he pleaded guilty to three of the charges. Five other weapons and drug-related charges were dropped after the Crown and defence jointly recommended the three-year sentence. Provincial Court Judge Bob Prince said the actions of the smuggler went beyond stupid and were actions that society would not tolerate.

* * *

In October 1995, an Ontario man was arrested at the Halifax International Airport after trying to smuggle 36.5 kg of KHAT into the country. A new substance listed in Canada's Food and Drug Act, KHAT is the green leaf of the Catha Edulis plant, a flowering evergreen shrub native to East

Africa that produces a stimulant effect similar to that of an amphetamine.

Customs officers discovered the KHAT in two large black suitcases belonging to a man and a female companion arriving from Amsterdam. The man was fined $7,000 for attempting to smuggle the illegal substance into Canada.

* * *

On November 18, 1995, Canada Customs intercepted 7,500 kg of hashish, worth an estimated $154 million, in a container of rice from Pakistan. The drugs were placed in vacuum-sealed gold foil and clear plastic packages, stuffed inside almost 200 to 500 jute bags. Some packages carried labels marked "Hamburger Helper" (chilli-flavoured), and each contained up to 40 kg of hashish. John Fagan, spokesman for Canada Customs, explained that the drugs were detected using X-ray equipment and drug dogs. There have been no arrests.

* * *

Biscuits from Jamaica were the hiding place for a cache of 484 kg of marijuana and 72 kg of hash oil found at the airport in December 1995. The drugs, valued at $4.5 million, were behind a wall in a 12 metre container of the biscuits. Sergeant Bill Parker of the Halifax RCMP drug section said the false wall was restored and the container sent on to Rexdale, Ontario. Meanwhile, RCMP officers from the Milton detachment waited for the conspirators to collect their cargo. On January 4, 1996, four men were arrested when they showed up for the drugs. They face charges of importing narcotics, possessing narcotics for trafficking, conspiring to import narcotics, and conspiring to traffic.

* * *

On February 28, 1996, a fifty-six-year-old man from Ontario was sentenced to five and a half years after he pleaded guilty to arson and possessing drugs for the purpose of trafficking. He was arrested February 13 after he was spotted setting fire to his 1984 Cadillac near Burnside Industrial Park in Dartmouth; his car was destroyed and three other vehicles in the Brownlow parking lot were damaged.

During the arson investigation, 30 kg of hashish were discovered in two briefcases in the Cadillac's trunk; the man's fingerprints were on the drugs, worth between $450,000 and $600,000. Police said he was acting as a courier for an unidentified accomplice, but cannot explain why he tried to burn the shipment.

* * *

Coffee did the trick in March 1996, when Canada Customs in Halifax announced another major drug interception at the Port of Halifax. This time, 8.6 tonnes of hashish with a street value of $172 million were stashed in packets marked "Coffee," destined for Montreal, and hidden in a container behind bales of cotton cloth from Pakistan.

Inside information led Halifax RCMP, working with Montreal police, to a container ship arriving in Halifax from Pakistan and Sri Lanka. X-rays revealed dark objects in the containers of cloth, so the cargo was more closely scrutinized. With the help of sniffing dogs, the hashish was found in seventy of the eighty-two bales of grey fabric. The drugs were packaged in small vinyl and foil packets stuffed inside large plastic-wrapped bundles; Colombian coffee and contact lens solution was also found in some packets. No arrests have been made.

* * *

Ten men, six Nova Scotians and four from Quebec, were arrested in June 1996, when Halifax and Montreal police busted an elaborate drug operation through which cocaine and hashish were brought into the province for distribution. More than $600,000 in cocaine and hashish was seized in the raid along with $340,000 in personal assets.

The following month, three Mexicans pleaded guilty to drug related charges and to a charge of being in Canada illegally following an April bust in Kings County. The men were arrested after police raided a farm and seized hundreds of marijuana plants and hydroponic equipment.

* * *

In October 1996, hashish again became the focus of a major investigation when RCMP in Cape Breton intercepted a mother ship loaded with 10 tonnes of the drug valued at approximately $200 million. The vessel was intercepted southwest of Chéticamp, about 14 km off the coast. The ship, with the drugs that originated from Africa, had been waiting for a week to rendezvous with another ship, RCMP said. Three men from California were arrested following the seizure and charged with possession for the purpose of trafficking and narcotic importation. They were also charged with conspiring to import and traffic a narcotic.

On October 17, more than fifty officers with the Halifax Regional Police Department arrested thirty-five people following a raid in a north-end Halifax neighbourhood where cocaine trafficking had been rampant. In the raid labelled Operation Crackdown police targeted street-level dealers.

* * *

In November, police raided homes in Shelburne and Boutiliers Point seizing 481 marijuana plants with an estimated value of $300,000 along with $50,000 worth of equipment. Three people were charged with cultivating a narcotic and possession for the purpose of trafficking. In April 1997, a twenty-six-year-old man was sent to federal prison for two years after he pleaded guilty to narcotics and electricity theft charges. He had been arrested in Shelburne in November when 186 marijuana plants were found growing in the basement of a rented bungalow. He pleaded guilty to cultivating a narcotic, possession for the purpose of trafficking, and theft of electricity from the Nova Scotia Power Corporation. Similar charges against a thirty-year-old woman were withdrawn by the Crown. The estimated street value of the drugs was up to $250,000.

*   *   *

In January 1997, Canada Customs intercepted $2 million worth of hashish and marijuana stuffed inside the wooden pallets of a shipping container unloaded in Halifax. Inside the container from Jamaica was a shipment of canned breadfruit and spinach. The container was destined for Toronto.

Also in April 1997, a twenty-five-year old Sydney Mines man was charged after RCMP seized 2,200 g of hydroponic marijuana along with 112 g of cocaine valued at an estimated $85,000. The man was arrested when a courier company notified Sydney authorities that a shipment of drugs was coming into the area. RCMP in Alberta and British Columbia assisted Cape Breton Regional Police in the investigation.

*   *   *

Kentville's *The Advertiser* reported that a twenty-two-year-old Wolfville resident was charged April 13, 1997, after police made what they described as one of the largest drug seizures made in the Town of Wolfville. The random raid by police of a residence in that community netted a large quantity of various types of drugs valued at approximately $17,000.

In a separate incident, a thirty-eight-year-old resident was charged with narcotic and firearm infractions as the result of an April 10 seizure by New Minas RCMP in Lower Wolfville. At the time RCMP said the seizure involved an indoor cultivation operation which yielded in excess of one hundred plants at various stages of growth. More than 1 kg of dried marijuana was also seized along with restricted firearms, *The Advertiser* reported.

*   *   *

In May 1997, Revenue Canada confirmed Halifax customs officers had seized 92 kg of cocaine valued at $18.4 million on the street. The drugs were found stashed in a false floor in a pickup truck brought to Halifax on a container ship from Panama. The truck was destined for Montreal. Three Quebec men were charged in connection with the seizure.

Later that month, Digby RCMP acting on an anonymous tip, seized more than six hundred marijuana plants along with hydroponic growing equipment from a residence in Bear River. A man and woman, each aged thirty-three, were charged in the incident, and police estimated the drugs were valued at approximately $400,000.

*   *   *

... And on it goes.

Pushing it to the Limit

SINCE THE WINTER OF 1989, the drug business had taken Ray Martin throughout Nova Scotia, delivering narcotics to secluded locations and densely populated city neighbourhoods alike. With each delivery, Ray began to feel more at ease with what he was doing, able to push aside his negative feelings about helping people to perpetuate the drug problem. He continued to do business with Frank, content with his new lifestyle but distancing himself from his family and friends. He continued to provide financially for his children, but he saw little of them. He made good money, and soon the loss of his children was his only regret.

By the summer of 1990, Ray had proven himself to the organization as a reliable, trustworthy front man. Larry told him the partners were impressed with his ability to keep his mouth shut while getting the job done; Ray, he felt, had a bright future with the syndicate. The added responsibilities were rewarded with more money, but it was making a good impression that mattered as much as the cash. For once in his life, he felt he was a success—even if he was doing something illegal.

Ray no longer asked Larry questions when he was sent on a job, just did what he was told without trying to second-guess the instructions. He knew Larry planned well and paid careful attention to detail. Like most people in the drug business, Ray had accepted the fact that eventually he would be arrested; it was inevitable. But Larry had been a good teacher and had helped Ray legitimately hide his money so he'd have a stash for survival. Someday, when the police caught up with him, Ray would find something legitimate to do after serving his time. But until then, he'd do as he was told and rake in the dough; he had long ago risen above the $2,000 starting fee and was making big money.

The one drawback was some of the people he dealt with. A few, like Frank, were okay, but most were losers and bums—like this one dealer, Buck. Ray had done business with him at least six times over the past few months, and each time he walked away feeling cheated—which didn't make sense, since Ray was paid by Larry. Still, it was a feeling, some-how, that Buck had gotten the better of him, and he didn't like that. He didn't like Buck, either.

He had first met Buck about a year before, at a small diner near Truro. A mysterious man who knew a lot about the drug business, he looked and smelled like street scum. His presence was overbearing: with his large frame and domineering physical stature, he commanded atten-tion. His eyes were cold; his fists were often clenched like hammers; his voice was powerful and assertive and his words obscene and vulgar. When Buck spoke, you listened, and Buck liked to talk. Their first con-versation had been a strange one. Ray liked to find out something about the people he dealt with, so he began by asking Buck about his involve-ment in the drug trade. It could have elicited a simple answer—or it could have been a mistake, if the man hadn't liked people asking ques-tions. But Buck liked to talk, and took advantage of the opportunity to brag about some of his experiences.

"So you want to know what it's like to work in the fucking drug busi-ness, do you?" Buck asked, his language, as Ray would learn, was more than colourful with slang and off-the-cuff observations of the under-ground drug world. "I've been involved in drugs for more years than I fucking well care to remember—probably around twenty or twenty-five, give or take a fucking year or two—and I've seen a lot of shit go down. Sometimes I think I'd like to get out of this goddamned shit, but I won't. Once you're in, you're in for life. That's just the way it is." As he talked, he glanced frequently around the small, nearly empty restaurant, then went on with his ramblings.

"I've done some things that I'm not particularly proud of, but I've learned to live with them. What the fuck, I say. Someone's gotta do it. You gotta learn to accept what you do or it will eat you up like a freakin' cancer. I've never killed anyone, if that's what you're thinking, but I have done some pretty disgusting stuff. It ain't a pretty picture, but you gotta survive sometimes when you're in this fucking business, especially when you're at the goddamned bottom of the fucking heap."

Buck stresses that drug dealers are ruthless and mean. "Don't let them fuck you around, Ray. Don't trust any of the pricks. They'll stop at nothing to get their stuff into the country, and they'll be twice as hateful until they get it out on the streets where they can finally see some return for their investment dollars. I remember this one guy who invested, I think, about three million in a shipment of hashish, but it never made it. Man, was he pissed. You ain't seen nothing until you've seen one of these fuckers pissed off at losing a shipment. I wouldn't say for sure—because I never saw nothing myself—but some of the other guys said heads rolled on that one. You can't really tell for sure if they were just shitting, or if something serious really did happen, because most of these guys were always wasted. You never know who you can trust and who you can't in this fucking business."

It was that incident, Buck admitted to Ray, that illustrated to him just how powerful these drug kingpins can really be. "The police never did trace the stuff back to this guy—you can't touch these pricks because they're so well connected right up the goddamned line. But the real funny thing about this was that he never skipped a fucking beat. The guy lost three million and kept right on ticking like it was just a few pennies or something. Man! These guys throw money around like it's loose change."

Buck acknowledges that his "career" in the drug trade happened mostly by accident, with a little help from a few "friends." Initially, he worked as a courier like Ray, and then as a pusher, but over the years he moved up through the organization. "I've seen it at both fucking ends. The bottom end can be pretty goddamned disgusting." Ray could relate. He'd seen a lot over the past two years. "The top end of the business is pretty goddamned good—that's where you want to be, Ray," he continued. These guys who are in charge live like fucking kings. We're talking big homes with a couple of cars in the garage. Drugs are good to those guys, while you and me bust our freakin' asses in the shit and puke. It ain't fair, but that's how it is, I guess."

Ray wanted to learn everything he could from Buck, although he disliked the guy and knew some of the stories were a lot of bull; somewhere in all of this were some valuable lessons. So he waited as Buck paused, lit a cigarette, inhaled deeply and began again, talking about his days as a drug user—his way into the business. "I'll tell you about this guy I used to know. We sort of hung around together and got high together, stuff like that. When you're using, you don't have any real friends, just people you see every day on the streets. Anyway, this guy must have gotten hold of some pretty bad shit. I can still see his freakin' face as he tried to catch his breath—his veins sticking out, his eyes popping out of his fucking head, his face turning blood-red and his lips dark blue. Then he began throwing up and frothing from the mouth—and then he up and died. They said it was a drug overdose. No fucking shit, we said. You could've fooled us. We were right there, after all. We saw it. We knew it was a fucking drug overdose. You didn't have to be a fucking rocket scientist to figure that out. Did it stop us from doing it again? No fucking way."

Buck had pretty much reached rock-bottom—living wherever he could crash, with anyone who would take him for a day or two. Mostly, though, he lived on the streets. "It didn't fucking much matter to me. All I wanted was a chance to get wasted." Then, one day, one of his suppliers asked him to run some errands, and he took the job. After that, he worked in various aspects of the trade, but now doesn't use drugs himself—like many dealers. Like Ray himself. "It's one thing to sell it, but another to use it," Buck said. "And most of them never think about what they're doing to other people. I know I never stopped to think about that over the years. All I wanted was the fucking money I could get from selling the shit."

Today, though, the big money is gone for Buck; he's scraping to pay the rent for his one-room apartment and put food on his table. "I still get involved in some little stuff every now and then, but I'm out of the big picture for good. The business is just getting too fucking big. The amount of drugs they're bringing into this market right now would blow your goddamned head away. Too fucking rich for my blood."

Buck admits he's afraid of today's drugs. "This is hard shit they're dealing in now. It'll blow you away. And the people are different. The guys I dealt with weren't wimps, but these guys play for keeps. They've got a lot of guys working under them, so if anything goes wrong, it's the guys like you and me who take the fall. It doesn't matter how much fucking heat the police throw their way, they can't touch these guys at the top. They're too well protected. They just vanish inside their big companies. It's like playing hide-and-fucking-go-seek, right out in the open."

Tapping his fingers on the small, square table, he recalls the risks of being a street pusher. He has been arrested seven times for possession, and almost as often for trafficking; he was jailed twice. "Once I spent almost fourteen months in jail. The second time, six, but I was out in less than three. Fuck, I was lucky." Jail was tough, Buck admits, "but the way I figure it, is that if you've been doing this all your fucking life, there ain't no goddamned way you're gonna stop. Shit, man. They can send you to jail but they don't tell you how you're gonna live once you get back out on the street. How in the hell are you gonna make enough to survive with a fucking prison record? I didn't have no fucking choice."

Buck buys from his suppliers and resells the drugs for a small profit. "It ain't enough to make you filthy rich, but it's enough to get me by. That's all. I'm done out there chasing the fucking pot of gold—won't find it anyway. If you're chasing it too, forget it. You'd be a lot fucking better off just walking away." Trafficking is relatively easy for Buck. "I can get the fucking shit whenever I want it and sell it anywhere I want. I've got my regular customers," and he smiles broadly, adding, "I guess you could call me a small fucking business owner, only I don't pay taxes or any of that shit."

One of his best customers, he says, is between twenty-five and thirty. "He's not a bad guy. Looks normal when you first see him. Clean-cut. But after you're around him for awhile, it ain't too fuckin' long before you can tell his head is pretty well fucked up." Buck estimates he's been selling to him for almost two years. "He'd come by to see me two, maybe three times a month with enough cash to buy a stash for a couple of weeks. He'd take grass, if that's all I had, but he'd rather have hash. Hash gave him a better high, he said." Eventually, though, he began asking for harsher substances. "But, like I said, I never deal with that fucking shit, so I sent him to another guy I know who deals with coke and shit like that. Last I heard, he was blowin' crack and on his way to a fatal collision with that stuff. If he stays with that shit long enough, it'll blow his fuckin' mind. But I guess that's his decision. I ain't nobody's fuckin' keeper and I don't ask no questions. That's just good fuckin' business—don't piss them off and they'll come back."

Another of his customers, a seventeen-year-old high school student, told him she thinks she can't get hooked on what she's using. "I've been selling to her for about three or four months. I'll keep supplying her as long as she keeps coming back. If she's got the fuckin' money, I've got the fuckin' stuff. Too bad she's so goddamned young, but the way I figure, I may as well sell to her as send her to someone else. If she wants the stuff bad enough, she'll get it and someone else will get her fuckin' money. Just call it supply and demand. If they demand it, supply it."

For the most part, Buck has a good business with steady clients of various ages and backgrounds, and a relatively steady supply of drugs. But deals can go sour. Buck has been physically assaulted only twice, but that was enough. "The first time was a long time ago—maybe fifteen years or even more," he said. "I thought I was selling to a guy I could trust [but] I come to find out he didn't have the cash to buy the fuckin' stuff, but he wanted it anyway." As the desperate and intoxicated customer pulled a knife and thrust it towards him, Buck used his right arm to deflect the blade. Rolling back the right sleeve of his faded brown jacket, Buck revealed a long, thin scar running from his elbow all the way down to his wrist. "This," he pointed, "is how he paid me."

The second time was about seven years ago, he recalled, when three young fellows ganged up on him and stole his supply. "I should have never trusted those little cocksuckers. There was something about them that didn't sit right from the start. When they started talking about taking all I had, I should have realized they were up to something." While one grabbed him and held his arms, the other two beat his face and ribs. "They damn near beat the fuckin' shit out of me. I was wasted for two weeks and I was really pissed. They took everything, six hundred dollars worth of hash and some grass."

Buck learned another valuable lesson. "You never go out on a deal by yourself when you're meeting more than one customer. Now, I never agree to meet more than person at a time, and if it's someone I don't know all that well, I pick the place."

Glancing at the clock on the restaurant wall, he told Ray they'd better get their business over with. "Time's a-wastin'. I gotta get goin'." Checking out the dimly lit diner to see if anyone was watching, Ray quickly slipped Buck a small chunk of hashish, which he wrapped in a white napkin. "Larry said to tell you this will be a $1,000 and he expects payment in three days. You know how to get him the money—just like the last time."

"Must be some pretty fucking good for this little piece of shit to cost that goddamned much," Buck responded, taking the napkin from Ray and pretending he needed to wipe his hands before slipping it into his pocket. "Tell Larry he'll get his fuckin' money. He doesn't have to worry about that. He knows I'm good for it. I ain't stuck him yet."

"Yeah, well I'm just delivering the message, Buck," Ray shot back. The meeting was over; Buck got up and left through the grimy glass door, disappearing into the night.

Ray saw Buck every few months after that, whenever he needed some extra drugs. But they never talked much again—not like the first night. And not like with Timmy, a regular contact with whom Ray truly sympathized, although he tried his best to keep his feelings out of the job—or he couldn't have gone on.

Timmy, only seventeen, started pushing when he was twelve, and considers himself an experienced dealer who knows the ropes, as he's quick to point out. He and Ray usually met in a wooded grove on the outskirts of the South Shore town where Timmy lives and plies his trade. He admitted to Ray that he doesn't like the kind of life he leads, but there are no alternatives. "There's a lot of tough shit goes on around here," he once told Ray. "But if there's one thing I learned from my years in this business, it's that you gotta keep your head together and you gotta be on your toes all the time. You always gotta be one step ahead of everyone else."

Scrounging through the pockets of his faded jeans jacket for a match, a cigarette resting between his lips, he told Ray that he once dreamed of graduating from high school, going to college, and getting a good job. "I had it all figured out, but things didn't go according to my plan—they never do." A friend introduced him to drugs. "We'd get the stuff right on the school grounds. I think the first time I smoked a joint, I was about nine or ten. It just sort of happened; it seemed like it was always available, so we kept trying it and I guess one thing led to another, until I ended up selling the stuff for this guy I knew." (Today "this guy" is doing time for trafficking in a narcotic.)

At first, Timmy said, he didn't consider himself a serious pusher. One Friday night, a friend asked him to deliver a package to a house on the other side of town. "I knew it was drugs, but I figured, what the hell. This guy was paying me five bucks to deliver a package, so I did it. I didn't figure it would hurt anyone." After that, his friend began relying on him regularly to deliver packages around the community. "I did it because it was good money. I mean, what the hell. These guys were going to get the drugs anyway, right? I figured I might as well make a few bucks off the deal."

Eventually, his friend became more trusting, and Timmy's courier services turned into small-scale, street-level trafficking. Timmy was twelve when he sold his first joint on the school grounds to a teenager three years his senior. "It didn't mean a whole lot to me who bought the stuff just as long as I could sell it. The more I sold, the more I made. Business has always been good. You never have trouble selling grass and hash— that stuff goes like hotcakes."

Timmy doesn't think of what he does as criminal activity, but survival. "Life's the shits," he said bluntly. "I don't worry about those guys who buy the drugs, and I don't think about the cops. If they want to bust my ass, I'll do my time. When I get out, I'll do it all again. I can't stop now. There's nothing else for me to do."

Unlike other pushers, Timmy is also a user, and realizes he no longer controls his future, his profits go to supporting his own habit. "It's what I do; it's what I have to do. I don't apologize for any of it. These assholes in government and in the police departments think they know what it's like, but they don't know shit. People who don't do drugs, have no fucking idea what it's like—it's fucking tough. It's easy to say 'Get out.' Get out and go where? I don't see any of those do-gooders inviting me to live with them."

Drug addiction, he told Ray, is a disease, like alcoholism and addiction to tobacco. Laws against it only intensify the problem and lead to violence. "I've seen some guys get beat up bad by the cops, just for passing a few joints. They nearly beat the shit out of this one guy I knew because he had a few ounces of hash on him. I guess that makes them feel like big shots or something, but all they're doing now is making the situation worse.

"I'm not afraid of the drugs," he continued, "I'm afraid the cops, or some other drug pusher trying to avoid the cops, will kill me someday. I don't trust anyone—not even you, Ray." The teenager has been beaten up more than once by buyers with no currency but their fists—and by missing a promised payment to his supplier a couple of times. One such mistake earned him three broken ribs and a fractured wrist. "But it taught me not to screw around with these guys, because they mean business. I got the message—you don't fuck with them, they don't fuck with you. Simple as that." As for the future—no change in sight, he said. "I'll just keep taking chances and see what comes of it. This business is all I know and I think it's worth the risks."

Ray always felt bad after seeing Timmy; he was reminded how pervasive the drug trade was, respecting neither age nor social boundaries. Sometimes he felt repulsed by his own involvement, but was always able to tell himself that he couldn't change the world, and he might as well make some money from it. The argument sounded weak even to his own ears, let alone when he dealt with pushers like Fred, a forty-seven-year-old convicted drug trafficker and another of Ray's regular contacts. Scarred, wrinkled, physically worn, and looking years older than his age, the balding man acknowledged at one of their meetings that drugs had ruined his life. "At my age, it's a little late to be looking back at all the things I've done wrong and, believe me, there have been many. I'd change a lot of things if I could, but you can't go back—you gotta live with your past.

"I was a bad cat in my younger days," he reflected. "I've lied, cheated, stole, and damned near killed a lot of people. There's times when I wonder, if I had been pushed hard enough, if I would've taken that final step." But to kill someone would be the final step to hell, for Fred, and he shivered at the thought of how close he came to doing it.

There was a time when Fred was living on Easy Street—driving big cars, living in fancy houses. At his peak, he had more than a dozen pushers working for him. "It was a good deal," he recalled. "Those boys— mostly kids—pushed the goods and took all the risks. I just sat back, getting all the benefits. It was a good life, but when it comes down, it comes down hard." In Fred's case, after the crash he was a convicted drug trafficker, homeless and penniless. Today, he survives on whatever he can get by doing odd jobs and selling small quantities of drugs. Most of the time he lives in shelters and eats at soup kitchens.

"I know what they mean when they say life's a bitch these days. I made a promise when I was in prison that when I got out, I wasn't going to do this any more. But it didn't take long to find out I had no other choice. I only got back into drugs because I had to," Fred continued, pointing out that he depends mostly on the charity of others—especially the Salvation Army—to get through each day. "You don't have any idea what it's like to have to live on the streets and go days without anything to eat. It ain't a pretty way to live. At least if I get caught selling drugs again, I'll have a place to sleep and food to eat. That wouldn't be as bad as the way I'm living now."

Fred blames his "worthless" existence on the drug trade. "If I hadn't gotten involved in drugs, things might be a lot different for me today. One thing's for sure, I probably wouldn't have a criminal record, and I might have a good job. If you're involved in drugs, then you're in for a whole mess of trouble. I speak from experience."

Drug dealers, Fred explained, have only one goal: to make the big score. "It doesn't matter how much stuff you've already moved or how much money you've already made, you're always looking for ways to do better; you're always looking for the one big deal that will finally put you over the top. In my case, I went back to the well one too many times. Look at where I am now."

And Ray looked. Fred's clothes should have been discarded five years ago, he thought. The man's eyes were sunken, his skin a greyish white. A doctor might prescribe some medication, but Ray knew without asking that Fred could barely afford to eat. The man's voice cut into his thoughts: "I think I've just about reached the end of the line. There's not much left to live for. If that's the case, then I hope I can get it over with quickly," he added matter-of-factly.

It was a risky, sometimes deadly, business, Ray could see; trafficking promised wealth, but delivered only pain, suffering, and self-destruction. He also realized that he too was in the loop—which would only end (if just temporarily) when he was busted. It would happen, he knew, and he was prepared for the inevitable.

* * *

Christmas of 1990 was tough for Ray. His ex-wife, Shirley, had remarried earlier in the fall, and she and her new husband wanted the children with them for the holidays. He agreed, but reluctantly. Since it was to be their first Christmas together in their new home, he didn't want to cause problems. It was a hard decision, but he hoped his children would finally enjoy being in a complete family again.

Putting his personal feelings aside, Ray had done what he thought was in the best interests of his children. Every year since the divorce, he had looked forward to the holidays, when he would have the children for the week after Boxing Day. It was the only time of the year that he got to spend more than a few hours with them. But not this Christmas. And it seemed proof that their bond was being severed.

Shirley did agree to a visit for two days over the New Year's holiday, but that was little consolation. Although he looked forward to their company, he would miss the joy their smiles brought at Christmas, reawakening his holiday spirit. This year, since the children weren't coming, he didn't bother with a tree. No need for a Christmas tree if you don't have anyone to share it with.

It came as no surprise when, on Boxing Day 1990, Ray received a call from Larry instructing him to make a drop to a new customer. If it had been any other Christmas and the children had been with him, he would have refused. But he had no other commitments this year.

The arrangements were simple enough. Ray was to meet his contact at 4:15 P.M. on December 28, ironically, at the bar where he had first met Larry and his two partners more than three years before. Rick Strictland was the guy's name, Larry said, describing the man as about 6'2" and weighing about 250 lbs. He would be wearing a black overcoat and a Toronto Maple Leafs baseball cap. After several years in the drug business, Ray hated cold calls. Established customers were a known element; meeting new contacts made him uneasy. Larry assured him that Rick could be trusted; he had been introduced to the organization by someone who had been lining up contacts for years and, Larry insisted, Rick had been thoroughly checked out. If this deal went smoothly, Rick would gradually be moved up to larger quantities; this meeting could lead to benefits for Ray.

Ray took in Larry's words, but decided to wait until after the meeting to pass judgement. He had heeded the warnings of the pushers and street people he had met: trust no one, even someone highly recommended by the organization; you don't have any friends in the drug business.

Cautiously entering the bar, he spied the tall, heavy-set man in a black overcoat and baseball cap, sitting at a corner table near the men's room—familiar territory, as it was a spot where he had made many deals in recent years. Ray carefully eyed the clean-shaven stranger as he approached the table. "You're Rick?" he asked, selecting a chair directly across the table from him. "Yeah," the man replied, staring sharply at Ray, making eye contact. "And I guess you must be Ray, right?" Ray sat down. "Right. Where you from?" There was no small talk. Ray liked to get right down to it. He wanted to find out as much as possible before any business was discussed.

Rick waited until the waiter delivered the beer he'd ordered just before Ray got there. Taking a swallow, he finally responded. He seemed friendly and talkative, but Ray remained guarded. The stranger began: "I've been around. You know, here and there. Nowhere for any length of time. Before I came here, I was up Cape Breton way for a couple months. Before that, Newfoundland and Calgary. Where you from, Ray?"

"Round here" was Ray's only response. "Round here's a pretty big place, Ray. What exactly is round here?" Rick persisted, mocking Ray's heavy South Shore accent. Ray didn't like talking about himself. His personal information was his business, and he liked to keep it that way with customers, especially new ones. Besides, he was the man with the goods; he should be doing the asking and Rick should be doing the answering. "I don't much like to talk about myself," Ray said flatly.

Rick turned back to his beer, then finally offered: "Geez, Ray, I didn't mean to piss you off. No need to be so touchy. I was only trying to be friendly." "Don't need any more friends—got too many friends now." "Yeah, well, everyone needs friends. It don't matter what you do, you gotta have people you can trust, people you can count on."

"Like I said, I don't need any friends. I don't even know who you are or what the hell you're all about. I don't trust anyone, especially people who ask a lot of questions!" Again, Ray felt Rick had turned the table on him. He didn't like that. Rick seemed too self-confident, almost cocky. That made Ray uncomfortable, too; it put him on the defensive. He had to watch himself, and the best way to do that was to lay his cards on the table. "I don't think I can trust you, Rick. I'm getting strange feelings about you. I don't know why, but something just ain't right."

"Now wait a minute; just hang on there, Ray. You just got here. How can you say that already? You're right; you don't even know me. So how can you jump to that conclusion already? I was only trying to be nice, so fuck you if you don't like friendly people," Rick retorted. "You've been here two minutes and you've already decided you can't trust me. That's not much of a chance. What gives?"

"I don't give people chances. Giving people chances leads to trouble," Ray replied, watching Rick's body language closely to see what kind of reaction he would get with this direct approach. Rick shrugged, regaining his cool, confident composure. "Can't say I blame you, I guess," he said. "I've been there, Ray. I know where you're coming from. I've been screwed one too many times myself, and it ain't no fun. But you can't just cut me off without giving me a chance. I was promised you'd deliver this afternoon. I'm counting on that. I've got other deals pending. If you're pissed at something, or if you're pissed at me for something, don't let it mess up this deal. I've got arrangements. You can't back out now."

After that exchange, the two men sat stone-faced, neither talking nor looking at each other. Minutes passed. It was almost as if they were waiting for the curtain to rise on the next act of some poorly directed stage production. For Ray, this was unfamiliar territory. Rick was proving to be a formidable opponent. Usually, he could find out a lot from first conversations with new contacts, but not this time. He felt Rick was either an experienced dealer or a seasoned drug operative who knew how to take charge; in fact, he was having altogether too much trouble assessing the man, which was making him extremely nervous. He wanted to leave, but that would take some explaining, especially since Larry had assured him that Rick had been cleared by the organization. He hadn't second-guessed any of Larry's arrangements before, but this situation just didn't feel right. Rick handled himself differently, and Ray didn't know how to deal with that. Well, maybe he was overreacting; Ray decided to push the conversation forward again. "So just what is it that you think I can do for you, Rick?"

"Don't be coy, Ray. I don't like playing games. We both know why we're here." Rick was upstaging him again. "I know what you're thinking. You're wondering if I'm for real, or if I'm some kind of cop or something. Well, it don't matter what I tell you, you can't know what I am, and you won't know until we do this deal. You got to decide if you can take a chance or not. You don't trust me and maybe you're right. Maybe I am a cop, or, then again, maybe I'm a man offering you a chance to make a lot of money if things work out. I've been where you are, Ray. I know what it's like not to trust anyone. Look at it from my perspective—maybe you're a cop, setting me up. Right? You and me both know you can't trust anyone in this business, so you gotta take a chance. Chances are what this business is all about. Your boss won't be happy if you blow a good deal. Those guys are gonna be pissed if you screw me up. It won't matter to them, Ray, what you've done for them in the past; they only deal in the present."

"You talk too much," Ray interrupted. Rick was making sense; it was already too late for Ray to back out. If Larry had sent him into a trap, then the scenario would have to play itself out. Ray felt cornered. "I don't want to listen to you running off at the mouth. I don't trust you, but we got business. I guess we may as well get on with it. What do you want?"

"You know what I want, Ray. Where is it?"

"It's safe. But you better have the cash," Ray responded. "When I leave, you stay here and finish your beer; I don't want us to be seen leaving together. Have another beer if you want. Wait about twenty minutes, then you come out. Once you get outside, turn right and start walking towards the little store down the road."

The minutes Ray spent in his truck waiting for Rick seemed like hours. He desperately wanted this exchange to be over. If Rick was a cop he wanted the waiting to end; then, finally, his secret would be out. Deep down inside, Ray hoped that Rick was an undercover cop, so the charade would be over. As he watched Rick leave the bar, he snapped back to reality. If he were caught, it would mean he'd go to jail and probably lose everything he had worked for. He didn't really want that; drug money provided him with a comfortable lifestyle, which promised to get even better if this deal worked out.

Ray pulled his truck up alongside Rick and told him to get in. "I don't like to do business right here in the open like some people," he told the stranger as he climbed into the cab. "We'll go someplace safe and do this—a place where I know we won't be seen."

As Ray headed out of town, he continued to feel uncomfortable dealing with Rick, and covered up with another question. "What brought you to these parts, Rick?"

"I got family around here and since I couldn't get work anyplace else, I thought I may as well try my luck around here."

Ray didn't buy it. "There ain't too many jobs around here either, so I guess you'll be heading out soon."

"Well, not right away. I'm staying with a cousin and his friend. They said I could stay as long as I want. I'll probably stick around for awhile to see what comes along."

"What's your cousin's name? This is a small town. I know a lot of people round here—maybe I know him."

Rick hesitated, then answered, "He's kinda new around here too. Name's Neil West, know him?"

"No. Never heard of him." Ray didn't buy the "cousin" story. He felt he had just poked the first hole in Rick's cover, but what did that accomplish? Even if Rick were lying about his cousin, that didn't prove a damned thing. Drug dealers often have fake identities and false covers, including elaborate schemes involving several people. But, then again, so do undercover cops. Searching for more information, Ray asked, "What's your cousin do?"

"He's in construction. But the work's slow around here, like you said. He's having a hard time getting jobs. But he's got a line on a couple of good things so hopefully something will come along pretty soon. He said he might even be able to find something for me."

Nice recovery, Ray thought. It became painfully obvious to Ray that he wasn't going to get any information from Rick that might shed some light on the man's true identity. He decided to drop the questions, for now at least. For the remainder of the trip the two men kept quiet. About ten minutes after they had left the outer town limits, Ray turned the truck onto an old, gravel logging road and parked behind a clump of spruce trees, out of sight. It was time for business.

"Okay, Rick, if that's your real name ... I gotta say this and get it off my chest once and for all. It's nothing personal. I never met you before and I don't like you and I don't trust you. I'm here to do a job. You might be a cop or something, but I'm kinda in a pinch, so I've got to take my chances. If you are a cop, let's just get this over with. The stuff's in the back of the truck."

"Take it easy, Ray," Rick said. "I'm not a cop. I'm just a dealer looking to connect with a steady supplier. I'm told you guys can get me the stuff on a regular schedule, and that's what I want. If I was a cop, I'd have busted your ass long before now. No amount of talking is going to ease your mind, so if you can't do this, just turn around and take me back to town. No hard feelings. But let's not waste any more time."

Ray began to feel a little more comfortable about Rick. Perhaps it was because they were away from the bar where people could see them, but whatever the reason, Rick was gradually winning Ray over. "I didn't say I wasn't going to do this. I just said, I didn't know if you were telling me the truth or not. You wouldn't be the first dealer to lie to me." He retrieved the drugs from the special compartment in the back of his truck. This time, Larry had told Ray to get the money for the shipment on the spot; it wasn't the first time, so he hadn't been surprised. Larry would arrange to get the cash later—almost $15,000, which Ray would stash in a safe place. He'd hear from Larry within two or three days.

Rick seemed satisfied with the goods and told Ray to expect more deals in the future. "This is just the beginning, Ray. Once I get things going the way they should, we'll be seeing a lot more of each other. This is good for starters. If you guys can handle it, I'm gonna want a lot more of this."

"You're talking to the wrong guy," Ray replied. "You'll have to make those arrangements through Larry. It's up to him who we deal with. But if I'm talking to him, I'll tell him you're interested." He headed back to town, silently recalling the night's events. Although the transaction had gone off without a hitch, he was still uncomfortable. He hoped the feeling would pass once he got to know Rick better—if Larry agreed to take him on as a regular. Ray dropped Rick off at a street corner about two blocks from the bar. He thought that would be safer. "I'll be seeing you later," Rick said as he jumped out of the truck.

With the night's mission now accomplished, Ray headed home. Rick was right. The transaction of December 28, 1990, was just the beginning. Over the next seven and a half months, Ray met Rick on eleven different occasions, delivering increasingly larger amounts of drugs. Despite the rocky introduction, the two men eventually found a mutual respect: Ray decided if Rick's directness gave him an edge, it also gave Ray an advantage over other dealers because it kept him on his toes.

Since the first $15,000 drop, Ray's deliveries to Rick had added up to almost $200,000. They never used the same location more than once, nor did they ever repeat their arrangements, many of which were organized by Rick. Ray had no objections, but he usually threw in a twist of his own to let Rick know he was still in charge.

On an early August night in 1990, the two men were on the phone planning the largest delivery yet. Rick had told Larry he could move a shipment worth about $100,000 if the organization could get it together. There was a customer willing to take on the shipment, but insisted that he and Ray work out the details. Larry trusted Ray after years of good work, and Rick was fast becoming a reliable mover, pulling in big money for the organization, so he had agreed.

"I don't think we should use anyplace that we've used before," Ray said. Such a large shipment would be difficult to conceal, and most of their other transactions had been in areas that were relatively public. "Where do you suggest, Ray? You know these parts better than I do. But it should be someplace where we don't have to rush. Pick a place where we can take the time to load it in the trunk of my car."

After a few years of drug running, Ray knew all the old logging roads, several with abandoned cabins on them; he thought of one that wasn't too far off the main road and was easily accessible. Rick liked the idea right away, and Ray gave him careful instructions on how to find the place. Ray would pick up the hash from his supplier in Halifax and bring it to the cabin; the two men agreed to make the exchange at midnight, August 21.

Ray's part went smoothly. He drove to Halifax earlier in the day and picked up the drugs—a trip he'd often made in recent years, returning with large quantities of contraband for distribution along the South Shore. This day, he believed, would be no different. At around 11:30 P.M., Ray drove to the cabin and awaited Rick's arrival. He was relieved to find nothing out of the ordinary; Ray had checked out the location three days before and everything seemed the same. Ray had even taken the precaution of placing a small twig on top of the door hinge; it was still there. As he waited, he imagined Larry's pleasure about this large transaction, and the reward that would be in store for him.

At almost 11:45, Ray heard Rick's car approaching. As usual, he was early. "Been waiting long?" Rick asked as he joined Ray inside. "Couple minutes. I just arrived, really. Got the money? Larry wants me to get it to Halifax first thing tomorrow. Guess he's not used to the idea of me handling so much money all at once," Ray joked.

The two laughed as they went outside. Rick had parked close behind Ray's van, so it only took about half an hour to move the drugs from one vehicle to the other. With money in hand, Ray jumped into the cab of his truck and prepared to turn on the ignition. He never saw the two dark figures emerging from the shadows behind the cabin. Within seconds, two RCMP officers, dressed in camouflage and armed with semi-automatic rifles, had flung open the door of Ray's truck and pulled him out of the cab, pushing him face-down onto the dusty ground. Ray had had no time to react or resist; he had been caught completely off guard. As one officer began reading Ray his rights, the second went over to Rick and congrat-ulated him on a job well done. So, Rick was an undercover drug operative, after all. It hit him like a tonne of bricks, as he recalled his suspicions during their first meeting in the bar, months before. Ray watched more police officers arrive and begin removing the hashish stowed in Rick's trunk. On the way to the patrol car, Ray caught Rick's attention. There was no need for words. Rick had set a trap and Ray had walked right into it. From the back seat of the patrol car, Ray watched the officers cor-don off the area around the cabin and begin taking pictures of the scene. He observed two officers as they flung open the back doors of his truck, and saw their excitement as they discovered the false compartments that Ray had so ingeniously constructed a few years ago.

Sitting in silence in the back seat of the police cruiser, the red and blue lights flashing like some hideous apparition, Ray realized he had finally reached his destination. It was over. He had been caught in an elaborate police sting, and now he would have to live with the consequences of his actions. He had always known this day would come. Clenching his eyes tightly, he thought of his children and wondered how he would ever face them again. He also thought of Shirley, almost pictured her saying "I told you so" when she heard that he'd been arrested for running drugs. Then there was Larry and the organization. What would they do? He knew he couldn't count on them for help. He was on his own.

And Rick. He had come to trust the guy over the past few months, and wondered how he could have been fooled. Ray didn't hate Rick—he had just been doing his job. Still, he thought they had become friends. He'd let his guard down; despite all the warnings, he'd allowed himself to trust someone in the business. But it had all been part of the plan—a good one—and he'd played right into the cops' hands. No, if he hated anyone, it was Larry, who had set up the first meeting, who had insisted that Rick checked out, who had emphasized that Rick was trustworthy. Ray sat stone-faced in the back of the police car, his world crashing down around him.

An officer joined Ray in the back seat, telling him he was facing several narcotics charges, including possession, trafficking, and conspiracy to traffic. Ray would be taken to the police station in town, where he could call a lawyer and give a statement. Later, he would be formally charged before a justice of the peace. Ray said nothing, acknowledging the information with a brief nod. The officer left, and Ray was alone with his thoughts. He kicked himself for walking into the trap, for getting involved in the drug trade, and for being so greedy. He recalled his first venture, when he had transported that hash shipment for $25,000. What good would the money do him now?

About ten minutes later, another officer got behind the wheel and they drove in silence, heading towards town. As the police car passed through familiar neighbourhoods, Ray studied the homes as they went by. He knew many of the people who lived there; some for many years. He wondered what people would say about him in the morning when word got out that RCMP had made a drug bust and he was involved. Rumours and half-truths would be rampant.

At the detachment, Ray was fingerprinted and photographed. His statement, which took almost four hours to complete, included every-thing he knew about the organization. They had him red-handed, so he might as well cooperate. After covering his entire four-year foray into the drug world, including every intimate detail he could recall, he was ex-hausted and mentally drained. Two officers led him to a small, square cell, where he slept for about three hours; in the morning he was taken before a justice of the peace and faced seventeen different charges, dating back to his early involvement in the drug trade.

Later that morning, he was informed that five others, including three in Halifax and two in Truro, had been taken down in the same under-cover police operation. He didn't yet know who had been charged, but they were probably some of the people from whom he had been receiving his supply over the years. No one from outside the province had been arrested—not yet, anyway—which meant that Larry and the other main players were still outside the police net. Again, he felt anger towards Larry, realizing that he and the other front men were the pawns. They had taken all the risks, just as some of the customers and dealers had told him; their voices flooded into his head, warning him once again that he was playing a dangerous game. Well, he'd played, and he'd lost.

The police eventually filled Ray in on their investigation, which had started months before he met Rick, who, as it turned out, was not from Nova Scotia, but worked mostly in the Montreal area before coming to the South Shore. He had connected with someone who had a direct link to Ray's organization, and thus was recommended as a drug dealer. Once his cover was established, he had to get a contact in Nova Scotia; with the organization's blessing, he was teamed up with Ray, and over the fol-lowing seven months he worked hard to win Ray's trust. From the moment Ray met Rick at the bar, he was watched and tailed, his every movement traced. His phones were tapped, every call monitored. His mail was searched, visitors watched. His family and friends were investi-gated. Every intimate detail of Ray's life over the past seven months was known to the police. He had led them to his contacts in Halifax and Truro, to the pushers and dealers, some of whom would eventually be charged. It had been a carefully executed investigation, and Ray, unknowingly, had cooperated fully.

Over the next five months, Ray appeared in court several times and was finally sentenced to three years in a federal penitentiary and three years probation. He accepted his punishment with what little dignity he could muster. The law had caught up with him, as he knew it would, but the reality was sobering.

After his release from prison, Ray struggled to get back on his feet, but the fallout from his conviction left him financially ruined. His house and truck were gone, his business destroyed. His personal life was in shambles; most of his friends refused to associate with a convicted drug dealer. Shirley wouldn't allow the children to spend any time with him; his elder daughter, Jessica, completely cut herself off, embarrassed to have a father convicted of such serious crimes. Indeed, Ray has had no contact with Jessica since before he went to prison.

Ray served twenty-one months of his three-year sentence and says the time in prison left him a changed man. "Going to jail was the lowest point in my life. It felt like I was some kind of mad dog that someone locked away in a cage and then forgot about. I lost everything I had the day they arrested me for dealing in drugs. My family. My friends. My business. My dignity. My self-esteem. Everything. I saw some pretty bad shit go down while I was in prison, and I ain't never going back. That's a promise I made to myself the first day they locked the cell. It changed my life. But I don't blame anybody but myself. No one forced me to get involved in the drugs. I did it because I wanted the money, because I was greedy. At first, I told myself that things were in such bad shape that I needed to get the money any way I could. Drugs provided me with that money, but I know now I took the quick way out."

Taking a deep breath, he continues: "I'd go back and change it all if I could, but you got to live with the decisions you make in life. I've had to face some pretty tough times since all this came out in the open, but the loss of my children was the hardest thing for me to accept. Some people around these parts are pretty forgiving, and over time I've slowly been rebuilding my business and finally getting together with many of my old friends. But I know things will never be the same for me and my kids, especially with Jessica. She'll never forgive me for making her life so miserable. That's hard for me. I love my children very much and I want to see them. But they're all old enough to know that their dad did some pretty bad stuff, so it's hard getting back in touch with them. They'll come to me when they're ready, I suppose, but I'm convinced Jessica will never forgive me."

Unlike many who have been involved in the drug business, Ray is dead-set against legalization. "It's true that if drugs had been legal I wouldn't have got into trouble, but that doesn't make it right. I broke the law and I've paid for it. People who push drugs should have to pay—I really believe that." There's more to the issue of legalizing drugs than just easier access, Ray points out. "You gotta stop and think about what

177

these drugs do to people's health and how they affect their lives. If you get hooked on the stuff, your life is ruined. I don't know of too many people who support the idea of legalizing substances that can destroy entire lives. It's just not something that we should even be thinking about. Making it easier for people to get drugs would be a giant step backwards, as far as I'm concerned. I don't think society is ready for that."

He recalls fellow inmates who'd been addicted to hard drugs. "They were really fucked up, really screwed in the head. If you want to see what drugs can do to you, go to a prison. Or go to the streets, where the pushers and users live. I've been both places and, believe me, it ain't no pretty picture. That's where you'll see just how harmful drugs really are. It makes no sense to me to be thinking about legalizing this stuff so more people can mess up their lives."

If certain drugs were legalized, Ray believes black-market activity would still thrive, as the demand for new and different substances emerged. "It don't make sense to me to think you can deal with a serious health problem by making this stuff legal. I think the answer is to find some way to wipe it off the face of the earth altogether—that's the only solution, as far as I'm concerned.

"I just wish someone had done that before I got involved," he says, his tone now tinged with sadness. "My life would be a whole lot different today if I hadn't been suckered into drugs because of the money."

In Plain-Clothes or in Uniform

SOME COMPARE IT TO an action-packed cloak-and-dagger movie, where heroes snare the villains in a foolproof trap. That is the Hollywood version, but the war on drugs is not fiction. It is a costly reality. Every day, the men and women who do battle in the war put their lives on the line. It is a responsibility they take seriously; they understand the importance of their work and the impact their efforts have on their communities. They also understand and appreciate the danger, although sometimes they choose to ignore that part of the job.

The police are on the front lines of the drug war, and as the years pass and the drug trade in Canada intensifies, the risks increase. Deals worth hundreds of millions of dollars now push the stakes even higher.

One undercover operative, called Al to protect his identity, says not a day goes by that he does not think about his decision to become a drug investigator. But, he adds, he never regrets it. What keeps him going is the certainty that he is doing something to make a difference, not only for his own children, but also for other young people.

A sixteen-year veteran of the drug war, Al stands almost six feet tall; sandy-coloured hair frames his weather-beaten face, and he smiles easily under a thick black mustache, now tinged with grey. In a uniform he would look like a typical police officer; but undercover operatives must look like ordinary people—they must blend in, easily convincing dealers that they are part of the underground system. Dressed in worn jeans, a faded dark-blue shirt, and cowboy boots, Al definitely looks the part.

Al and hundreds of other undercover officers across Canada lead double lives. They try to separate truth from fantasy, stepping in and out of the drug world as if crossing an imaginary border between fact and fiction. It isn't easy, especially for a family man. Some assignments have kept Al undercover for months at a time, away from his wife and children. "How can you step back into your normal life after you've dealt with such creeps for that length of time? It's hard. Sometimes you find yourself practically living with these assholes for weeks on end, without a break.

179

BUSTED! NOVA SCOTIA'S WAR ON DRUGS

I often find myself wondering how long I can keep this up." But he continues to do the job because he wants to make a contribution, to do something positive. To be an effective undercover agent, everything about him must remain a mystery, for his own protection and the safety of his family. Secrecy is his best ally, false identities his best protection.

"There's a lot of shit going on out there on the streets of our towns and cities," Al says. "If it wasn't for people like me and hundreds of other dedicated police officers in this country, these drug dealers would be making the rules and running the show. They'd be controlling our lives, and it wouldn't be a very nice place to raise children. In fact, it wouldn't be much of a place for any of us. It'd be hell."

Since his earliest memory, Al has wanted to be a police officer, but he hadn't initially planned to work as an undercover agent. "I just sort of fell into it purely by accident. It's one of those things that I just found myself doing and discovered I was really good at it." Indeed, Al has the type of personality that drug traders will trust; he gives the impression that he has something to hide—shies away from eye contact, remains evasive and aloof when questioned, seems jumpy and edgy, as if constantly watching over his shoulder. He calls that his "sixth sense," and it has served him well over the years. His language is peppered with street slang and thick with a gutter-style accent that disguises his good education. Having a brooding, mean disposition and being a good talker are traits Al says make him an effective operative.

"The trick is to be able to talk your way into a situation and then convince the dealers you're one of them. That's not always easy, and sometimes it's taken us months to infiltrate these organizations. These guys are suspicious of everyone, and they are protective to a fault. They're tight. They look out for each other. You gotta be fast and quick on your feet, because they'll try to screw you around pretty good until you prove yourself to them. The first thing I do is try to come across like I want to get in on the action just for the money. I never let them think I want to be a friend. I think that's why it works so well, because these guys aren't out to make friends; they want the bucks. If you can convince them that you're just like them, then you're on the right track. Sometimes it doesn't take me long to get into their organizations, other times it's a hard sell, but eventually I get there."

Proudly, he notes that in the dozens of cases he has worked, he has never failed to make his mark: all his cases have ended with arrests. "Some have been touch and go, but I've been lucky enough to pull them all off."

Sure, the work is dangerous, but Al says he avoids dwelling on that aspect of the job. "The way I figure it is that when your time is up, it's up, and there ain't no use worrying about it. That sounds pretty simplistic, but how else could you do this kind of work if you didn't look at life in simple terms? What are you going to do when someone's holding a gun at your head? It's no use crying about it then. If you can't accept the danger, you can't do this kind of work. I figure I may as well be doing something I like and helping to get rid of these scum at the same time. I like my job, very much, even though I know that each time I go out on an assignment, it could be my last one. I think that's maybe why police officers doing this kind of work are able to stay on their toes; they know it's so dangerous and that they're putting their asses on the line. When you're protecting your life, you're going to stay sharp and that comes in handy in this line of work, where these guys would just as soon cut your throat as look at you, especially if they find out you're a cop."

Al's first marriage broke up because his wife could not bear the pressures and worries that came with his work. But despite the personal toll undercover work has exacted, he feels compelled to continue. "It's just in my blood, I guess. I've seen the damage that these drug dealers can do and I want to make a difference. I want the bastards stopped. If that means going undercover to do it, then that's what I do. It does have personal costs, but I don't let myself get caught up in that any more. I've got a job to do, and that's all I think about; I stay focused on my job. I can't be effective if I'm worrying about what my wife is thinking or what someone else is doing. It comes with the territory."

Recognizing and accepting the dangers is part of the process, Al points out. "When you go running headfirst into a situation where you're trying to take down five or six guys in the middle of a drug deal, you really are putting yourself right in the line of fire. We hope that these guys will use their heads and realize they have nowhere to run, but we really don't know how they'll react. After all, we're talking about millions of dollars, and people will do some drastic things to protect that kind of money. We really don't know if they'll start firing on us, but we go rushing in there anyway. No one's been seriously hurt or killed yet in Nova Scotia, but it only takes once for some guy to think he's invincible, and we could have a tragedy on our hands. You really don't stop and think about that when you're doing this—you just do it day after day and hope for the best."

The officer remembers one incident that could have ended differently. "I was involved in a take down where this one asshole thought he could hold us off. There we were, this one guy with dozens of armed police officers breathing down on him. This guy was just crazy enough to do anything, because I guess he thought he had nothing to lose. It's those kinds of guys you really have to be careful of, because you just don't know what they'll do; they're like a time bomb just waiting to explode, and you don't want to be in their line of fire when that happens. Eventually, we got the drug dealer and he was successfully convicted. But it was hairy there for a few minutes; it could have turned out really badly."

But in general, Al finds drug work personally rewarding. "I like being a police officer," he says. "I wouldn't want the kind of job where you're stuck to a desk all day or out handing out parking tickets. I like knowing I'm out there beating the streets and helping to take these guys out of action. I figure the more I do this, the fewer drugs there'll be to get onto the streets." However, he is quick to point out that the work is far from glamorous. "I've been involved in some cases where I've had to go undercover for weeks, and that's a hard thing to adjust to. But I survive. Some of the situations you find yourself in may leave you asking why in hell you're doing this, but you know why you're doing it—it's your job, and beyond that, you feel it's your responsibility. That's the only explanation I have, because you wouldn't go crawling around in some of the shit we face unless you felt you were doing something very important—or at least I wouldn't."

In recent years, undercover agents have played major roles in some major drug investigations. In December 1994, the RCMP paid two undercover agents a total of $800,000 in connection with two spectacular drug busts off the east coast. One of the operatives was involved in a case in which 700 kg of cocaine was recovered off the floor of the Atlantic Ocean near Sheet Harbour, Nova Scotia; the other led Newfoundland authorities to the *Luciana*, which sank in 1992 with 3 tonnes of cocaine on board.

Canadian Press quoted RCMP sergeant Lawrence Grant as saying the payments were awards for services rendered. "Police don't pay agents to testify. They are provided an award based on several factors, including their level of involvement in the case and the level of the target."

Retired RCMP member Gary Grant, once an undercover operative himself, says he truly believes all police officers are a special breed of men and women who recognize the risks but do their jobs because, like Al, they want to help solve a serious problem. "For most of these guys, the real payoff comes in knowing that you made a difference, that you did something positive to help make the community a safer place for people to live and raise a family. It isn't the money, because you can make better money doing something else that's not as dangerous as police work. And it isn't for the glory, because, usually, police work is the least glamorous type of job you can have." He should know— Grant did the job for more than twenty-three years, most of it spent in drug enforcement.

In 1969, the Dartmouth native saw a recruitment notice for the RCMP. He had no pressing urge to become a police officer, but decided to enlist anyway. "It's not like I had this lifelong wish to work in law enforcement, because I really didn't. However, I had just graduated from Prince Andrew High School and was looking for something to do," he recalls. "I'd tried a few odd jobs around the city, but noth-

Retired RCMP officer Gary Grant says working in the drug trade is a risky business, but also rewarding.
VERNON OICKLE PHOTO

ing seemed to click, so when this opportunity came along, I guess I saw it as a chance to do something interesting and exciting, and I never regretted my decision."

Following the traditional six months of training at the RCMP depot in Regina, Grant was posted to Ottawa, where he served as a member of the Governor General's special forces unit. In 1971, he returned to the east coast—Newfoundland, where he first became exposed to the drug trade just beginning to show signs of becoming a force to be reckoned with. "Even back then, we recognized that the drug problem was going to get worse, because there was big money to be made, and whenever there's that kind of money, then you're going to have people who are willing to take risks."

Grant spent five and a half years in Newfoundland, the first three in Whitbourne, a small community about 100 km west of St. John's, the rest in an even smaller place, Ferryland, on the island's southern coast. The RCMP force in Ferryland consisted of two officers—the corporal in charge and one constable. Between them, the officers shared a patrol car and worked out of a small cubicle they called "the office." He learned a lot during those years, Grant recalls. "Basically, the two of us had to do everything that had to be done in the area when something happened, because backup was over an hour away. If there's one thing I learned in Ferryland, it's that you should know how to use your tongue just as good as you can use your fists. Over the years, I've found that good police work is a lot of good public relations and that means if you know how to talk to people, you can avoid a whole lot of shit."

Grant also learned how to initiate a drug investigation: it was in Ferryland that he experienced his first drug bust, which turned out to be one of the first major seizures in Canada. The drug dealer was a well-known and highly regarded doctor, trafficking marijuana on the side. While the seizure was minor compared with today's standards, Grant says it was big enough to get him hooked on drug investigations. "It was from that point on that drug activity just seemed to follow me wherever I went, and I wouldn't have wanted it any other way. It just seemed like I was destined to be involved in the drug scene in one capacity or another."

The experience and knowledge he gained from his Newfoundland posting would come in handy for his next assignment. Grant says it is not an exaggeration to describe the South Shore as the drug capital of Nova Scotia in those days. "There's no question about it, this was the place to be if you wanted drugs back then. We're only talking about grass [marijuana] and hashish, because the other stuff, like cocaine and crack, hadn't arrived yet, but there were enough drugs to tell us we had a major problem." One of the best-known locations for drug activity was Liverpool, where, in 1976, Grant—who by then had developed a reputation as an effective drug operative—was transferred. He was not yet known to the drug dealers in the province, and his imposing stature and ability to fit in with the drug crowd, gave him an edge. His job was to infiltrate the drug rings along the South Shore. Working undercover, in street clothes, Grant would never be suspected as an RCMP officer. Indeed, it wasn't long before he won the trust of the town's drug dealers.

Eventually a series of arrests blew Grant's cover, but the war had begun. For three and a half years, he led the fight in Liverpool against the drug trade and developed a reputation as a tough, no-nonsense police officer who backed down from no one. He developed an attitude and disposition that sent a clear message to drug dealers. The message was simple: "If you're doing drugs in my town and you get caught, you can expect to pay the price. People knew that if they did the crime, they were going to do the time." Drug dealers recognized and feared his authority, while the public saw his gentler side, and respected him as a person who truly cared about his job and his community.

Today, law enforcement personnel and people who live on the South Shore still speak highly of him as they recall his exploits. Sheriff Bob Brogan says Grant was one of the toughest officers he has ever worked with, and one of the most dedicated. Grant, for his part, returns the compliment. "I enjoyed my three and a half years in Liverpool. The people there were very good to me. They were very supportive in helping us to get the job done. Naturally, there were other officers who worked just as hard and who were just as dedicated to the job as I was."

In particular, Grant refers to the detachment's sergeant, Bob Brogan, as another officer who wanted to make a difference on the local drug scene. "In fact," Grant explains, "it was Sergeant Brogan who first gave me the specific duties of a specialized drug enforcement officer. He recognized that the situation was so serious, that at least one officer should have nothing else to do but concentrate on the drug problem. With his support, I literally threw myself into the job. The drug trade had my total concentration and everything else was secondary. I believe that's the only way a successful drug investigator can work."

His efforts in Liverpool ruffled a few feathers, he knows, but he is unrepentant. "I know that some people hated me and saw me as a son-of-a-bitch, but that's all right by me, because it tells me I was doing my job. If these guys liked me, then I wouldn't have been much good as a drug enforcement officer, now would I? When you're working in drug enforcement it's like you lead a double life, where you're hated and feared by the people in the drug communities, but you're also seen by the public as a champion of the family way of life. That's why I was in the job in the first place."

Following his success in Liverpool, Grant was sent to Bridgewater, about a thirty-minute drive away. There, authorities were trying to come to grips with the escalating drug trade in the province, and Grant became part of a newly created three-man anti-drug squad. Their duties included investigating smuggling operations, cracking importation conspiracies, and coordinating undercover operations with the goal of infiltrating drug rings. "We're talking about a whole new ball game here where we now see the police placing a major emphasis on drug enforcement," Grant points out. "I think this was a major turnaround for the force and for the war on drugs in general. I have felt all along that if we are going to be effective in this war, then we need to have strong street enforcement along with strong deterrents against illegal importations. That's the approach we started in the early 1980s, but I'm afraid now they're pulling back from that. Today, the streets are vulnerable again, because the police have eased off and taken the pressure off the pushers. Economically, they say they cannot afford to police the streets; I say economically they cannot afford not to do it."

For authorities to win the war on drugs, Grant says they need to win the battle on the streets. "If you're losing it there, you're also losing the bigger battle—and today, I think we're losing that battle. If we let the dealers win, then it's game over. The police and politicians had soon better wake up to the reality and get going."

During his posting in Bridgewater, Grant saw the drug trade bloom from bud to flower. "In less that ten years, we saw the damned thing grow into a monster, to the point where, today, the drug trade touches every man, woman, and child in this country in one way or another. These are the people that police have to get involved in the war, and I don't think the police today are doing that. If this war is going to be won, the public has to be on our side. To get the public on your side you must show the people that you're making progress. Right now, we're not making much progress."

From Bridgewater, Grant moved out of the drug scene to the Cole Harbour detachment, where he worked for a year as a shift supervisor— a rewarding job, but it lacked the opportunity for him to do what he liked best—investigate the drug trade. In 1989, when he was asked to be drug awareness coordinator for the province, he jumped at the chance. In that position, which he held for three years, Grant travelled throughout Nova Scotia, talking with the public and promoting his "get-involved" philosophy on battling the drug trade. During his last few years in the force, Grant fulfilled the duties of media relations officer and drug awareness coordinator for the province. "These years were all very rewarding for me because, again, I felt I was making a contribution in doing something positive about the drug trade."

In September 1992, he decided to leave the RCMP to become director of loss prevention for Atlantic Canada with Bolands/IGA. In retrospect, he says, he became disillusioned with the direction in which the force was moving. "Do I miss it? Some aspects of it, I do, without question. But today I think the force is putting more emphasis on money than on people, and I think that's wrong. I didn't want to be a part of that. The thing that you have to keep in mind is that when you're a police officer—not just a member of the RCMP, but any police officer—it gets in your blood; it becomes an addiction. You live it, you sleep it and eat it. When someone is putting money above you, then there's a reason to become disillusioned"— particularly in these volatile times. "The drug situation right now is more dangerous, more violent, and more volatile than ever before because of the arrival of harder drugs, like cocaine. You can't expect success when you're taking away resources from this area of enforcement while the situation is escalating on the other side. It just doesn't work that way."

Looking back on his own experience, Grant recalls many close calls. "You're always trying to be careful when you go out on these jobs but there's so many variables that you can't control that you never really know what to expect. All you can do is prepare yourself as best you can. In my day, there were many times when the situation got somewhat hairy, but we always knew how far we could go, and money was never an obstacle. If the job had to be done, then we did it. That's not the case today."

Legislation, he adds, is also making police work more difficult. "It's almost like the laws are stacking up in favour of the criminals. But I believe that if we're going to make a positive change, then the lawmakers are going to have to get back in step with the reality of the situation." Perhaps coming from the "old school" has influenced his line of thinking, "but I still believe the important thing is to make sure the public and their communities are protected. That's what policing is all about for me, as I'm sure it is for most of the police officers. I know you can't win them all—but you have to at least make sure you're in the running. The most important lesson I learned from my time in the drug trade is that you don't gloat over your wins and don't cry over your losses."

As drug smugglers improve and vary their techniques and skills, Canadian authorities, like Grant, see enforcement efforts as inadequate, and that drugs must be seen by the public as a major threat to this country. The number of people charged by the RCMP with cannabis-related offences showed a downward trend in the 1980s, yet it remains a problem of major proportions. Authorities say fewer charges illustrate that while the drug trade is growing, police enforcement is less successful.

Probably the lack of regular offshore patrol vessels accounts for the country's vulnerability, especially for a province such as Nova Scotia. Furthermore, the number of RCMP officers assigned to drug enforcement in Canada is relatively small, considering the size of the problem. Drug-law enforcement here is not a top political priority. It gets an undisclosed—but relatively small—portion of the RCMP's $65-million national budget. By contrast, the United States Coast Guard alone has a $600 million budget exclusively for drug enforcement.

In comparison to the Canadian forces, the United States Coast Guard conducts a rigorous anti-drug campaign, with as many as twenty ships patrolling the Atlantic Ocean, with special attention given to the Caribbean. This effort does not include the United States Customs, Drug Enforcement Administration, navy, military, and a variety of other agencies watching for smugglers elsewhere. While all RCMP members in Canada are responsible for enforcing drug laws, only a few are assigned exclusively to the task. In Nova Scotia, which has one of the country's highest rates of drug interceptions per capita, police resources rank at the lower end of the list.

Even with limited resources, authorities are addressing the problem as best they can. Today, police place particular emphasis on seizing, freezing, and forfeiting to the Crown the proceeds of drug crime, but admit there is no way to seriously infiltrate the multibillion-dollar underground industry. They must rely heavily on public support and investigate all complaints concerning the illicit possession, trafficking, or importation of illegal substances. Coastal Watch and Neighbourhood Watch programs are other effective tools.

The RCMP also maintains a close liaison with Interpol, the United Nations, Organizations of American States, provincial and municipal police departments, the Departments of National Defence, Canadian Coast Guard, and customs authorities. Because of Canada's proximity to the United States, RCMP also promotes a close relationship with that country's enforcement agencies, including the Drug Enforcement Administration, the FBI, and customs and immigration. Such cooperation has helped to identify drug sources, smuggling routes, and entry points.

J.P.R. Murray, RCMP Commissioner, said in the 1994 National Drug Intelligence Estimate that Canadian police agencies face several challenges in combating drug traffickers. "The law enforcement community faces budgetary restrictions and must be increasingly resourceful in its fight against the international drug trafficker. The drug problem demands effective law-enforcement strategies coupled with creative education programs, aimed at encouraging drug-free lifestyles for Canadians."

In the same document, J. T. G. Ryan, Assistant RCMP Commissioner and Director of Drug Enforcement, said that the RCMP's enforcement strategy is to take aim at the disruption of major international trafficking operations. "Record heroin seizures, the dismantlement of large-scale cocaine smuggling operations, the continuing focus on the apprehension of major clandestine chemical drug manufacturers, and the large seizures of domestic and imported cannabis products continue to dominate the

RCMP's enforcement agenda. The law enforcement community also continues to focus on the forfeiture of drug money as traffickers expand and diversify their money-laundering networks. The RCMP Drug Awareness Program has successfully worked in partnership with government and non-government organizations to curtail the illicit drug demand."

Ryan said that rising heroin purity levels, the growing trade in crack cocaine, chemical drug abuse among Canadian youth, and the prevalence of potent, domestically grown marijuana, all translate into a significant challenge for law enforcement agencies. "These trends also suggest that our education and prevention programs must not only keep pace, but must be expanded to provide Canadians with alternatives to drug abuse."

It remains to be seen if the challenge can be met.

A Legacy of Suffering

AFTER ALL THE TALES of drug seizures on the idyllic Nova Scotia coastline, drug interceptions in the air, months-long undercover police operations, sordid dealings on the streets of big cities and rural villages, and disturbing statistics outlining the growing presence and undeniable destructiveness of narcotics in today's society, the story of the illicit drug trade comes down to one word. People. It is the suffering caused by these substances—the lives ruined by them—that remains the fundamental concern, and the ultimate vindication for the police's continuing efforts to combat the drug trade.

Here are just a few accounts of the experiences endured by individuals who have become enmeshed in a nightmare world through the use of drugs. Perhaps their stories may influence others—especially young people—from going down the same dangerous road.

MATTHEW

The door slammed shut. The damp and dirty basement room of the derelict building was quiet. A good meeting place, away from prying eyes.

The distinctively sweet, pungent smell of freshly smoked marijuana hung in the air, burning the young man's eyes. Through the dim light, Matthew could make out the familiar figure of the tall, slender man he knew only as his supplier. As he crossed towards the man he had met only seven months earlier, he thought about his predicament. How did he get trapped in such a vicious circle of drug abuse and sadistic sexual practices?

It was a question Matthew asked himself a lot these days. Even though he knew the answer, a voice inside him told him that as long as he felt remorse, he might hang onto his sanity.

Getting high gave Matthew an escape, a way to forget about life. He understood that drug abuse was a vicious, all-consuming disease. He knew the wrong turns he had taken on his painful journey to addiction.

Now, stealing was routine, nor was it beneath him to give up his body when he needed money for some acid or a gram of cocaine. It was a sad, disgusting lifestyle, but for an addict, these were often the only alternatives.

As he reached the other side of the room, the man, masked by the dim lights, lit a joint and handed it to him. It was a starter, but he'd want more. Marijuana no longer satisfied the burning within him; he needed something stronger. Matthew had graduated to the world of cocaine, crack cocaine, and LSD. He had even tried heroin once, but it had been a bad experience; nevertheless, he'd probably try it again—it was supposed to offer the ultimate escape.

Matthew wasn't living, really. He was just surviving in an unnatural, unhealthy environment. Money was always a problem. He could not find a job: who would hire a known drug addict? The only alternative, at least for today, was to exchange sex for the drugs he needed. The scenario had been played out many times in recent months. As word spread, men seeking sexual pleasures from other men knew they had lucked on to someone who would do anything they desired if they provided him with drugs.

The frail young man did not pull away when his supplier pushed him to his knees; it was a position in which he had found himself on many occasions. When it was over, the man slipped Matthew a palm-sized plastic bag of cocaine: payment for services rendered. As he opened the bag and snorted the drug, he suffered the usual pangs of remorse. Sex for drugs, or sex for money to buy drugs, had become his only means of supporting his habit.

Matthew was born in rural Nova Scotia, into a comfortable world. His parents were good to him, he did reasonably well in school, but at thirteen, his world changed forever when a friend introduced him to drugs. At first it was an occasional marijuana joint, then hash, and eventually cocaine and crack cocaine. Gradually, his world fell apart; his grades fell, and his parents became concerned. Ignoring their pleas to discuss his problems, Matthew left home before he was sixteen, seeking freedom on the streets. He had no money, no place to live, nothing to eat, and no friends to count on. He could have gone back home, but he was ashamed of what he'd done and too proud to admit it and just go home. Life on the streets of Halifax, with no money and with a habit to support, is mean and cruel. Matthew, weak and inexperienced, went from shelter to shelter, taking whatever help he could get and hoping to find a way out of the trap.

Soon after his seventeenth birthday, Matthew took that all-important first step on the road to recovery. Today, he wonders how he managed to stay alive as long as he did. Body language betrays his tough facade. His posture stiffens as he speaks and he visibly shudders when he thinks of some of the horrors he escaped, such as AIDS or a life of crime. At twenty-two, living comfortably with friends in rural Nova Scotia, he talks with compassion and honesty about his addiction and his struggles to recover. "I know it may sound like all of this is just a bunch of bullshit," he says, "but people must begin to understand that this stuff is happening every day in every town of Nova Scotia. It's easy to say it only happens in Toronto or places like that, but I'm living proof of what drug abuse can do to people right here in a small town. It hurts to admit it, but I became a bum and a prostitute, living off the streets and being used. It wasn't living, really. Just getting by."

Matthew now recognizes that he reached his lowest point when he began using sex to support his drug habit. "I was young and alone with nowhere to go or no one to turn to for help, or so I thought. I was confused. I was scared and needed the stuff, just like an alcoholic needs booze or a smoker needs cigarettes. When you're hooked on something as bad as I was, you'll do anything you have to do to get it. That's what I did. If it meant having sex or stealing to survive, then that's exactly what I did, and I don't apologize for that. I believe I had no other choice."

Even though he admits to performing what many consider unnatural sexual acts to get money to buy drugs, Matthew says: "I have nothing to be ashamed of. By that time, I was out of control and really didn't know what I was doing. It was like a disease. All that was important to me was getting high, and I never really stopped to think about what I was doing. But I am ashamed of myself for getting myself involved with drugs in the first place."

Anyone thinking of using drugs should reconsider, Matthew advises, adding that drug addicts come from every segment of society. "I came from a good home and had parents who would have given me anything or done anything for me. I know that now. You see, a lot of people think that to be a drug addict, you have to come from a bad home or be abused by your parents or something like that, but that's just not the way it is. I'm sure that happens a lot, but it wasn't what pushed me to drugs."

Nor should people fool themselves into thinking they can stop whenever they want. "At first, I thought I could do drugs whenever I wanted to, but it doesn't work that way. Once you start using drugs, they will eventually take over your life and make you do things that you would never think you were capable of."

At his worst point, Matthew says, his only reason for living was to get high. "My mind was numb. I had no feelings, and I couldn't think clearly. It was like something else was thinking for me; like something else had control of me. The drugs had a hold on me that I just couldn't get away from. That's an awful feeling, you know. You just feel so helpless.

"I did some pretty disgusting things," he recalls. "When all you care about is getting your next fix, you don't stop to think about the repercussions of your actions. When I was in that basement with all those guys, I never thought about what I was doing; it was like I wasn't even there; like I was outside my own body watching someone else do all those things."

Today, Matthew says, he feels extremely lucky to have been able to turn back. "I really believe that if I hadn't gotten out when I did, I'd be dead now, either from an overdose or something even worse," he says, adding, "It's a wonder that I didn't pick up some sort of disease like AIDS or something because I never took any kind of precaution. I couldn't think clearly enough to even think about that. I badly abused my body and I know I was lucky to get out alive."

His road to recovery has been a tough one. Many times he felt like giving up, but he knew there might never be another chance. "It's such a painful thing to keep going sometimes. Even after five years it's still hard. There are days when I still want those drugs; days when I want them real bad, so bad that it hurts right to the bone. I have to be on my guard all the time or I could screw up. If I do, it's all over for me."

Matthew was rescued from the streets by a caring counsellor working at a Halifax shelter. Largely because of his gratitude, he fights not to give in. "I know I shouldn't do this for him; I should do it for myself," Matthew explains, "but I guess I use my friend as a crutch to give me strength to resist the urge to go back to drugs." No matter how much counselling he receives, Matthew says it would still be easy to go back to using drugs. "I'd just as soon blow my brains out than to go back using drugs, because that would be a death sentence anyway. But even though I know that, I don't think it would take much to get started again." He ponders his next comment and fiddles with the cigarette lighter on the table in front of him. "If things are going bad in your life, I could see an addict going back to drugs. I hope I would be strong enough to resist the urge, but I don't fool myself. I fight the ghosts every day and relive the pain just like it happened only yesterday. Getting cleaned out was one of the hardest things I've ever had to do. Just imagine how it would feel to take something away from your body that you really need. When you're an addict, that's what drugs are—something you really need, and you really don't think there's any way you can live without them.

"If I ever got hooked on drugs again, I'd just as soon die than go through that agony again," he repeats, emphatically. "I don't think I could handle that much pain any more. It tears you apart, like someone ripping your guts out. Recovering was like being lost in a strange world; like you've lost your way. You want something so badly that you'd kill for it, but you just can't have it. You get sick; you can't breathe, and you literally lose control of your body. You can't think properly; you really wish that someone would just cut your throat and get it over with."

Today, Matthew concentrates all his energy on staying clean. "For a recovering addict like me, the best thing I can do is just avoid it. If any of my friends do drugs, I stay away from them and tell them that's not my scene any more. If I had one piece of advice to give anyone about using drugs, it would be simply to stay away from them altogether. There's no such thing as a 'soft drug,' and it doesn't take much to get hooked on them." Matthew says he knows there are young people on drugs in every Nova Scotian community. He is sympathetic because he can relate to them; he understands them. "I feel bad that they think they have to do drugs to survive, and I feel bad that they have no idea what kind of trouble they're heading for. They think that they can control the drugs, but they're sadly mistaken. If something is not right in your life, drugs are not the answer. In fact, they may be the problem."

BOBBY

Drug use, for Bobby, began at home, under the tutelage not of a stranger on some dark, abandoned street, or a friend at school, but of his parents, right in his own rural Nova Scotian community.

Now twenty-four, the troubled young man with thick, curly black hair recalls his first memories of experimenting with drug use—when he was six or seven. "Things are pretty cloudy from those times back then. It seems like they happened so long ago," he explains, hanging his head. "I think things are so hard to remember because that's the way I want it. I don't think I want to remember, so I put all that stuff out of my mind. It's painful to think about what happened to me and my sisters back then, especially when it was our parents that got us hooked on drugs in the first place."

Bobby was about eleven when he finally became hooked on drugs. His parents had started giving it to him at parties, until finally he became hooked. "It was 'only' grass and hash; I know people don't think you can get hooked on that stuff, but I'm telling you that you can. I don't care what anyone believes or says, I know that I needed it and I'd do anything to get it—I did do anything to get it."

He doesn't believe his parents set out to turn him and his two sisters into drug addicts, but he does blame them for the way his life has turned out. By the time he was twenty, he had a record "a mile long" and he had been incarcerated three times for a variety of offences. "Perhaps it isn't right to blame someone else for the things you do, but me and my sisters were only kids; we really didn't know any better. If you can't trust your parents, who in the hell can you trust? Our parents have a lot to feel guilty for, but I can't say that I really hate them for what happened to us."

His father, a mechanic who seemed to be home more often than he was at work, was the person who most often supplied the children with drugs, until they were old enough to get it on the streets themselves. "Maybe he thought it was funny. I really don't know why he would do something like that. Maybe he thought he was being nice to us kids by giving us something that he thought we wanted. It is hard to accept the possibility that maybe your own father would give you something that would destroy your life someday. But that's what he did even though I don't think he really knew what he was doing. I'm not making excuses for the man, but you got to understand that I don't think he knew any better. I'm not so sure he was smart enough to figure out he was doing anything wrong. In his own way, I believe he thought he was actually helping us. I know that doesn't make sense, but I can't figure it out any other way."

Bobby remembers seeing his mother using drugs, which, he says, set a very bad example for her children. Even so, he sympathizes with her plight. "Mom worked hard because Dad didn't seem to work much. She had a hard life with him. She did odd jobs like cleaning for other people or working as a waitress—anything she could find, even if it didn't pay much. Maybe she needed the drugs to help her get by." It does bother him that his mother, the one person children should be able to trust and count on for guidance, would allow her children to be led down a road that would take them nowhere. "She was really no better than he was. I can't say that our mother gave us any drugs, but she knew what was going on in our home. She had to. Dad never physically abused us, or hit us, or anything like that. I can say that much for him. But he did yell at us a lot, and I think that maybe he gave us the drugs we wanted to make up for those times that he got mad at us. But Mom was just as bad for letting him do that. She may as well just have handed the stuff to us

195

as to turn her back when we got it from Dad. I hold them both responsible for the way things turned out. And I blame myself—I have to take some of the responsibility, don't I?"

By the time he was twelve, Bobby was already stealing and breaking into homes to get money to buy drugs. Shoplifting became second nature to him; he considered himself an expert. "I could steal anything you wanted in a few minutes flat and be out of the store quicker than you could shake a stick," he proclaims proudly in his thick, rural Nova Scotian accent. "I don't want to sound like I'm bragging or anything, but I was good at it, and that was the truth." Stealing was also a family affair. "My sisters were almost as good at it too. They weren't quite as good as me, but they could keep up. Actually, though, my younger sister was the sneakiest when it came to shoplifting. Some of the stuff she did would make your head spin."

Pausing for a moment as if searching for some forgotten memory, Bobby then continues, an impish grin on his ruggedly handsome but strangely old-looking face. "I remember this one time we were in a big department store downtown and she wanted a [cassette] tape. It was really amazing how quick she got that tape down her pants and out of sight in just a few seconds flat. I don't think anyone could have seen her do it, because it happened so fast. And if anyone did see her do it, were they going to take a chance and put their hands down her pants looking for a tape that might or might not be there? I don't think so." Less than half an hour later, the ten-year-old girl sold the tape for $5 and used the money to buy 2 joints.

Bobby was closer to his younger sister than his elder sister, perhaps because there was only two years between them. The eldest child was almost six years older, and didn't have much in common with her siblings. "Mom and Dad had to get married. Everyone knew Ellen was an accident, and sometimes we teased her about that. But she was different than us; she seemed able to resist more than us. She never really got into the drugs, like me and Sara, but she did try it every now and then." It was Bobby and Sara who became the addicts, though. "I think that happened because we had so much in common and did so much together, like stealing and getting high," he explains, turning his head to gaze out of a window. "We just liked hanging around with each other. We grew up together and developed some kind of bond."

Bobby and Sara are no longer close. Their lives have pulled them apart. He lives in Nova Scotia where they grew up; she lives on the West Coast, and the separation bothers him. "We don't stay in touch. I think it's been maybe two or three years since I got a letter from her. I used to get phone calls once in awhile from Sara, maybe around Christmas or on my birthday, but not any more." His voice cracks as he says that, in fact, he has lost touch with most of his family. He hardly ever sees his parents, even though they live only about thirty minutes away. "I don't have much use for parents. They didn't do too much for me when I was a kid so why should I expect anything from them now that I'm grown up? We just aren't close and that's fine by me. They've got to live with what they've done."

As for Ellen, he hasn't seen her in years. "It's like she just left home and never looked back. I guess maybe she was ashamed of us all or something. I don't know, and I can't really say that I care very much about where she is or whatever happened to her. I miss Sara a little, but the rest of them can go square to hell for all I care. Ellen was too good for me and Sara when we were kids, so I never expected her to be around much when we got older. She waited for her chance to get out and she took it—that was that. Good for her, I say." He thinks she might live in Calgary, but only maybe. "I'm not sure if I'll ever see Ellen again and, you know what, I really don't care."

Bobby has paid a high price for his abnormal childhood. "I'm not making excuses for anything. I did a lot of bad things, and I don't blame anyone for anything that has happened, or for the way things turned out," he says, matter-of-factly. "Did I know what I was doing when I was breaking into those houses to steal the money I needed to buy drugs? Yeah, I guess I did. I can't claim that I didn't know what I was doing because I was high or something. As far as I'm concerned, I think that's a cop-out that a lot of people use to cover their asses."

Half-laughing, he says: "I might be rich today if I would have just stuck all that stuff away or saved all that money. But I was even too stupid to do that. I would have done anything to get drugs. And you know, even today, although I like to think I've kicked the habit, I still think about them a lot. They really did have a hold on me and it was hard to get away—if I really am away." He considers himself "clean," but admits to smoking the odd joint every now and then. "I know that's dangerous because it could just be the beginning of something bigger, but what the hell. My life's shit anyway. I can't get a job because no one wants to hire a recovering addict with a criminal record long enough to choke a horse. As Mom always said, I've made my bed, now I've got to lie in it. That's funny when you think about it, because I did have some help spreading the sheets along the way."

197

Bobby has no false expectations about the future. "What do you think?" he asks slyly. "I really ain't got a snowball's chance in hell of getting my life together. You hear all these people who are supposed to be recovering users talking about how they're going to do this and that, but it's all talk. It's not easy, and if anyone does manage to turn things around, then they've done something really special. Giving up drugs is hard work, and that's the bottom line."

Bobby has one regret, that he didn't understand earlier what he was getting involved in—the world of drugs, all-consuming, in which children lose their way and adults lose their minds. "My parents were sick. It's just not normal that a father would give his children drugs. I know there had to be something really wrong with his head for him to do something that stupid, but I can't change anything. You can never go back and undo what's been done; that's why it's important to walk carefully as you set out on your life's journey. You gotta know that every decision you make will impact on your future and that you got no one else but yourself to look out for you. You got to tread lightly, as they say."

Bobby recalls times when he and his sisters rejected their father's offers, but eventually he wore down their resistance; he broke their spirits and turned them into little drug addicts. "While most kids were out playing catch with their dads, we were in the house getting stoned with our father. Today we're carrying the baggage with us."

LOUISE

Louise, a thirty-seven-year-old recovering addict, now lives in Nova Scotia. She may be just another statistic in the annals of law enforcement and social services, but her story illustrates the seriousness of the drug problem.

For Louise, drugs were an escape from a life of hell. More than thirty years ago, her father began sexually abusing her; she thinks she was about six, although any earlier memories may have been blurred to blankness. "It's painful to remember, and most of the time I just try to put it all behind me," she says, sitting in a big armchair and shifting her fragile-looking frame to get comfortable.

Indeed, she does not talk much about the abuse or the drugs, especially since her father died in 1989. In a way, she pities him; she may even be ashamed of herself for making his last few years miserable by confronting him with the past. At least, he seemed miserable, she recalls. "It's an awful thing to live with. I almost feel like I may have killed him by finally telling him how I felt about what he had done to me when I was a kid. I was his only daughter—his only child, for that matter—and he ruined my life. Telling your father that you can't forgive him for what he has done is like cutting off one of your arms or legs. It's like part of you dies, or at least that's what it was like for me." Fighting back tears, she adds: "After all, no matter what he did, he was still my father, the man who was supposed to love me and protect me. But it turned out that he hurt me real bad, and how do you forgive something like that?"

At first, she recalls, the abuse was only subtle—gentle rubbing of her bum or the occasional grabbing at her genitals. But as she grew older and her body matured, the abuse became more severe. By the time she was thirteen, she was having sex regularly with her father, including intercourse. "Back then I was ashamed of myself for what he was doing to me and for what he was making me do to him, but now I know that it wasn't my fault. That doesn't make it any easier, but at least I know I have to blame him, not myself."

When Louise was nine, her mother went away for a few days, leaving her at home with her father. That was when the abuse went from touching to more serious sexual activity. "I can't remember where Mother went, not that that's important now, but it's just something that always bugged me. It's like I might be blaming her for leaving me all alone with him. I think that maybe if I could just remember where Mother went, it might not make me want to blame her. If she had a good reason for not being home when I needed her, then I think I could accept that." However, Louise never asked her mother where she had been; she died twenty years ago, long before Louise summoned the courage to face her father with the truth. "But even today, I wish I knew. It just might make it easier to cope with."

The memories are vivid. It was cold that October. Winter had arrived three months earlier than it was supposed to. She recalls the events clearly, even the date. When her mother was away, Louise tried to avoid her father, staying in her room with the door closed and playing with her dolls. That's where she was on the night of October 24, when she heard her father calling. "'Louise, come here, I need your help,' he was calling to me from the bathroom. I ignored him at first, but he just kept calling louder and louder, until I couldn't resist his pleas any more. I knew that if I didn't go to him, he'd come looking for me anyway, and that would be worse because by then he'd be really mad and rough with me."

Reluctantly, she opened her bedroom door and crept down the hallway towards the bathroom. In the light escaping from under the door, Louise could see his shadow. She paused, trying to build up courage and trying to fight back tears; her father didn't like it when she cried. Then, in a

199

whisper, she asked what he wanted. He told her to come in. She waited another few minutes, then, taking a deep breath, opened the door and entered, keeping the door open a crack in case she needed to make a quick escape.

Inside, the walls seemed to close in around her; the room was warm and damp from her father's recent shower, and she found it difficult to breathe. Her father explained that he had cut himself shaving and wanted her to help with the bandage.

"'You do want to help your Daddy, don't you?' he said as he gave me the Band-Aid. I remember that I didn't say a word, but just took the Band-Aid from him and waited to see what was going to happen next.

"'Here, Louise,' he said, 'put it here,' as he reached out and put his hands around my waist." At that moment, Louise knew she was at his mercy. "I had to look at him; I had no other choice. But it made me sick to my stomach just to be that close to him." After she had obeyed him, she tried to leave but could not break free of his grasp. "'You're not done yet, Louise,' he said to me. 'I need more help from you than that.' At that point he reached behind me, closed the bathroom door tight, and locked it. I didn't know what to do and I surely didn't know what was going to happen next, but whatever it was, I knew it was going to be bad. He just had that look about him."

Getting back up on his feet—he stood almost six feet tall—he said, "'Now, Louise, I think you're getting old enough that you can help Daddy even more. I've got something really special that you can help me with, and it will make Daddy feel really good,' he said to me while he was undoing his pants. I had touched him down there before, many times, but it was always in the dark so I had never seen his penis before. I was a little nine-year-old girl; I didn't know what to expect and it's hard to explain what I was thinking or feeling when he pushed his pants and underwear down to his ankles and then kicked them off."

Louise recalls she tried to protest and pull away as he pulled her hand towards his penis. But his grip tightened. "How does a skinny little kid fight a big man like that? You can't. But I never really expected what he would do next." He pulled her forward, and holding her head firmly in his powerful hands, forced her to perform oral sex on him. "It was the worst thing that had ever happened. I was crying and pushing at him, but he was just too big and strong that I couldn't stop him. The harder I cried, the harder he pushed and the more insistent he became that I should like this. But I didn't. I knew this wasn't natural."

That night, Louise lost any remaining love she felt for her father. "I hated him with every ounce of my body; he repulsed me. I repulsed myself for letting myself get caught in his trap." The assault lasted less than five minutes; its impact has lasted a lifetime.

After that night, things got worse between Louise and her father. "I don't know if Mother ever knew that something was going on, but I never told her. I felt too dirty and ashamed for what he was making me do. And when he finally forced me to have intercourse with him, I just felt like a piece of dirt; it was for that reason that I turned to drugs." For Louise, drugs became an escape from her father's torment and abuse. She realized that if she got high, the sexual abuse would seem more of a bad dream than reality. "It became a way for me to hide from him. He could have my body, but he couldn't have my mind. I guess you might say that I thought the drugs would make it more tolerable and more easy to live with, but I didn't know I was only hurting myself even more."

Within a year, Louise was becoming dependent upon the highs and falling deeper into a cycle of despair. Getting the money to buy the drugs was no problem—her father gave her anything she asked for as long as he could get what he wanted. Nor was it difficult to find the drugs. "This was only twenty years ago, so you could get them anywhere you wanted— in school or on the streets, it didn't matter. I usually got mine from this guy I knew in school. He'd sell them to us right in the hallway and he never got caught: at least, not when I was in school."

Louise dropped out of school in Grade 10, and after her mother died, she left home to live at a friend's apartment in another town—as far away from her father as she could get. "I just couldn't stay there with him and let him do those things any more; I had to get away. With Mother gone, there's no telling what he would have done." Unfortunately, she could not escape her cravings. "I was hooked—grass, hash, acid, cocaine, anything that I could get high off, I used and ruined my life. I know now that drugs were not the only way to escape the abuse I suffered from Father, but it was the only way I knew how back then."

She needed drugs every day, just to make it from morning to night. As for sex with anyone else, that was another story. She brushes back her long hair and shifts her slender body again to find a more comfortable position. "It got so bad that when I finally got away from Father, the only way I could have sex with another guy was to get high first. I know now that it was because of the abuse I suffered that I couldn't face sex, but I thought the drugs were going to make it better for me. Sex was never any good, and it still isn't today, as far as that part goes. It didn't matter if I was high or not, but I thought the drugs helped me to get through it.

Maybe they did for a time, but it didn't last long."

For years, Louise moved from town to town, doing odd jobs. "There I was, an addict stuck in a city with no regular job and nowhere to go. But I always seemed to find drugs, somehow. I guess it was a matter of priorities." Everything changed, however, when Louise overdosed on cocaine. "I thought it was the end of my life. My body felt like it had been pulled through the wringer, and thankfully some doctor in the hospital told me right out straight that if I didn't get some help for my drug problem then I was going to die. He told me like it was; he didn't hold anything back. He said if I wanted to kill myself, there were quicker and cheaper ways than doing it slowly, using expensive drugs. He told me if I didn't want to die, then I had better get hold of my life and turn things around before it was too late. He told me to smarten up. It was good advice. It saved my life.

"I'm not going to begin to tell you that it was easy, or that I didn't have times when I was weak and went back to using the drugs again, but I am going to tell you that I am alive today because that doctor gave me a good kick in the ass. It was hard, real hard, but I made it through. Trying to kick a drug-addiction habit is the hardest thing I've ever had to do, except finally facing the abuse that I suffered from Father."

Today, Louise is a recovering addict, but she is still haunted by memories of her childhood. "I had a horrific childhood, and things got even worse after I got hooked on the drugs. Turning to drugs is not the answer, no matter how bad the problem might be. You can't help yourself by hiding behind drugs, because they take away your ability to think straight; they only compound the problem and make matters worse. I know now I should have sought help somewhere else other than from drugs, but I guess I had to learn my lessons the hard way."

KATE

A seventeen-year-old high school student, Kate is certain the drugs she uses won't turn her into an addict. "I can control drugs and give them up any time I want to," she says of her habit: over the past five years, she has used drugs on a semi-regular basis. Not hard drugs such as cocaine or crack cocaine, just popular and easily obtainable substances such as marijuana and hashish. "That stuff's easy to get. Me and my friends know where we can get it anytime we want it. We haven't tried crack or anything like that, but we might someday."

Kate seems carefree and non-apologetic. "I use drugs every now and then, but that doesn't make me an addict. I just do it sometimes when I'm depressed or when I'm with my friends or when things aren't going right. You know, just to help me forget my troubles. That's all there is to it, nothing more."

A pretty brunette who wants to study business when she finishes high school, Kate admits it was peer pressure that got her using drugs; she wanted to fit in with a certain crowd. "They were doing it and I didn't want to be an outsider, so I just joined in. It hasn't hurt me." Although not an academic superstar or outstanding athlete, Kate does well in school, which, she says, proves her point that "soft" drugs aren't a problem. "I think drugs are getting a bad rap and that people are blowing things way out of proportion. They're misleading us when they talk about the drug war and telling us that drugs are bad for us. If you use them in moderation, I believe that certain drugs could be just like alcohol. It's only those people who abuse them who have trouble down the road. I don't ever plan on getting myself to that point, because I can control it."

Kate believes marijuana should be legalized; then, she says, people wouldn't have to sneak around like criminals to get it. "I understand they have to keep some control over the harder drugs, but marijuana—and maybe even hash—wouldn't be a problem. It's really too bad that kids who smoke grass or hash are portrayed as bad kids, because we're really not. It's just that sometimes we want a break. I don't mind sneaking around to get them if that's what I have to do, but I don't like being called a criminal because of it."

She and her friends have even gone to school stoned, and that too, she says, is all right. "We didn't hurt anyone; we were just having some fun and you can't blame us for that. People need to lighten up." Same goes for her parents, who have often taken her to task about coming home stoned and hanging around with the wrong crowd. "They think I'm going to be a good-for-nothing drug addict by the time I'm twenty. They don't give me credit for anything. All they do is get on my case about how I'm wasting my life and about how they didn't do stuff like that when they were my age. There's more pressure to succeed, and it's hard to do that when you can't afford to go to university and you can't get a job. Our future doesn't seem very bright, so maybe we need to use drugs just to help us cope."

TOM

A thirty-three-year-old recovering drug addict infected with HIV, the virus that causes AIDS, Tom is not gay, nor has he been sexually promiscuous. He did not receive a transfusion of bad blood. He caught the virus sharing dirty needles.

203

Today, a time bomb ticks away inside his body: he doesn't know when he will get full-blown AIDS, just that he will. Tom thinks he picked up the virus in 1987, when public education about AIDS was practically non-existent in Nova Scotia. He blames himself for the death sentence, but urges other drug users to be careful.

"I'm not the preaching type," he says, lighting a cigarette and pushing his long, stringy, sandy-coloured hair out of his eyes. "I know I'm going to die before too long, and I can't change that. I don't know how much longer I've got left, but I hope that today, with all the education they have about AIDS and the use of drugs, along with the needle exchanges, other people won't fall into the same deadly trap. When I stuck that needle in my arm, I may as well have put a gun to my head and pulled the trigger. It's going to end the same way; it's just going to take more time and be a lot more painful this way."

But Tom doesn't give up hoping and praying that someday his situation might change. "I'm not waiting for any kind if miracle cure or anything like that, but I do try to get along as best I can and try to take better care of myself." After he was diagnosed with HIV four years ago, he kicked his heroin habit. "I don't want to sound like any kind of saint or martyr, but I haven't touched the drug for almost four years. It hasn't been easy, but I figure the longer I stay away from drugs, the stronger I'll stay and the healthier I'll be. So maybe I'll live a bit longer. No one really knows for sure how much time I've got, but I hope to make the most of it. Being stoned all the time wouldn't be any way to cope with my situation.

"People might think that getting high would be a good way to forget about what's going to happen, but that's not a positive way to deal with the reality. Actually, that is how I handled it at first. I'd get high, and the truth would disappear for awhile; but then I'd come down again and there it was, the truth—ready to pounce on me like a rabid dog. And I think that coming down from a high actually contributed to the depression. You just can't hide from something like I've got; it's with you all the time." While his approach may sound bravely intelligent, he says he's really scared and has been very stupid. "I was stupid to try drugs in the first place, and then I just got hooked. It was one of those things that you would go back and change if you could—but you can't." With a heavy sigh and a deep drag on his cigarette, he says: "All you can do is play the hand you've been dealt. Unfortunately for me, it seems like the game's going to be cut short."

Tom was born and educated in Nova Scotia. As a teenager, he fell in with the wrong crowd. "Somehow," as he puts it, he managed to complete high school and find a good job in Halifax. Under the facade, though, Tom was an addict; over the years, he grew more dependent on drugs— marijuana, hashish, cocaine, crack cocaine, and finally heroin. "It's not hard to get any of that stuff, but it sure is hard as hell to get away from it," he says, taking another drag of his cigarette and swiping at his hair with agitation. "Man! If whatever comes with AIDS is only half as bad as giving up the drugs was, then I'm in for a tough time. Surely, if it's that bad, they'll be able to give you something for the pain. No one can even imagine how you feel when you're trying to give up something, while at the same time your body is telling you it's something you need so badly. It's like hot lava rushing through your veins; it's utter agony."

The intravenous method of using heroin infected him, but Tom blames himself for deciding to use drugs in the first place. "Sometimes you just kind of fall into things, and that's what happened with me and heroin. The first time I tried it I was at a party, and someone said, 'You want to try some of this good stuff? It won't hurt you.' What an understatement that was. If only he knew how much it would hurt me someday; if only I had known what was going to happen. It's stupid to even think about that any more."

Tom cannot change the past, so he tries not to dwell on his mistakes. "Things are the way they are, and I've got to accept that and live with it as best I can. I only hope that I can convince others to stay away from that stuff—all drugs, for that matter—because one way or another, it's going to kill you. I wish I would have listened; it's too late for me but hopefully not for the kids that are now growing up."

The day will come when doctors will tell Tom he has full-blown AIDS. That will be the beginning of the end for him. "It's painful in a way, knowing that you did something to yourself that is eventually going to kill you. I have dreams that wake me up in the middle of the night, dreams where all I see is me sitting in a dark corner somewhere, I don't even know where, using this same needle over and over again, just sticking it into my body over and over and over. More communities should really consider starting needle exchanges to help prevent the spread of HIV."

The best solution is to convince people not to use drugs at all, but, Tom adds, "We're not going to do that so it seems to me the best thing to do is admit that some people have this drug problem and at least help them avoid getting this deadly illness. Making sure heroin users have clean needles will be the least of the government's worries if they don't do something to address the AIDS crisis."

Tom tries to be brave, but he becomes sad thinking about all the young people in Nova Scotia who are going to turn to drugs. "The problem is that stuff is so easy to get. How can they really be stopped? I'm not so sure they can." Addicts find themselves in some pretty depressing and even life-threatening situations. "It really bothers me that there could be children out there just like me, using dirty needles and getting AIDS. When they tell you that you've got HIV and you know you got it because you shared a needle with someone, it's like getting kicked in the guts and having the shit knocked out of you. All I kept thinking about at first was that I could have prevented this if only I had not been a drug user. Man! It's a nightmare."

Tom learned he was HIV positive when he fainted at work a few years ago. He was taken to the hospital, and while doctors were carrying out a battery of tests, they discovered the infection. "I certainly had no idea that I would have had the virus. I never ever thought about the possibility, because I wasn't gay and I never had sex with that many people. It didn't take us long to eventually figure out that it was through the exchange of dirty needles that I got infected."

Tom is already preparing for his death. "It will come; I accept that. I don't hide the truth any more, and I've gone beyond the stage of blaming everyone from myself to my friends, my parents, and even the teachers I had in school. I just kept asking why hadn't they stopped me from using drugs, but it's not their fault. Trying to find someone to place the blame on is a waste of time and energy." Butting out the cigarette that has burned down to the filter, he says, matter-of-factly, "I'm not afraid of dying. People live all their lives thinking about dying, but I'm not frightened. On the other hand, though, I am afraid that once I'm gone, people will forget me. I have not had the chance to do anything meaningful with my life; it's like my life didn't count for anything. That's what bothers me the most—being forgotten."

Today, Tom concentrates on a healthy lifestyle, eating the right foods and following a regular exercise routine. He also spends time with other HIV-infected addicts. "Actually, I just try to be their friend. I can do that because I understand what they're going through. I don't really offer much advice, just let them use me as their sounding board. Everyone needs that when you've got something heavy on your mind." There are no statistics on HIV-infected addicts in Nova Scotia, but Tom believes there must be hundreds. "Probably more than we really want to admit. If we did know, it would probably scare the hell out of us. Maybe it's time the government did something to try and find out just how many of us there really are. But they won't do that, because then they'd have to admit there was a problem and they might have to take action."

Time is running out for Tom. "It's going to be all over for me in probably a few years, but we must never lose hope that an answer will be found. I can accept the fact that I'm going to die in a couple of years, but it bugs the hell out of me that no one seems to be doing anything to help these people; that no one seems to care. The time for action has long since passed, and we still have got a long way to go."

There are a few individuals and groups helping addicts and HIV-infected users, but not enough. Tom praises a group of concerned people in Halifax who have taken action to address the problem. In May 1992, the Main Line Needle Exchange opened to fill a void in the drug and AIDS communities. Valerie Firth, program coordinator and director, said at the time the needle exchange program operates under the management of a board of community-based agencies. Over time, it identified a need in the Halifax area for a non-judgmental clean-needle service.

The People With Aids (PWA) organization first promoted the program. "The PWA recognized that while some people were looking at AIDS and drug abuse, all the issues were not being addressed," she explains. "There is the realization that some people use drugs and will not change their habits. It was the belief that, if that was the case, there should be some service available which would ensure these individuals were not going to get infected with a deadly disease."

With some funding from the Nova Scotia Department of Health, the Main Line Needle Exchange has been operating since 1992. Its goal is to reduce blood-borne infection such as HIV and Hepatitis B in those engaged in high-risk activity. Since its doors opened, Firth estimates, the exchange had served more than 650 people a month. Initially established as a city service, the program now serves users throughout the province; some people come from as far away as Yarmouth and Sydney to take advantage of the safe exchange. Every month, Main Line hands out between three and five thousand needles, and three thousand condoms. "While needles are our main focus, it is our objective to reduce health risks, so we also provide condoms to those who cannot afford to buy them." Because drug addiction and prostitution are closely related, the distribution of condoms is an essential component of the program.

Despite these numbers, Firth says health officials estimate that Main Line Needle Exchange reaches only about 15 per cent of the IV-using community. "That's likely due to the fact that most addicts will not admit they have a problem, or, if they have a health problem, they don't recognize it as serious because they really don't know what it's like to feel healthy. Statistics are difficult to determine, because addicts are not exactly known for going in for HIV testing. They spend most of their lives running away from the fact that they are killing themselves, so we may never really know just how many people are infected through drug use."

In April 1996, the Government of Nova Scotia provided $55,000 to the AIDS Coalition of Cape Breton for a needle-exchange program in Sydney. The money was for public education, counselling, treatment referrals, and the distribution of needles. In a six-month period starting at the end of 1995, ten cases of HIV infection were reported on the island. Half of those were a direct result of sharing needles.

KURT

On the surface, Kurt Smith was just a teenager, struggling for acceptance while growing up in rural Nova Scotia. But he felt torn between family beliefs and the pressures of his peers: the freckle-faced fifteen-year-old had a tough time finding his own place. Gradually, he became a loner, torn apart inside while putting on a brave face for his unsuspecting parents.

His mother and father do not think they were overly strict with their son; they just wanted the best for Kurt. They expected him to do well in school, find some type of extracurricular activity that would keep him happy, and associate with "good" kids. That last stipulation still haunts them today.

As they sit in the modest yet comfortable living room of their bungalow, the Smiths share their painful story in the hopes of helping other parents avoid the pain they are now enduring.

The room is neat; Mrs. Smith is a good housekeeper. At sixty-one, she is a stately woman with greying hair; the lines on her forehead are the scars of her burden of grief. Her eyes are full of pain, but she struggles to appear strong. Hesitating, she says, "I am a clean freak. I guess I got that from my mother." As she glances around the room, a hint of smile crosses her face. "My mother was a clean woman and so was her mother. I think that sort of thing runs in the family. The house is about all I have these days to keep me busy. I clean it every day, just to keep my mind off things."

The stocky Mr. Smith, fifty-eight, joins the conversation, gently touching his wife's shoulder in a comforting gesture. "I can tell you her mother was a nut when it came to keeping the house clean. I've always appreciated the fact that I had a comfortable place to come home to every day after work, and that our kids had a clean home to grow up in." Motioning towards his wife, he continues, "I think if she didn't have this house to look after, she'd just about go crazy or something, and I'd lose her too. I just wish I could get her out of here more often."

On the surface, the Smiths are an odd couple. She is taller than her husband. She is slender; he shows signs of a middle-age spread. She is three years older than he, and hails from western Canada, while he was born, raised, and lived all his life in Nova Scotia. She has a university degree in education. He learned about life as a construction worker. However, below the surface a close bond has stood the test of time. Their relationship has survived many difficult challenges, and they rely upon each other for comfort and support.

Throughout the room are photographs of the family—the Smiths' wedding picture, taken thirty-seven years ago; their first-born son, Allen, who now lives in the United States with his wife and their two children, whose pictures are strategically placed there. There is a picture of the Smiths' daughter, Marie, who died twenty-eight years ago, at seven months of age, from a degenerative heart problem. And there are the pictures of Kurt, the son they lost five years ago, when he was fifteen.

The Smiths exchange painful glances as they begin talking about their youngest child. Thinking about the past brings back all the memories, all the pain. "It's not right, you know," she whispers, her voice trembling. "It's not right that a mother should outlive her children. I know I can't bring them back, and I know I can't change anything that happened back then, but it just seems so unfair. When you have children, all you want is for them to be happy, healthy, and do well for themselves. A parent wants no more or less than that for their children. We didn't expect Kurt to be more than he wanted to be, but we did hope that he would be happy."

Kurt was never a high achiever in school, sports, or any other activity; the Smiths accepted the fact that he would never go to university, but they always hoped he would graduate from high school, get a good job, settle down, and have a family. That may sound idealistic, she acknowledges, but asks, "Why should we not want what is best for our children? I don't think that's expecting too much."

In school, Kurt struggled just to get by, Mr. Smith says: "I know now that our hopes for him might have put added pressures on our son. But you just try to do what you think you need to, to guide them in the right direction. We didn't see anything wrong with that, but I guess maybe it was just too much for him to handle. We loved Kurt very much. I just can't believe that he would have done something so terrible because of us, or to get back at us for something he may have concocted in his head. It just doesn't seem right. It doesn't seem natural, and I haven't gotten any good explanation from anyone yet to try to help us understand what might have been going on in his head."

The Smiths began seeing a change in Kurt when he turned thirteen and was in junior high school. At first, they dismissed the rebellious behaviour as puberty or growing pains. They had not had any trouble with Allen at that age, but they realized that the two boys were different. Some youngsters have a hard time coming of age.

Then they learned that Kurt was using drugs. For a family with a strong Baptist background, that discovery started a chain of events that the Smiths now relive every day. Drawing a deep breath, Mrs. Smith suggests their insistence that Kurt avoid certain people led to constant squabbling. "He was a proud boy," she explains. "When he started hanging around with these other kids, he felt that he finally found a place where he belonged. We know it was through those kids that he became exposed to drugs, although we are not blaming anyone else for what he did. We had always taught Kurt to be his own person, to make his own choices but to make those judgments based on what was morally and legally right. If he chose to get into drugs, then I don't think we can blame anyone else. That might be convenient or cold, but we cannot cope with what Kurt did by placing blame on someone else."

Mr. Smith admits they had suspected Kurt was doing drugs long before they ever confronted him with their suspicions. "It's just one of those things that you don't ever want to admit to yourself. No parent ever wants to find out that their kid is on drugs. We saw the changes, but we didn't want to admit what we knew was the truth. He was lying to us, and we were lying to ourselves."

Late nights, slipping grades, a confrontational attitude, denials, and trouble with the law for minor vandalism and shoplifting, finally convinced the Smiths to speak to their son about the situation. "We tried talking to him many times," Mrs. Smith says, her throat constricted with emotion. "But it didn't matter how many times me and his dad tried to talk to him about what he was doing, he always felt we were trying to run his life or tell him what to do. Sometimes we'd get angry with each other, but anger didn't help solve the problems. If anything, it probably made them worse. If I could do it over, I'd give him a hug instead of arguing with him."

She pauses to wipe away the tear trickling down her cheek, while Mr. Smith takes over the conversation. "Kurt had this attitude, this feeling that we were his enemies. I really believe that, for some reason, he saw us as the bad people and his friends as the saviours. I'm not surprised that the more we tried to talk to him, the further apart we grew and the deeper he became involved with those kids. I don't mean to make those others out to be bad kids, but they needed help too. Today, some of those kids are in big trouble."

The Smiths agree that talking with Kurt was an exercise in futility. However, the day Mrs. Smith found some hashish in Kurt's jacket pocket, they knew the time had come to take drastic steps. "It's a hard thing to tell your kid if he ever brought drugs into your house again, or if you ever found out they were using drugs, that you would put them out on the street," Mr. Smith explains. They hoped that threatening him might scare Kurt into going straight. "That is what we told him. Right or wrong, we just couldn't take it any more. We loved him with all our hearts, but the constant arguing was just too much to take. We felt that we had to let him know how serious this was, and we had no idea that our actions might lead to something that we would regret for the rest of our lives."

After that confrontation, Kurt withdrew from his parents and his friends. Mrs. Smith, who has regained her composure, recalls that her son did not go out much, even though it was summer. "He just seemed to hang around the house all day long. He spent a lot of time in his room with the door closed, and he hardly talked to me or his dad. I guess we never knew just how strong our words had been to him."

The Smiths would gladly take back those words if they could. They would have taken a different approach if they had known how deeply rooted Kurt's anguish had become. But, as Mr. Smith points out, "You can't go back and change the past, no matter how much you regret what you did. The past is gone and so is our son."

Kurt slipped deeper and deeper into his shell. As the Smiths considered getting some help for their son, they ran out of time. On Sunday, it was customary for both Mr. and Mrs. Smith to attend church. When the boys were younger, the Smiths insisted they go with them, but when they turned twelve, the children were given the option of going to church or staying home. The Smiths are devout Christians, but they did not believe in pushing their beliefs onto their children. Allen continued to attend church until he was seventeen, the year he graduated from high school; Kurt stopped going the first Sunday after his twelfth birthday. Mrs. Smith says she accepted his decision, because it was his to make. "I really had hoped that he would continue with church, but I knew it was his way of expressing his independence. I accepted that, but I always thought, deep down inside, that he would eventually come back—but he never did."

One Sunday morning, a little over five years ago, the Smiths left for church at 10:30. They were both concerned about leaving Kurt alone, as he had seemed extremely depressed for a number of days and had been unresponsive to their pleas to let them help. Today, they know his behaviour was a sign that something was terribly wrong; today, they wish that one, or both of them, had skipped church that day to stay home with him.

When they returned, shortly after lunch, Kurt did not respond to their calls. Mrs. Smith went upstairs to his bedroom; the door was unlocked. She went in when he still refused to answer, and discovered his decapitated body sprawled across the blood-soaked carpet. Kurt had killed himself with one bullet fired from one of his father's rifles. While his parents were at church, Kurt had gone to the basement, where his father kept the guns he used only for target shooting. He took a rifle from the rack, and loaded the gun with one shell. In his bedroom, he sat on the floor, propped his back against the foot of the bed, put the barrel into his mouth, and pulled the trigger. He died instantly.

Fighting tears again, Mrs. Smith says she and her husband had no idea that their son was in such a deep state of depression. Later, when they were cleaning Kurt's bedroom and packing away his things, they found drugs stashed in various hiding places. In addition to the hashish and marijuana, Kurt had also been taking various chemical drugs, which doctors said were more likely to have caused his depression than had the confrontations with his parents. However, the Smiths wonder if their harsh words could have contributed to his state of mind. His death was so violent, and there was no note; to the Smiths, this is confirmation that Kurt was angry with them when he committed suicide.

"I can't help but wonder why he didn't talk with us or leave us a note to explain what he was thinking," Mrs. Smith says. "To me, this means that Kurt was mad at us and wanted us to suffer. Why else would he do this where we would find him? Maybe it was the drugs that clouded his judgment, but I still believe he wanted to get even with me and his dad for what we tried to do. In his mind, I think he saw us trying to interfere with his life, and he wanted us to get the message. This was his ultimate revenge."

Mr. Smith nods in agreement. "I knew Kurt, or at least I thought I did. I think he would do that to us if he was angry enough and wanted to get back at us, particularly if the drugs were not letting him think clearly.

That's one of the reasons we find it so difficult not to blame ourselves."
Mr. Smith also regrets having kept guns in the house. "There's just so
many things we'd do different if we had the chance again, but that's not
possible. So we have to try and find a way to accept things. We have to
try to go on.

"Drug use is a disease," he says. "We always hoped our kids wouldn't
get into drugs, but our hopes never became a reality. Someday, though,
we hope that everyone who thinks about using drugs will stop and consider what they're doing to themselves and to the people who love them.
There must be a way to stop this madness, to get the message out there
so that other kids don't end up like our Kurt."

Mrs. Smith glances at Kurt's picture. "It's too late for our boy, but hopefully others can learn from what happened to him," she says. "It makes
me sad that there are others out there just like Kurt who could end up
the same way. The time has come to put an end to this monster before it
claims any more victims."

Unfortunately for Canadian society, Kurt's story, and those told by
Matthew, Bobby, Louise, Kate, and Tom, are only a small sample of the
horrors of drug addiction in communities across the country. The use of
illicit drugs touches every neighbourhood, town, and city in Canada.
Drugs know no social, economic, racial, or ethnic boundaries. Every
Canadian, in one way or another, is affected by the drug trade. This is
the on-going struggle, between authorities and the drug dealers,
between the users and the money-hungry pushers, between mainstream
society and the underground world of the drug trade.